Manchester Medieval Sources Series

series advisers Rosemary Horrox and Janet L. Nelson

This series aims to meet a growing need among students and teachers of medieval history for translations of key sources that are directly usable in students' own work. It provides texts central to medieval studies courses and focuses upon the diverse cultural and social as well as political conditions that affected the functioning of all levels of medieval society. The basic premise of the series is that translations must be accompanied by sufficient introductory and explanatory material, and each volume, therefore, includes a comprehensive guide to the sources' interpretation, including discussion of critical linguistic problems and an assessment of the most recent research on the topics being covered.

THE TOWNS OF ITALY
IN THE LATER MIDDLE AGES

Manchester University Press

Medieval Sources*online*

Complementing the printed editions of the Medieval Sources series, Manchester University Press has developed a web-based learning resource which is now available on a yearly subscription basis.

Medieval Sources*online* brings quality history source material to the desktops of students and teachers and allows them open and unrestricted access throughout the entire college or university campus. Designed to be fully integrated with academic courses, this is a one-stop answer for many medieval history students, academics and researchers keeping thousands of pages of source material 'in print' over the Internet for research and teaching.

titles available now at Medieval Sources*online include*

Visit the site at *www.medievalsources.co.uk* for further information and subscription prices.

THE TOWNS OF ITALY
IN THE LATER MIDDLE AGES

translated and annotated by Trevor Dean

Manchester University Press
Manchester and New York
distributed exclusively in the USA by Palgrave

Published by Manchester University Press
Oxford Road, Manchester M13 9NR, UK
and Room 400, 175 Fifth Avenue, New York, NY 10010, USA
www.manchesteruniversitypress.co.uk

Distributed exclusively in the USA by
Palgrave, 175 Fifth Avenue, New York, NY 10010, USA

Distributed exclusively in Canada by
UBC Press, University of British Columbia, 2029 West Mall,
Vancouver, BC, Canada V6T 1Z2

British Library Cataloguing-in-Publication Data
A catalogue record for this book is available from the British Library

Library of Congress Cataloging-in-Publication Data applied for

ISBN 0 7190 5203 3 hardback
     0 7190 5204 1 paperback

First published 2000

14 13 12 11 10 09 08 07 06 05   10 9 8 7 6 5 4 3 2

Typeset in Monotype Bell
by Koinonia Ltd, Manchester
Printed in Great Britain
by Bell & Bain Ltd, Glasgow

CONTENTS

ACKNOWLEDGEMENTS

I am very grateful to Drs Frances Andrews and Kate Lowe for reading and commenting on this book in draft. Their criticisms and corrections have shaped the final work in many ways, though I am responsible for all the remaining errors.

The author wishes to acknowledge the following copyright-holders:

Accademia della Crusca for document 105b; Accademia nazionale dei Lincei for documents 34a and 55c; Adelphi Edizioni S.p.a. for document 68; American Philosophical Society for documents 44 and 63; Archivio di Stato di Firenze for documents 73b, 76 and 85a; E. J. Brill for document 92a; Davaco Publishers for document 14; Deputazione di storia patria per l'Umbria, for documents 8, 17d and 91; Deputazione di storia patria per le province di Romagna, for documents 58a and 86b; Deputazione di storia patria per le Venezie for document 104; Deputazione provinciale ferrarese di storia patria for documents 52, 78 and 103a; Edizione Athena for document 95; Istituto storico italiano per il Medio Evo for documents 5, 11, 12d, 13, 14, 18b, 31b, 32b, 40, 42b, 57b, 61, 69, 71, 73c, 74, 79, 97, 106 and 108; Istituto veneto di scienze, lettere ed arti, for documents 51, 54c and 55a; Jouvence Società Editoriale for documents 16a, 49a, 80 and 87; Leo S. Olschki for documents 47 and 73a; Monumenta Germaniae Historica for documents 4, 18a, 30, 31a, 34b, 36, 39, 65, 66a and 85b; Rusconi Libri for document 81; Società napoletana di storia patria, for document 67b; Società storica pisana for documents 10 and 100b; State University of New York Press for document 64; Ugo Guanda Editore for documents 9, 17a, 17b, 32a, 35, 43, 45, 67a, 98 and 101.

All other extracts are believed to be out of copyright. Every effort has been made to contact copyright-holders. If any proper acknowledgement has not been made, copyright-holders are invited to contact the publisher.

LIST OF ABBREVIATIONS

MGH *Monumenta Germaniae Historica*
RIS   *Rerum italicarum scriptores*

Frequently cited sources

Corpus chronicorum bononiensium, ed. A. Sorbelli, in *RIS*, 2nd edn., vol. 18, pt. 1, 4 vols

Salimbene de Adam, *Cronica*, ed. G. Scalia, 2 vols (Bari, 1966); *Cronica fratris Salimbene de Adam ordinis minorum*, ed. O. Holder-Egger, in *MGH, Scriptores*, vol. 23 (Hannover and Leipzig, 1905–13)

Cronache senesi, ed. A. Lisini and F. Iacometti, in *RIS*, 2nd edn., vol. 15, pt. 6

Statuti di Perugia dell'anno MCCCXLII, ed. G. degli Azzi, 2 vols (Rome, 1913–16)

Statuti di Bologna dell'anno 1288, ed. G. Fasoli and P. Sella, 2 vols (Vatican City, 1937–9)

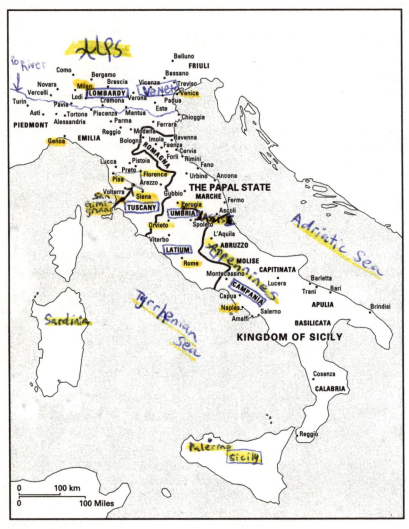

Map of Italy, *c.* 1300

INTRODUCTION

The towns of later medieval Italy were one of the high points of urban society and culture in Europe before the industrial revolution. They also produced huge amounts of written material, which is exceptional in quality and quantity for the Middle Ages: 'More source materials survive than a hundred scholars could adequately master.'[1] For almost every town in the north and centre there survive chronicles and voluminous collections of statute-law; for many cities there are the records of executive decision-making, of taxation and of trials; from Tuscany especially there is a wonderful outpouring of poetry and stories (*novelle*); for the history of the church and religion there are sermons, and records of the trials of heretics and the canonisation of saints, as well as the more humdrum deeds of property-owning; for private individuals there are letters, diaries, and mountains of notarial contracts. Guilds and confraternities produced statutes, membership lists and registers of their activities; men of the church and the universities produced works of law, theology and political theory; businesses produced account books and commercial correspondence; governments produced legislation, treaties, proclamations, letters, tax lists. Little of this huge mass of material has been translated, or ever published. The only areas to receive any sort of consistent coverage are Florence and the artistic/humanist 'Renaissance': translations include some early chronicles and later diaries,[2] art historical documents,[3] humanism,[4] and Florentine society.[5] This means that, for most of Italy,

---

1 J. Larner, *Italy in the Age of Dante and Petrarch 1216–1380* (London, 1908), p. 11; and see P. J. Jones, *The Italian City-State: From Commune to Signoria* (Oxford, 1997), pp. 156–7, 202–3.

2 *Dino Compagni's Chronicle of Florence*, trans. D. E. Bornstein (Philadelphia, 1986); *Villani's Chronicle*, trans. R. E. Selfe (London, 1906); *Two Memoirs of Renaissance Florence*, ed. G. Brucker (New York, 1967); *A Florentine Diary from 1415 to 1542*, trans. A. de Rosen Jarvis (London, 1927).

3 E. G. Holt, *A Documentary History of Art* (New York, 1957); D. S. Chambers, *Patrons and Artists in the Italian Renaissance* (Columbia, 1971); *Italian Art, 1400–1500: Sources and Documents*, trans. C. E. Gilbert (Eagelwood Cliffs, 1988).

4 *The Earthly Republic: Italian Humanists on Government and Society*, ed. B. G. Kohl and R. G. Witt (Manchester, 1978); *The Three Crowns of Florence*, ed. D. Thompson and A. F. Nagel (New York, 1972).

5 *The Society of Renaissance Florence*, ed. G. Brucker (New York, 1971).

for most of the thirteenth and fourteenth centuries, there is little available in modern English translation. This volume is intended to fill that gap, by providing a more inclusive and balanced coverage of Italian urban life in the period.

There are of course difficulties with such volumes, at both practical and theoretical levels. Roberto Lopez and Irving Raymond, editors of a previous collection that drew heavily on Italian material, observed: 'Our task was not easy, to pick a mere few out of an immense number of records.' A small number of documents cannot give a complete picture, they warned, no matter how carefully selected, and they hoped that readers would 'not look for what is missing, but for what is included'.[6] Such sentiments are shared by this editor. Bordone, editor of a similar collection of documents in Italian,[7] identified two risks faced by compilations of documents: that they construct, with fragments of real cities, an inexistent city; and that they flatten development over time.[8] Similar objections have been made, at a more general level, regarding anthologies: that, in making 'a single book out of clippings from many books', they create 'an illusion of composite authorship', and take extracts out of context, forcing them into association with other extracts, devaluing each with 'the same negative poison'.[9] These risks and objections can of course be avoided and answered. The risk of creating an inexistent city can be addressed through the use of contrasting extracts, as is attempted in places here. The risk of flattening development can be addressed by including several documents from different periods from the same cities, again as attempted here. The charge of putting texts into 'forced associations' is willingly acknowledged: it is precisely in such associations that the value of a selection of sources lies. In an era of critical theory in which the author is seen less as the sole and deliberate creator and more an orchestrator of divergent voices, such objections to anthologies fall away. It is worth remembering, too, that medieval writers loved anthologies.

In looking for the chief features of Italian communal cities, we might point to the following: the unity of city and dependent countryside (*contado*), the stability of population, urban functions (religious, economic, military and political), the development of public spaces,

6 *Medieval Trade in the Mediterranean World*, ed. R. S. Lopez and I. W. Raymond (New York, n.d.), pp. 4, 7.

7 R. Bordone, *La società urbana nell'Italia comunale (secoli XI–XIV)* (Turin, 1984).

8 *Ibid.*, p. 21.

9 L. Riding and R. Graves, *A Pamphlet against Anthologies* (London, 1928), pp. 67–76.

social composition (the coexistence of landowners, traders and artisans), the development of autonomous institutions, and civic culture.[10] All of these elements are also present in this volume, though within five broader thematic chapters. The buildings and their decoration, and urban 'social services' form the subject of Chapter I: the cathedrals and town halls, the towers and palaces, the paintings and statues, the prisons, street-paving and fountains; the hospitals and schools, and the efforts to control and regulate activities and waste. Civic religion is addressed in Chapter II: the feast-days of urban patron saints, the devotion of urban inhabitants as manifested in the cult of official and unofficial saints and in the performance of miracles, the conflicts between communes and the local church, the problem of heresy, the clerical attack on usury, and the confraternities that relieved urban poverty. Chapter III explores production and commerce: the effects of monetary affluence, the guilds and markets, government interventions to stimulate production, to regulate exchange, and to control the city's population. The longest chapter – Chapter IV – deals with social groups and social tensions: *popolo* against magnates, noble clans against each another, men against women, young men against city elders, Christians against Jews, freemen against slaves, food riots and tax revolts, acts of resistance and indecency. Finally, Chapter V examines the great variety of political regimes in late-medieval Italy: from consolidated communes such as Florence or Venice, to stable or unstable 'tyrannies' in Pisa, Ferrara or Verona, and finally to the creation of regional states in which communes with their own traditions of proud independence – in this case Pisa and Padua – were absorbed by their greater and more powerful neighbours.

Every selection of documents bears the editor's imprint. Three principles have underlain the choice of documents in this book. The first is a desire to present material from as many different cities and as many different writers as possible. Thus material from the great cities – Milan, Florence, Venice, Genoa – is naturally included, but alongside it are documents from second-rank cities such as Padua or Ferrara, and from small towns such as Fermo and L'Aquila. I have also attempted to include some documents from the south (doubtless insufficient in number and range to satisfy its historians) to illustrate some of the ways in which urban life there was different from that in the communes of the north and centre: though historians of southern

10 Bordone, *La società urbana.*

towns speak of their autonomy,[11] it is autonomy of a different order when Brindisi had to petition the king in order to appoint a new physician [22], or when Chieti had to seek the king's support against a neighbouring count pursuing his vassals [72]. Second, my search for inclusiveness and balance has meant avoiding the familiar. It might seem to some critics that I have produced an 'Italy in the Age of Dante and Petrarch', but without either Dante or Petrarch. My answer would be that these canonical authors have translations enough already: Dante's great poem, the Divine Comedy, though arguably untranslatable, has recently received numerous versions in English. The same reasoning excludes Boccaccio.[12] I have, though, included considerable material from two prose authors where existing translations exist, but for good reason: the selections from Villani published in 1906 are now old-fashioned and out of print;[13] the full translation of Salimbene's chronicle published in 1986 is unfortunately defective, with many omissions and misunderstandings.[14] Finally, a third principle is to reflect some of my own concerns in the 'minor' history of Italy (Ferrara), and in the behaviour and mores of the nobility (vendetta, knighthood).

I have aimed for fairly literal translation, while often reshaping sentences in order to obtain smoother effects (turning passive into active verbs, and adjectives into adverbs, for example, or breaking up lengthy preambles with their many subordinate clauses). I have also lightly edited some texts in order to remove repetitive or obscure material and to clarify the sense. There are two important words that I have frequently left in Italian or Latin, and they cause all translators problems: one is *stato/status*, which has a meaning combining government, regime, power and state; and the other is *popolo*, and its derivatives *popolani/populares*, which never included the whole people, and was sometimes restricted to 'the better sort'.

11 R. Caggese, *Roberto d'Angiò e i suoi tempi* (Florence, 1922), pp. 357–466; G. Galasso, *Il Regno di Napoli: Il Mezzogiorno angioino e aragonese (1266–1494)* (Turin, 1992), pp. 407–46. Cf. Jones, *City-State*, p. 260: 'there were no autonomous communes or renascent city-states' (and generally, pp. 258–63, 289–90).

12 See the new translation of *The Decameron* by G. Waldman (Oxford, 1993).

13 See above, note 2.

14 *The Chronicle of Salimbene de Adam*, ed. J. L. Baird, G. Baglivi and J. R. Kane (Binghamton, NY, 1986). There was an earlier, partial translation: G. G. Coulton, *From St Francis to Dante: A Translation of All that is of Primary Interest in the Chronicle of the Franciscan Salimbene (1221–1288)* (London, 1906).

I: THE PHYSICAL ENVIRONMENT AND SOCIAL SERVICES

City descriptions

In the period 1280 to 1340 a number of descriptions of Italian cities – Milan, Florence, Pavia, Padua, Genoa – were written which describe those cities at the height of their medieval development, before the crises of the mid–late fourteenth century.[1] This volume starts with three of these: Bonvesin da la Riva's innovative description of Milan, Giovanni da Nono's more conventional, but lively description of Padua, and an anonymous, verse description of Genoa. Like the famous description of Florence by Giovanni Villani,[2] these praise the sheer size of the urban population and of their daily food needs, the great numbers of city churches and their clergy, the wide range and value of productive activities, the abundance of foodstuffs on city markets, the impressive buildings erected both inside and outside the city, and the power of the local nobility. They focus on gates and walls, churches and monasteries, schools and hospitals, mills and markets, rivers and ports, roads and bridges, places of execution and places of pleasure: all those physical aspects of Italian cities that made them resemble Rome in contemporary eyes, and all those opportunities for employment and consumption that have made them famous ever since ('here every man can earn money'; 'anything you want you can have at once' [1 and 3]).

All of these aspects of city life were closely supervised, guided and controlled by city governments. Cities gave attention to all physical aspects. First the walls: successive circuits of walls were built to incorporate rapidly expanding suburbs, and the numbers and size of gate-towers were a source of pride, 'an expression of beauty, force and economic power'.[3] Secondly, governments addressed problems within

---

1 J. K. Hyde, 'Medieval descriptions of cities', in *Literacy and its Uses: Studies on Late Medieval Italy*, ed. D. Waley (Manchester, 1993). Hyde does not deal with the verse description of Genoa.

2 *Cronica*, XII.94. For translations, see *Social and Economic Foundations of the Italian Renaissance*, ed. A. Molho (New York and London, 1969), pp. 19–22; Lopez and Raymond, *Medieval Trade*, pp. 70–4.

3 D. Balestracci and G. Picinni, *Siena nel Trecento: Assetto urbano e strutture edilizie* (Florence, 1977), p. 25.

the city of circulation, security and hygiene.[4] Narrow, dark or winding streets impeded the passage of people, animals, carts or soldiers, and attracted criminals. Latrines that discharged within view of the street, and sewage that flowed from alleyways between houses onto the thoroughfare were both unsightly and unhygienic. So communes issued laws setting minimum widths for roads, forbidding the obstruction of public roadways, and restricting projecting platforms that robbed the street of light. They also carried out works to straighten and widen streets, using compulsory purchase where necessary, in order to improve access to cathedral, market or fountains. They legislated to oblige householders to close alleyways where sewage collected and to route their drainage underground. They issued laws to control traffic (requiring carts to be led at walking pace by dismounted riders). They paved the streets in brick. Third, they were concerned with moral and physical cleanliness: they acted against air- and water-pollution caused by the waste, stench and noise of industry and processing by restricting the location and working hours of productive activities such as tanning and butchery. They ensured water supplies for domestic use and for drain-cleaning. They tried to confine lepers to suburban hospitals, Jews to inconspicuous areas and prostitutes to the public brothel (though the latter had a constant tendency to spill over on to the streets and into private rented accommodation).

Lastly, they embarked on *grands projets*, creating 'an almost entirely new secular architecture'.[5] Chief among these was the public palace or town hall, incorporating a residence for the chief executive and judge (*podestà*) or for the executive committee of Priors, rooms for communal officials, a large first-floor hall for council meetings, ground-floor loggias for popular assemblies, balconies for proclamations and speeches, and a bell-tower. More than building a town hall was involved here, as shown by the example of Perugia, where the commune's decision in 1275–6 to embark on what has been described as a 'grandiose project of radical urban renewal',[6] involved over the following decades the construction of an aqueduct and fountain to bring water

4 F. Bocchi, 'Regulation of the urban environment by the Italian communes from the twelfth to the fourteenth century', *Bulletin of the John Rylands Library*, 72 (1990).

5 H. Wieruszowski, 'Art and the commune in the time of Dante', *Speculum*, 19 (1944), 15.

6 M. R. Silvestrelli, 'L'edilizia pubblica del commune di Perugia: dal "palatium communis" al "palatium novum populi"', in *Società e istituzioni dell'Italia comunale: l'esempio di Perugia (secoli XII–XIV)* (2 vols, Perugia, 1988), p. 490.

to the city centre (symbolising the city's ability to supply its citizens with essentials), new or enlarged residences for the government and the Captain of the *popolo*, improved road access, and a new cathedral. Communal projects thus both impinged on and promoted the church: churches, hospitals and cemeteries were moved, land was bought from the church to build palaces, walls and housing, cathedral-building was sponsored and controlled, squares were improved for sermons or relic-displays.

Images in the city

Italian cities were also full of images. Images of saints, especially the Virgin Mary, were dotted around the city 'like fountains' on the gates, at street corners, on the facades of churches.[7] At Bologna, figures of saints were painted in the city treasury and scenes from the life of St Dominic on the city walls. Scenes of judgement and symbols of justice were depicted in the lawcourts (Florence, Padua). Noble families and their clients displayed their coats of arms on buildings. Political heroes and military champions were commemorated in public portraits (King Robert of Naples in Florence, Guidoriccio Fogliani in Siena), as were significant moments in civic history (the history of Pope Alexander III and Emperor Frederick I in Venice). Such images were fixed, permanently visible; others were mobile, such as the flags of guilds and confraternities, or the miracle-working images paraded in procession at times of disaster, or the painted war-wagons (*carrocci*) housed in the cathedral.

Such images performed various positive functions: celebrating achievement, holding up exemplars, encouraging 'reverential behaviour', asserting ownership, identity or group-membership, invoking a saint's intercessory power. Painting was also used, however, to defame and harm public enemies, through *pittura infamante* which depicted fugitives from justice, usually traitors, in humiliating poses (wearing mitres, hanging upside down), alongside base animals (pigs, asses, etc.) or creatures with evil associations (basilisks), and with insulting captions listing the traitor's vices. Such art, none of which survives, flourished in many towns of north and central Italy in the

7 E. Muir, 'The virgin on the street corner: the place of the sacred in Italian cities', in *Religion and Culture in the Renaissance and Reformation*, ed. S. Ozment (Kirksville, 1989), p. 26.

late thirteenth and fourteenth centuries, though it died out in the fifteenth [15].[8]

There was, however, a clear distinction between the civic art promoted by communes and the art promoted by city lords, the so-called 'despots' who took control in many cities from the late thirteenth century onwards. City lords too embarked on beneficial public works, such as street paving (as too did the king in Naples), but they regarded *pittura infamante* as bringing disrepute to the city. Instead, they went for 'effects that would excite a sense of wonder' (Green), building palaces that made 'lavish use of precious materials' and housed collections of rare animals. The paintings described by Fiamma in Azzone Visconti's palace in Milan associate Azzone with heroes and state-creators of history and legend (Aeneas, Charlemagne), while also developing the novelty of ruler-portraiture (perhaps deriving from its revival under Frederick II). Azzone also, according to Fiamma, planned to have an equestrian statue of himself placed on the cathedral. Other *signori* followed a similar pattern in asserting the warrior, chivalric and dynastic values of lordship. At Padua, the da Carrara lords used art 'both to advertise their wealth and prominent political status ... and also self-consciously to validate their dynastic claims to Padua':[9] through prominently-sited tombs bearing full-length, carved effigies and lengthy inscriptions; through the decoration of their large palace with heraldic devices, animals, scenes from classical history or myth (warfare, heroes, emperors, generals) and portraits of the da Carrara themselves and their military victories. In Verona the tombs of the della Scala lords of the city bore equestrian statues and reliefs of their military *gesta*, while their palace had paintings of Roman emperors and a park containing both domestic and exotic animals.[10]

Grands projets, however, ground to a halt with the Black Death of 1348. This was most clearly the case at Siena, where work on the cathedral was suspended, where other projects (walls, Fonte Gaia) were not finished until the next century, where one suburb, developed for immigrants in the 1320s, was abandoned and apparently returned

---

8 S. Y. Edgerton, *Pictures and Punishment: Art and Criminal Punishment during the Florentine Renaissance* (Ithaca and London, 1985), p. 71.

9 D. Norman, "'Splendid models and examples from the past': Carrara patronage of art', in *Siena, Florence and Padua: Art, Society and Religion 1280–1400*, ed. D. Norman (New Haven and London, 1995), p. 155.

10 *Gli Scaligeri*, ed. G. M. Varanini (Verona, 1988), pp. 264–5, 318–19.

to cultivation. The smaller scale of Sienese building projects can be gauged clearly in the local chronicles. There is reason, however, for seeing the Sienese case as extreme: elsewhere, after an interval, old projects were brought to completion, and new projects were started – in Venice the Hall of the Greater Council, cathedrals and other church buildings in Florence and Milan, in Bologna the new church of San Petronio, public clocks in many cities [6, 11].

Education

In late-medieval Italy 'a revolution was taking place in the way in which education was organised: state intervention was increasingly extended into this area'.[11] Both Villani and Bonvesin da la Riva give precise statements about schooling, Villani claiming that in Florence in 1336–8 there were as many as 10,000 pupils, girls and boys, in elementary reading schools, and hundreds more in abacus and grammar schools.[12] Villani's figures have been largely dismissed by historians as an impossible exaggeration: they would mean that Florence achieved higher schooling rates than any other European state for centuries. However, in other respects, Villani has been corroborated, in the possibility of female education (there were even female teachers in fourteenth century Italy),[13] and in the relative ranking of subjects has been shown to be accurate: most pupils learned reading; next in importance came abacus; last and least came grammar, a minority subject, argues Bob Black, limited probably to the élite and to those intended to proceed to university.

Denley and Grendler put a certain emphasis on public provision of grammar teaching. They note how ecclesiastical schools had disappeared by 1300, under a variety of internal and external weaknesses: mainly because they were unable to meet the public and private demands for education in Italian urban societies. To meet the needs of both business and public administration, a combination of communal

11 P. Denley, 'Government and schools in late-medieval Italy', in *City and Countryside in Late-Medieval and Renaissance Italy: Essays presented to Philip Jones*, ed. T. Dean and C. Wickham (London, 1990), p. 94; and in general see Jones, *City-State*, pp. 157–8, 203.

12 Giovanni Villani, *Nuova cronica*, ed. G. Porta (Parma, 1990–1), vol. III, p. 197 (XII.94).

13 P. F. Grendler, *Schooling in Renaissance Italy: Literacy and Learning, 1300–1600* (Baltimore and London, 1989), p. 90.

and private schools sprang up, especially in the fourteenth century. Communes declared education to be part of the common good, asserted that Latin grammar was the foundation of all virtue, and subsidised grammar teachers through contracts, stipends, rent-free housing, tax exemptions and so on. Some communes, such as Lucca, went further, funding teachers in logic and philosophy, and providing grants for university students. However, Grendler does recognise the limits of this: 'The governments judged public education to be beneficial to the community, but saw no reason to offer it gratis.' Most pupils still had to pay. Communal schools taught only a minority of pupils: the private sector was still the major provider, with parents contracting directly with teachers who either lived in, taught in rented rooms or kept boarding schools. And Denley draws the distinction between small and middling towns, where government intervention accelerated from the early fourteenth century, and the larger cities (Florence, Venice, Genoa), where such intervention was 'much delayed and much weaker'.[14]

Petti Balbi, by contrast, puts more emphasis on private schooling and abacus-teaching.[15] She argues that private schooling preceded public in time, as parents sought the utilitarian, business-oriented skills they valued (accounting, commercial letter-writing), and that the driving force behind the proliferation of private schools was not the public good, but private profit – that of both teachers and pupils. Second, she argues that communal interventions were less commonly to establish public schools (as in the exceptional case of Bassano [23]), than to stimulate the immigration of private tutors: provisions of the Bassano type, though multipying in the fourteenth century, were characteristic of small towns, marginal to the areas of greatest educational demand in the big cities. Third, whereas the communes intervened only rarely in primary education (for example, in circumstances of plague in Lucca in 1348 [21]), they would commit public funds to attracting and retaining abacus teachers, who were more in demand and better paid. Whether provision was public or private, education in Italy produced the most literate and numerate society in Medieval Europe.

14 Denley, 'Government and schools', p. 99.

15 G. Petti Balbi, 'Istituzioni cittadine e servizi scolastici nell'Italia centro-settentrionale tra XIII e XV secolo', in *Città e servizi sociali nell'Italia dei secoli XII–XV* (Pistoia, 1990).

1 'A world in itself': Milan, 1288

Bonvesin da la Riva (*c.* 1250–*c.* 1313) was a grammar teacher in Milan and member of the Humiliati. His writings, in both Latin and Italian, combine the religious and the didactic. In the most famous of his works, he enthusiastically describes his native city.

Bonvesin da la Riva, *De magnalibus Mediolani*, ed. M. Corti (Milan, 1974), with the corrections and suggestions of the new edition by P. Chiesa (Milan, 1997).

To all men joined in the catholic faith whom this work reaches, fra Bonvesin da la Riva, citizen of Milan, gives greeting ... As I have noticed that not only foreign peoples but also my compatriots are asleep in a desert of ignorance and are unaware of the marvels of Milan, I thought that they should be assisted and advised in their view, so that they see with open eyes and, seeing, recognise how and how much our city is to be admired. Therefore, in the year of Our Lord 1288 ... after determinedly investigating the truth of things with great diligence and much labour, I have written this little work ... at no-one's request or suggestion, and in expectation of no reward on earth, but rather by divine inspiration. And I have written with the intention that, when the pure truth of this eulogy of Milan is read and understood, three useful things will result: first, that all the friends of this city ... reading and hearing of its marvels will glorify God in thanks, and that the envious will either be converted or be saddened and consumed by their own envy; second, that all foreigners, learning of the nobility and dignity of the Milanese, will everywhere come to honour and respect them, love and defend them ...; and third, that my co-citizens, seeing themselves in this mirror, and considering into what a city they are born, will not degenerate from such nobility, nor stain and malign their *patria* with dishonourable conduct ...

Among all the regions of the earth, universal fame extols, distinguishes and places first Lombardy for its location, its density of towns and inhabitants, its beauty and its fertile plain. And among the cities of Lombardy, it distinguishes Milan as the rose or lily among flowers ... or the lion among quadrupeds and the eagle among birds ...

To make it easy to find material presented here, we shall divide this work into eight chapters: first in praise of the location of Milan and its *contado*; then, in praise, second, of its buildings, third of its inhabitants, fourth of its fertility and abundance of goods, fifth of its strength, sixth of its constant loyalty, seventh of its liberty and eighth of its dignity.

[From chapter 1] By reason of its site this prosperous city is recognised as glorious, because it is located in a rich and fertile plane, where the air is temperate ... between two wonderful rivers (the Ticino and the Adda) equally distant from it ... Are there marshes or putrid lakes corrupting the air with mists and stench? Certainly not. Rather, there are clear springs and fertile rivers ... In the city there are no cisterns or conduits bringing water from afar, but natural, fresh water, marvellous for human consumption, clear, healthful and close-at-hand, never failing in times of drought, and in such abundance that almost every decent house there has a source of fresh water, which is called a well ...

[From chapter 2] The houses with doorways onto public streets have been found to number about 12,500, in very many of which several families cohabit with a multitude of servants ... The courtyard of the commune ... occupies an area of 10 square perches[16] ... In the middle stands a marvellous palace, and in the same courtyard is a tower in which are the four bells of the commune. On the east side is the palace where the offices of the podestà and judges are, at the end of which is the podestà's chapel built in honour of our patron saint Ambrose ... On the south side is a loggia where judicial sentences convicting the guilty are read out ... A ditch of admirable beauty and width circles right round the city, containing not a swamp or putrid standing water, but fresh spring-water, full of fish and crabs. This ditch runs between a marvellous wall and an internal embankment ... Beyond the walls are so many suburban dwellings that they form a city by themselves. The main gates of the city are very strong and number six; the secondary gates, called posterns, are ten ... The main gates each have a pair of towers ... The saints' shrines ... number about 200 in the city alone, with 480 altars ... and it is wonderful to note how and how much the Virgin Mary is venerated in the city, for there are thirty-six churches built in worship of her alone ... In the city the bell-towers are about 120, and the bells over 200 ...

[From chapter 3] Both in the city and in the *contado* ... the number of the population grows daily and the built-up area of the city expands ... In the city there are ten houses of canons, not including the house of the cathedral canons ... and ninety-four chapels ... and six houses of monks and eight of nuns ... most of which, in terms both of numbers

16 The Milanese *pertica* was equal to about 650 sq. m.

and property, prosper ... There are also in the city and suburbs ... ten hospitals for the sick poor, almost all well-endowed with property. Among these the chief is the hospital of [Santo Stefano in] Brolo, very rich in valuable property and established in 1145 ... Here, as the brothers of the hospital attest, are sometimes counted, especially in times of food-shortage when numbers are recorded, more than 500 sick poor on the beds, and a greater number not on beds. All are fed at the expense of the hospital. Besides these, there are in its care over 350 infants in the hands of wet nurses. All of these ill poor people, except the lepers for whom another hospital is dedicated, are received there and are made strong again through kindly and copious provision of food and board. All the poor in need of surgery are diligently treated by three surgeons specially seconded for this and in receipt of salaries from the commune. No one in misery is turned away or refused ...

There are also in the city and *contado* houses of the second order of *Humiliati*, of both sexes, reaching the number of 220, in which a large number of people lead a religious life while working with their own hands. Among these the chief is that of Brera ... There are also large numbers of houses of poverty [i.e. mendicant houses]: first the numerous convent of the Dominicans, then the Franciscans (besides their main convent, there are nine houses of these in the *contado*), third the Eremitani, fourth the Carmelites ... All are fed by alms. There are also some houses of poor nuns; among them the most noble nuns of Sant'Apollinare of the order of San Francesco excel for their honesty, sanctity, nobility and numbers ...

I shall leave counting how many human souls live in such a city to whoever can accomplish it. If he could do it accurately, he would arrive at a number, I firmly believe, of about 200,000, as it is proven sure and diligently established that over 1,200 *moggia* of corn are consumed in the city alone every day; the truth of which can be certified by those who collect taxes on milled corn ... And why should the number not be as great, since in the city alone there are without doubt 115 parishes, among which are certainly some in which over 500 families live, and some in which about 1,000 live?

How many knights ready for war this city can field, I can say, because in the city and *contado* over 10,000 can with ease maintain war horses at the commune's command ... There are in the city alone 120 lawyers in civil and canon law, and their college is believed to have no equal in the world for size and learning ... There are more than 1,500 notaries ... [and] 28 expert medics, commonly called physicians ... [and] over 150 surgeons, of various kinds ... [and] eight grammar teachers, each with a crowd of pupils under their rods ... [and] over 70 teachers of elementary reading. The book-scribes, though there is no university in the city, exceed 40 in number, who earn their daily bread by copying books in their own hands. The ovens in the city, cooking bread for the citizens, are 300, as can be seen from the communal registers ... The retail wine-merchants, selling a wonderful wine of all kinds, are without doubt over a thousand ... [and] the butchers are over 440 ... [and] the fishermen who almost daily bring ... fish of almost every sort from the lakes and rivers in the *contado* are over 400 ... The innkeepers who accommodate foreigners for profit are about 150 in number. The smiths, who shoe horses, are about 80, from which number can be reckoned the number of horses and horsemen ... The makers of sweet-sounding, brass bells, which are fixed to the chests of horses (we don't know that they are made elsewhere) are more than 30, each of whom has many co-workers under him ... If I also wanted to describe the number of all manner of artisans, of weavers of wool, linen, cotton and silk, of shoemakers, tanners, tailors, smiths of all sorts, of the merchants who travel to all parts of the world for their merchandise and who play an important part in fairs in other cities, and of the peddlers and auctioneers, I believe that those reading and hearing this would be struck senseless in wonder ...

[From chapter 4] In our territory, fertile in fruitful produce, are grown such a large and so wonderful an abundance of many forms of grain, wheat, rye, millet, panic-grass, from which a sort of polenta is made, and every kind of vegetable, beans, chickpeas, lentils ... that they not only supply the food shortages of the city of Como, but, exported, also nourish the peoples of northern Europe ... An abundance of rape and cole are also grown, which bring not a little benefit to rich and poor alike in the winter. Our fields also produce an infinite and incredible abundance of flax ... Cherries, both bitter and sweet of every kind, are grown ... in such great quantities that sometimes over 60 carts a day are transported into the city, and from mid-May to mid-July they can be found for sale at any hour there. Likewise plums ... which are sold from the end of June until October. And at the same time as the plums begin to appear, so too abound the pears and summer apples ... then follow filberts, cornel-berries more suitable for women, jujubes and peaches ... figs and grapes of various kinds, almonds and nuts in incredible quantity, which citizens enjoy throughout the year after every meal ... There also grow chestnuts, both common and noble varieties, ... which are abundantly available throughout the year to both citizens and foreigners ... There are also gardens, flourishing throughout the year, producing abundantly all manner of fruitful aromas: cabbages, beets, lettuce, orachs, celery, spinach, parsley, fennel, dill, chervil, calamint, gourds, garlic, leeks, parsnips ...

The meadows are watered by fertile rivers and infinite spring brooks, and supply almost infinite amounts of hay for oxen, horses, mules, sheep and cattle ... because in the *contado* of Milan the meadows are so many that they supply us each year with over 200 cartloads of hay ... The numerous vines produce wines both sweet and sharp of all sorts ... white, golden and rosé, in such quantity that some families harvest from their own vines each year 100, 500 or 1000 carts of wine ... I have no doubt that there are many cities in whose territories all the vines could not produce the wine drunk by our flies alone ... The woodland and forest and river banks provide wood of various kinds suitable for building and other uses, and also the necessary firewood ...

The city overflows with ... the meat of all kinds of quadrupeds. It is noteworthy that, as I have carefully calculated with some butchers, on the days when Christians are allowed to eat meat, about 70 beefcattle are slaughtered in the city alone every day. As for pigs, rams, lambs, goats and other forms of quadruped, both domestic and wild, slaughtered by the butchers, I shall put a figure on them to whoever can tell me the number of blades of grass ... Moreover, the lakes and rivers in our *contado* bring to us all sorts of fish ... and enrich our tables during Lent. The rivers provide not only an abundance of fish ... but also, with their mills, which are over 900 in number ... feed so many Milanese ... And note that each mill wheel ... is said to mill so much grain each day as to feed over 400 men from the bread made from it ... I believe that there are many cities in Italy in which not as much bread is eaten by the inhabitants of both sexes as is eaten by Milanese dogs alone ... Salt fish of various kinds is brought in great quantities from afar by merchants from various places, as too is precious cloth of wool, linen, silk and cotton of all kinds, and salt, pepper and other spices from overseas ... All of which this most fortunate city, which might almost be called a world in itself, separated from the rest of the earth, distributes to other cities near and far ...

Within the city, general fairs are held four times a year: on the day of the ordination of St Ambrose [7 December], on the feast day of San Lorenzo [10 August], on the Ascension of the blessed Mother of God [in spring], and on the feast of San Bartolomeo [24 August]. To all these, countless numbers of merchants and customers come. Moreover, on two days each week, Friday and Saturday, in various parts of the city, there is an ordinary market; and, what is more, everyday, almost all things necessary to man are brought in great abundance to the piazzas and put on sale with shouting ... From which it is clear that, whoever has sufficient money in our city lives extremely well, for all things congruent to human pleasure are known to be at hand. It is also apparent that here ... every man, if he is healthy, can earn money and honour according to his own station ...

[From chapter 7] Many foreign tyrants have tried to install here the seat of their tyranny, yet the divine goodness, with the constant intercession of the blessed mother of our Lord Jesus Christ, in whose honour our cathedral is built ... together with that of our patron St Ambrose ... has often defended the city from tyrannical rage.

[From chapter 8] Two are the particular defects of this city, if I may say so: namely the lack of civil concord and of a port through which ships would be able to reach it from the sea ... To which I hope that the speeches of the just will remedy the first; the second could be remedied if the powerful of the city would apply the force in accomplishing this task that they exercise in destroying each other and in extorting money from their co-citizens to feed their own ill-will ...

It is clear from what has already been said, that our city has no equal in the world ... that it is almost another, separate world ... that it not only deserves to be called a second Rome ... but also that the seat of the papacy should be transferred here ...

2 A vision of Padua, c. 1318

'Padua is one of the few cities for which there exists a literary description from the medieval period'.[17] This description, by the early fourteenth-century

17 J. K. Hyde, *Padua in the Age of Dante* (Manchester, 1966), p. 29, and for the description, pp. 29–32, 42–3.

judge Giovanni da Nono, comes in the form of a vision given by an angel to comfort Egidius, the defeated legendary king of ancient Padua. The description needs to be handled with care, however: it is strongly stylized in its generic concentration on walls and public buildings; the walls mentioned are the old ones, which by the early fourteenth century enclosed under half the built-up area, and some of the 'palaces' mentioned are no more than covered markets. Moreover, the text has a 'strong sense of political mutability', with divine punishment for sin often being seen as the dynamic.[18]

G. Fabris, 'La cronaca di Giovanni da Nono (Visio Egidii regis Patavie)', *Bollettino del Museo civico, Padova*, n. ser., 10–11 (1934–9), 4–18.

I asked the angel in what form the city of Padua would be built. He told me: 'The fine wall of the city built by your Paduans will ... curve round for a mile like a horse-shoe ... and the water of the Bacchiglione and 'Tusena' rivers will flow round it ... The Paduans will place four royal gates in the wall. The first will be called the gate of the mill-bridge (Pontemolino), because thirty-four wheels, milling all sorts of grain, will be built alongside it. The bridge at this gate will exceed the other bridges of the city in beauty ... The second gate, towards the west, will be called the gate of San Giovanni delle navi ... outside this gate, at the head of the bridge, will be built of brick and stone a church of brothers and knights of the Hospital of St John the Baptist. It will also be near the port, for boats in which one can travel to Monselice, Este and the Euganei hills ... Through this gate will be led robbers and murderers and other criminals to a field, called Holy Field, in which justice will be done and they will be punished according to their crimes. The third gate, to the south, will be called the Gate of the Toricelli, for in this part of the city will be built many more towers than in any other part. By this gate will be built eight mill wheels which will belong to the city ... The fourth gate will be called the Gate of the Altinate bridge ... From here the road will go to the Porto Ognissanti, from where boats will go to Venice ... and next to this will be the Salt Port, for boats to Chioggia. From this gate merchants and others, both citizens of Padua and foreigners, will illegally and secretly transport foodstuffs to Venice ...

There will also be another fifteen minor gates ... Of these, the first will be called the Porta San Leonardo, which will have a most beautiful bridge, of one large, fine arch ... Beyond the cemetery of the church of San Giacomo will be a stone bridge, by which the commune

18 N. Rubinstein, 'Some ideas of municipal progress and decline in the Italy of the communes', in *Fritz Saxl 1890–1948*, ed. D. J. Gordon (London and Edinburgh, 1957), pp. 167–8.

of Padua will have two mill wheels, which eventually will be allowed to fall into ruin through rot ... The second will be called the Porta San Pietro, because a nunnery will be built at that church inside the city walls, almost next to the gate ... The third will be called the Porta de' Tadi, because that family's descendants will have their houses next to it. And there will be a large, beautiful bridge, with three wide arches, of white stone and brick ... The fourth will be called the Porta San Tomaso e Sant'Agostino, because opposite it, beyond the river in some marshland, a great church will be built by the Paduans for the Dominican order ... The fifth will be called the Porta del Castel di Ezzelino, for Ezzelino during his tyranny will build a castle there with a great tower ... The sixth will be called the Porta San Luca, for there will be built a church in honour of this saint ... The seventh will be called the Gate of the Counts of Padua, who will build their houses next to it. The eighth will be called the Porta Sant'Egidio on account of the church ... The ninth will be called the Porta Santa Giuliana ... The tenth will be called the Porta Santo Stefano, because of the monastery of nuns who walk elegantly in black habits and veils ... Through this gate Paduans will go ... to the great church of St Antony ... This great church will be built by fra Antonio, of the Franciscan order, first out of reeds, and later of stone. And on the eighth day after [the anniversary of] his death ... the citizens will recover Padua in June [1256].[19] On account of this act of divine grace received through the prayers of the blessed Antonio, the Paduans will establish that every year the friars there will receive L 4,000 to build this church, and that every year on 14 June, this saint's feast-day, all the clergy of Padua and all the guildsmen must carry large candles [there] at Vespers; and that on the octave of this feast-day ten horses must run a race for a prize of scarlet cloth [palio], and the fastest horse to the prize will win it, the next horse will have a hawk, and the third a cock ...

The eleventh gate will be called the Porta di Falaroto, after a man unable to achieve his ambition ... The twelfth will be called the Porta Braida ... The thirteenth the Porta San Matteo, because his church will be built nearby ... The fourteenth will be called the Porta Contarini, from the family of that name who will have their houses there ... Through this gate will be the road to the festival of San Bernardo, and to the district which will be called Porcilia, from which a great abundance of vegetables, pumpkins, cucumbers, gourds, onions and

19 Padua was occupied by a papal army on 20 June 1256 as part of the crusade against the allegedly vicious tyrant Ezzelino da Romano, who is later referred to in the passages by da Nono and Salimbene. St Antony of Padua died on 13 June 1231.

other foods will come to the Paduans. Oh, how many of the Paduan people on the first Sunday in May will go to the church of San Bernardo near the monastery of nuns ... I tell you in wonder that noble and common women, both on feast-days and work-days, will continue to go there, more to sin with men than for remission of sins, until the octave of this festival. And they will say that this is a beautiful festival, not out of love of pardon, but rather out of lust. Outside this gate, and also within the city walls, will be wooden houses in which countless women will live who, for modest sums of money, will indecently submit their bodies to any men whatever. The fifteenth gate will be called the Porta San Fermo, because of the church that will be built there ...'

After the angel had showed me the outline of the city, I said to him 'Lord, show me also what public buildings will be built by the Paduans'. And he told me: 'Fourteen public palaces will be built, some before the lordship of Ezzelino, some after. And of these some will be destroyed, and others will be altered. First will be the royal or communal palace, with a red tower, and in this great palace the Paduans will administer justice to all (which they will observe for only a short time, because love of money will turn them into perpetrators of every type of falsehood and stealers of other mens' property).

Second will be the Palace of the Council, which will be built after Ezzelino's death ... Also with this palace will be built a red tower, in which will be a place called the chancery, conserving all the public records. And in this palace, at appropriate times, a thousand men will assemble, and by a majority of those present all public business will be firmly approved. Under this palace[20] will be the shops of traders who sell grey Veronese cloth and other cheap cloth.

Third will be the podestà's palace, in which he will reside with his staff. And within this palace will be a courtyard, in which a water fountain will be set up. Under the palace, iron, both plain and worked, will be sold, as will cotton and all kinds of linen. But as one enters the first door of the palace ... one will find a terrible, fetid place, called Basta, where men will be placed who owe money to others, and almost all the criminals. And there will be ropes in place for torturing the criminals ...

The fourth palace will be called the Palace of Senators [*Anziani*] of the city of Padua, who will number eighteen ... and will advise the city, nor can anything be confirmed in the Greater Council unless it has been through their hands.

20 That is, on the ground floor.

Between this palace and the Palace of the Council will be a large tower, which will be called the Old Tower of the Anziani. This tower will be built by a family called the Campo Sam Piero and will in time be sold by them to the commune. At the top of the tower will be placed a bell, taken from the castle of Este, to ring the hours. When this bell breaks another will be put in its place and take its name from the Paduan *popolo*, and when it is rung hammeringly the whole *popolo* will assemble; but this name will perhaps not last long, for the Paduan magnates will organise offences against the *popolo*. Under this palace will be the stalls of salt-sellers and of men collecting gabelles and tolls for the commune of Padua. And inside the old tower will be the workshop of the goldsmith Silvestro, who will supply each year the lead ballots which will be necessary for taking votes.

Another ten palaces will be built around the Lawcourt (Palazzo della ragione), under which many kinds of things will be sold: under the two northern palaces, silk belts, gloves and things made with silk thread; under two others, to the west and north, salt pork, edible oil, Apulian and Paduan cheese.

One of the palaces, to the west, will be called the New Prison, and it will be very strong. This palace will be divided into three parts: in one will be placed men who owe others money or who owe the commune for fines or taxes, and this part can be likened to Limbo; in the second will be those who have committed some [minor] crimes, and this can be equated to Purgatory; in the third will be placed homicides, robbers, marauders and other criminals, whose crimes are manifest, and this dark part, where no light ever penetrates, you will truly be able to liken to Hell.

In front of and near this prison building, to the west, will be one of two palaces under which will be sold all manner of shoes and clogs ... and behind the prison will be the butchery, where will be sold fresh beef, wethers and pork.

Under the other two palaces, towards the east, cloaks and blankets will be made and sold. One of these two palaces ... will be demolished ... so that the piazza on which corn is sold can be widened, and later a fine palace will be built, opposite the doors of the podestà's courtyard, which will commonly be called the Fondaco delle Biade [Cornmarket] ...'

As my spirit delighted in these things that the angel of the Lord was showing me, I asked him again 'Show me, Lord, the main palace of the Paduans, in which they will administer the law'. And then he told me: 'Shortly before the arrival of Emperor Frederick, the Paduans will build their communal palace in some marshland, in which fisher-men used to catch many fish.[21] This palace will cover as much ground as a *campo*,[22] and its foundations will be laid of large, squared stones, tied together with lead and iron ... Around the outside will be balconies with paired columns of red stone. Four stairways of red marble will lead up to them ... At the top of each of these will be a door with a tabernacle supported on two large, red-marble columns. Halfway up the stairways will be doors, four in all, leading to the intermediate floor, between the ground and the large hall where law is administered. At the ground-floor level, looking north, will be shops selling "noble" cloths and sendal. And to the south will be the shops of leather-sellers. At one of the short sides will be built a prison, later called the Old Prison, with dark and horrible vaults ... On the north side of the intermediate level will be placed the shops of tailors who sew new garments, to the south the shops of men who scrape parch-ment and of some furriers. And at both ends of this side will be two store-rooms of the commune, in which its revenues will be placed ...'

3 Genoa in the late thirteenth century

The anonymous author of a poem on Genoa was a layman, but close to the church, resembling his contemporary Bonvesin da la Riva. His poems, some 150 in all, range in date from the 1290s to 1311, and include many on the themes of religion and work. His materialist enthusiasm for trade and trade-stuffs here, though, is only just contained within his religious orthodoxy.[23]

'Anonimo genovese', in *Poeti del Duecento*, ed. G. Contini, 2 vols (Milan and Naples, 1960), vol. 1, pp. 751–9.

Returning from Venice, the author lodges in Brescia and is asked by his host to tell him about Genoa, which the author readily does.

Genoa is a city full of people, and well supplied with everything. With its port on the sea it is the gateway to Lombardy. It is protected by narrow passes, and near and far by great hills which prevent it falling

---

21 This first palace is dated to *c.* 1160: C. G. Mor, 'Il Palazzo della Ragione nella vita di Padova', in *Il Palazzo della Ragione di Padova* (Venice, 1963), pp. 2–3. It was enlarged and made more 'majestic' in the early fourteenth century: C. Semenzato, 'L'architettura del Palazzo della Ragione', *ibid.*, pp. 31–2.

22 The Paduan *campo* was equal to about 3,863 sq. m.

23 On this poet, see most recently S. Epstein, *Genoa and the Genoese, 958–1528* (Chapel Hill, 1996), pp. 166–71; also L. Martines, *Power and Imagination: City-States in Renaissance Italy* (New York, 1979), pp. 87–93.

into foreign hands. No prince or baron has ever been able to bring it into subjection or to take away its freedom. It has a fine, beautiful circuit of walls, that circles it right round, with a bank outside the wall, since there is no need for a ditch. To the sea the city is much more accessible and it looks towards the West. The port in my opinion is beautiful ... but because nature gave it little anchorage, our ancestors and contemporaries have done such work as to create a marvel: to improve the port, a mole is built into the sea with stones, mortar and lime, and it cost more than a whole city is worth. On it always stands a great beacon, showing the entrance to ships ... There are mooring poles put in place, where ships lie, and a fine, clear fountain overflows with water. There is a church and an arsenal, which gives lodging to Pisans, and a great palace to one side which houses prisoners of war. The city is full from top to toe with palaces and buildings, and many other amenities of great value and splendour, with towers in great number, all adorning the city. In the city there is always a great abundance of merchandise from the Levant, overseas and all other places. Who could list all the types of precious brocades, sendals, velvets, cloth of gold, feathers, ermine, squirrel and other furs? Who could list all the goods that are brought there, the pepper, ginger and musk, the spices large and small ... the pearls and precious stones and marvellous jewels and other things that merchants bring from all parts? Whoever wanted to describe them would have too much to relate. And how the shops are set out along the streets! Those of the same craft are nearly all together. The shops are full of this fine merchandise ... And indeed, it pleases me more to see the shops open with goods on show, than to see them shut: on Sundays and feastdays, if it was decent, I would never want them shut, as I have great desire to look inside. There are so many different craftsmen, that anything you want you can have at once. If you have money on you, you can fit yourself out beautifully, such that when Lombards or others come here unexpectedly, the sight of these fine things empties their purses before they leave. The great delight of buying plucks their money away. One spicer here often has more pepper ... than another great city. Many are the men of mercy who aid the needy, giving great alms to friars and foreigners. [The poor of] all the cities of Lombardy, out of poverty and hunger, turn to them for pennies and ha'pennies to survive. And I believe that for this reason God has always defended and supported this city against many cruel events, and maintains it in great honour. So packed is the city with crossbows, and so skilled are its people in using them, that to

win wars it has enough for two other cities. Its shipping is so great
that it sails all over the seas, and so rich are its ships that each is
worth twice any others. And there are so many Genoese, and they are
so scattered across the world, that wherever they are they make
another Genoa. By their fine dress and furnishings, each man seems a
marquis; their maidservants and squires resemble ladies and knights;
their wives are so well-adorned that they truly look like queens, so
well supplied are they with *haute couture*[24] ... Of their feastmaking and
banquetting, their courts and revels, their nobility and honour, you
have never seen the like. The city is so packed with people ... and so
many are the foreigners, from inland towns and the coast, with ships
large and small, coming in loaded with goods, every day morning and
evening, that the roads are overcrowded ...

4 Public buildings in thirteenth-century Parma

The Franciscan friar, Salimbene de Adam, describes with ecclesiastical
emphasis the major building projects of his home town.

Salimbene de Adam, *Cronica*, ed. Scalia, pp. 759–60; ed. Holder-Egger, pp.
518–19.

1283: In this year the Franciscan friars of Parma built a beautiful
refectory in the *Prato di Sant'Ercolano*, where they resided, and where
Parma used to hold its markets and during carnival to have mock
fights with weapons.

In the same year, the Parmesans built a stone bridge over the river
Parma ... from the house of the Humiliati to that of the Dominicans.
They also built the city wall towards the hills by the river near the
hospital of San Francesco. Over the preceding years the Parmesans
had done many fine things in their city. They had completed the
upper part of the baptistery, up to its topping out; and it would have
been finished long before had not Ezzelino da Romano, then lord of
Verona, prevented it, for the baptistery was built only from Verona
marble. They also had the great [marble] lions made and the columns
in the main doorway of the cathedral, by the baptistery square and the
bishop's palace. Three great roads, wide and beautiful, were laid out:
one runs from the church of Santa Cristina to the communal palace;
another from the new piazza (where the podestà convenes public
assemblies) to the church of San Tommaso; and the third from the

24 *gran vestir.*

communal palace to the church of San Paolo. And along all these roads houses and beautiful palaces were built. They also built the very fine palace of the Captain [of the People] near the old palace, which had been built under podestà Torello da Strada [1221] ... In the same year they enlarged the new communal piazza and bought up, for the commune, all the buildings around the piazza; and they had to build another palace, with shops bringing revenue to the commune, on the site of the old palace of the Pagani family, a very beautiful building which I saw with my own eyes. Then the commune bought the very fine palace of lord Manfredo di Scipione, afterwards the meat market, and finally all the property in the area of the church of San Pietro, including the houses and tower of lord Ruffino de' Vernacci.

5 Public buildings in fourteenth-century Siena

Excerpts from two of Siena's rich series of chronicles allow us to follow its public building projects during the fourteenth century. Agnolo di Tura's chronicle covers the years 1300–51, while that of Donato di Neri continues from 1352 to 1373.

Cronaca senese attribuita ad Agnolo di Tura del Grasso, pp. 412, 415, 416, 428, 453, 454, 455, 457, 458, 488, 490, 498, 500, 507, 513, 518, 522, 525, 526, 537, 546, 547, 550, 551, 557–8, 561; *Cronaca di Donato di Neri e di suo figlio Neri*, pp. 569, 570, 585, 590, 591, 593, 594, 603, 634, 636, 646, 652, 654, 663, 679, in *Cronache senesi*.

1324: Siena was much grown in population, such that the city walls had been extended at Val di Montone ... and a gate, now called the Justice Gate, and many houses had been built on the city side of this gate. Now in May the Sienese decided that there should be more houses there, and that the 'savage', country-dwelling citizens created sixteen years ago, and those created in future, should live there.[25] So, many houses were built for new citizens ...

Siena bought from the prior of San Martino many plots that the church had outside the Val di Montone gate, that is between the gate and the new walls ... These cost L 500, and on these plots the commune of Siena built many houses for those who came to live in the city ...

In this year the drinking- and washing-troughs at Fonte Branda were made by the commune ... as was the roof-vaulting of the palace

25 Jones, *City-State*, p. 159; W. M. Bowsky, '*Cives silvestres*: Sylvan citizenship and the Sienese commune (1287–1355)', *Bollettino senese di storia patria*, 24 (1965).

housing the communal Biccherna[26] ... and the road from the old gate at Val di Montone to the new gate (called the Santa Maria gate) was paved ...

1325: The Sienese began to build a tower on the corner of the road called Malcucinato, which goes to Salicotto. This was begun on Saturday 12 October, and there was a great celebration in Siena. The canons and cathedral clergy came to bless the first stone, and they said prayers and psalms. The head of the cathedral board of works put some coins into the foundations as commemoration, and at every corner was placed a stone with Greek, Hebrew and Latin writing, so that the tower would not be hit by lightning or storm. With these foundations underway, the foundations were also laid for the palace of the podestà ... And on this site had stood the church of San Luca ... which the commune rebuilt shortly after on the Val di Montone road opposite the fountain.

1326: The commune of Siena bought nine houses in Salicotto from various people, at a cost of 2,500 florins. These were demolished to build the new communal prison ...

The Sienese began new city-walls, which start in Follonica and reached the Ovile gate, beyond the church of San Francesco, which will be within the walls, and the walls will then continue to Sant'Agostino and join the San Marco gate. And they have established the sites of the main gates. One will be on the road to Rome, and will be called the San Martino gate; to build this they bought the land from the monastery of San Barnaba at a cost of L 225, and today this is called the Porta Nuova. The second gate will be in Val di Montone, and is today called the gate of Justice, and is kept locked, for it is only used when executions are performed outside. And the third gate will be at the church of Sant'Agostino ...

The Sienese began a new, large prison, with a great circuit of walls, at the Malcucinato end of Salicotto, behind the podestà's palace ... And at the start of the work, almost all the clergy and religious of Siena were present, with musical instruments, saying psalms and prayers.

1327: This year the brick paving around the Campo was laid for the first time ...

Thursday 13 August, the Sienese began the foundations of the gate called the San Martino gate ... on the road to Rome. This gate will

---

26 The chief financial office of the commune.

join the new walls, which have been begun in order to enlarge the city because the population had grown so much.

1328: The new gate of the city of Siena, called the San Martino gate ... is now almost finished, and it is large and beautiful, a greater building than any gate in Italy ...

1329: Work continued on the walls of the prison that the Sienese were building in the via di Malcucinato: work had already progressed beyond the vaulting.

1330: The Sienese used to have a prison under the Alessi palace ... towards the Campo, and there were so many prisoners held there that they could not be numbered. So the Sienese pressed on with building the new prison in [the district of] Malcucinato, and it was now finished as far as the roof, so the prisoners were taken from the palace and put in the new prison on the night of 28 July. And the old prison became the salt office ...

The first podestà took up office in the new palace alongside Malcucinato and the Palazzo pubblico. There reside all the podestà's officials and judges, and there they administer justice. The palace was sufficiently finished for the podestà to go there, though work continued and it was soon finished. And the tower at the corner of this palace was not yet finished: work continued.

1332: The park running from the Porta Nuova to the Porta dell'Uliviera was made: it was small with large embankments, and was levelled and made as it is now.

1334: On the Campo, facing the palace of the podestà was a stone column called *El petrone*, at which corporal punishments used to be done, and there was a chain for holding those who were to be whipped. In May this column was destroyed by order of the commune. [Later the chronicler adds:] In former days, there was a column on the Campo, where those who were whipped were placed, and they were tied to it and stayed there for a time, then they were taken back to the prison or released ... and this was in the years before 1340.

1337: Above the council chamber [of the Palazzo pubblico], rooms were constructed for the Signori and their staff, and scenes from Roman history were painted outside them by Ambrogio Lorenzetti.

1338: Siena was at this time in a great and happy condition, and accordingly the Sienese began the great and noble enlargement of their cathedral church ... The commune bought many houses in the piazza Manetti and towards the road to build the entrance to the cathedral.

1339: The water conduits that collect and bring water into the Campo were begun this year, and the cost is to be met out of the revenues from the town of Grosseto.

1340: In the communal prison in Siena twenty-two prisoners, poor people, died in the two months of January and February ... Seeing that in the prison there were large numbers of prisoners and great sickness there, the Sienese established and built a hospital for the poor and needy in the prison, and many alms were offered to them. Nineteen poor men died in the prison in March and April, and another ten in May and June.

1340: Maestro Ambrogio Lorenzetti, painter, from Siena, painted Our Lady with the cardinal virtues, in the loggia of the Palazzo pubblico.[27]

1343: The Sienese had made many large conduits below ground to find water and bring it into the Campo. These conduits were started some time ago and run below ground for four miles outside the city. Many of these have not found water, but many draw it up in abundance ... and in April the Sienese began to build a fountain, not very big, in the Campo.

1344: The tower of the commune of Siena, which is at the corner of the podestà's palace, was finished this year, and is regarded as the most beautiful tower in Italy ... The communal bells, which were in the Mignanelli tower, were taken down in February, and in April the bell of the *popolo* was put in the new tower, while the other bells were put in the cathedral *campanile*.

1345: The Mappamondo in the Palazzo pubblico was done in this year by Maestro Ambrogio Lorenzetti.[28]

1346: The new walls of Siena, to enlarge the city, began to be built, on the perimeter of the park outside the castle of Montone ...

The livestock market used to be held on the Campo and was removed in October by order of the commune to the *piano di Fontebranda*, and then from there to the *piano di Val di Montone*, inside the gate and behind the Palazzo pubblico ... And many houses were bought up and demolished by the commune in December.

27 One of a series of *Maestà* paintings – the Virgin Mary in Majesty – made for the Palazzo pubblico in Siena, the most famous of which is that by Simone Martini.

28 A rotating map, now lost.

1346: The paving of the Campo was finished on 30 December, and it is regarded as more beautiful than any other piazza in Italy, with its beautiful and abundant fountain, its fine and noble buildings and shops all around.

1347: The paving of the *piano di Val di Montone* near the fountain was newly done in brick and mortar by the commune. 41,000 bricks were used. The commune bought land from several people at the market place behind the church of San Salvatore ...

1348: The great and noble building work of enlarging the Duomo of Siena was abandoned this year. It had been begun a few years earlier and the facade of the main entrance had already been erected ... and half of the columns and vault had been done ... And the masters who had contracted to build it were still owed 8,000 florins for their craftmanship, labour and workmen ... And because of the plague, it was suspended and taken no further because of the small population remaining in Siena, and also because of the low spirits and distress of those who remained. And the masters who had contracted to do the work almost all died, as did the citizens on the board of works ...

In Siena there was a miracle performed by the Virgin Mary, for which the commune began the chapel of the Campo at the base of the communal tower. Also at this time were begun the church of Santa Maria delle Grazie in Siena, in Camollia, and the church of Sant' Onofrio ... and many other oratories and shrines. The large bell of the commune of Siena was cast at this time ... weighing 17,777 lb [*sic*] ... and it stood on the Campo for quite a while, and then was installed in the communal tower.

1349: The paving around the Campo, up to a point marked by stones, was done by the commune in 1347. Now most of the paving on the lower side was done. Women carried earth to fill the Campo, which was very uneven, and a garland of stones was laid around the paving.

1350: The Sienese built a loggia in the market of Val di Montone, costing more than 500 florins.

1352: The fountain at Mandorlo, behind the hospital of Santa Maria della Scala in Siena, outside the gates, was begun at this time, and took one year to complete. The commune paid 50 florins, and seven neighbouring groups of inhabitants paid L 223 ...

In July the foundations for the chapel on the Campo were begun, and the [government of the] Nine put two gold florins into the foundations. And six large candles were lit there. It was dedicated to the Madonna's feast day in September.

1357: The commune built the Santa Lena hospital, near the Ovile Gate, and paid all the costs.

1359: The conduit of water to the Biccherna was laid at this time, made of lead, at a cost of L 58.

1359: The clock of the commune of Siena was installed at this time. It cost L 858 and is placed on the communal tower on the Campo.

1360: The fountain in the communal prison was built, costing L 144.

1361: The internal window spaces of the council chamber of Siena were painted. The masters were Giovanni di Benedetto and Lippo di Memmo, painters, of Siena. It cost L 152 ... The Madonna painted at the top of the portal outside the Camollia gate was painted: the commune had this done.

1363: The [government of the] Twelve had the Sienese defeat [of the 'English company' in Valdichiana] painted in the palace in the crossbow room. The painter was [Lippo di Vanni].

1370: The choir of the Duomo of Siena was finished in August ... it took four years to do ...

The loggia of the bishop's palace, which was at the corner of the cathedral and extended into the road, was demolished, so as to have more space for the display of reliquaries, and the commune compensated the bishop. And it was decided that the neighbours who benefited from this should pay, and a farm was bought for the bishop.

1372: The *Signori* and captain of the *popolo* of Siena ... had placed over the door of the Palazzo pubblico [statues of] two she-wolves with a lion in the middle. This was on 27 June.

1373: The livestock market began to be held on the *piano* of Fonte Branda, outside the gate, and a large ditch was dug and a pen made, on land belonging to the canons and the shoemakers' guild.

1374: The bishop of Siena had 1,356 florins from the commune to compensate for the loggia that the commune had demolished to build the chapel of San Giacomo in the Duomo ...

1376: The commune built the house for the prison warders. It cost 134 florins.

6 The enlargement and decoration of the Doge's Palace, Venice, 1297–1422

A sequence of deliberations from Venetian councils here provide an outline of the development of the Doge's Palace, including the enlargement of the Hall of the Greater Council – an 'enormous chamber' and 'one of the largest great halls in Christendom'.[29]

G. B. Lorenzi, *Monumenti per servire alla storia del Palazzo Ducale di Venezia. Parte 1: dal 1253 al 1600* (Venice, 1868), pp. 6, 7, 12, 17, 20, 26, 27, 31, 33–4, 34–5, 38–9, 48, 52, 56, 57.

29 August 1297

The motion was carried that all the prisons that are above the Palace, because they corrupt the air and bodies with infirmity, are to be removed and placed under the Palace, where the Doge, Counsellors and leaders of the [Council of] 40 think best ...

14 July 1301

Because the Hall of the Great Council is not sufficient for those who are members of the Council, the motion was carried that the said Hall be enlarged over the courtyard, and it is added to the statutory duties of the Rialto Officials that they are to enlarge the Hall with the income of the commune's rents, beginning as quickly as they can ...

11 December 1319

Because the church of San Niccolò of the Palace is totally devoid of paintings, the motion was carried that the proceeds from the property of the deceased madman, Andrea Coppo, which the commune is heir to, should be spent on the work of painting, in the said church, the history of the pope [Alexander III] when he was in Venice with the emperor [Frederick I].[30]

28 May 1323

That to ornament the Palace entrance, it is entrusted to the Procurators of St Mark that they are to have the images and the [figure of

---

29 A. Martindale, 'The Venetian Sala del Gran Consiglio and its fourteenth-century decoration', *Antiquaries Journal*, 73 (1993), 79. For the history of the Palazzo ducale, see most recently P. Fortini Brown, 'Committenza e arte di Stato', in *Storia di Venezia* (7 vols, Rome, 1992–7), vol. 3, and the bibliography there.

30 This 'history' – in fact 'an almost entirely fictitious version of the events' (Martindale, p. 98) – was an important part of Venice's sense of itself as a 'third force', able to pacify pope and emperor, and subject to neither.

the] lion, which are above the door to the stairs ... gilded, with the revenues of the Palace rents.

11 March 1326

To alleviate the prisoners who are excessively cramped in our prisons, more prisons are to be created below the Palace ... and if space is taken from the stewards' lodgings, they are to be provided with a residence elsewhere ...

17 December 1340

As various opinions are voiced in the matter of a new hall for the Great Council, some saying that it should be built over the hall of the Lords of the Night,[31] others that the present hall can be enlarged by removing the lodgings, chancery and small courtyard ... such that the hall would grow by a third and more, which would be sufficient for all time ... in order that it can be decided which of the two paths it is better to take, it is proposed to elect three expert advisers[32] to examine and advise which is better ...

28 December 1340

The said advisers, having examined the conditions of the present hall of the Great Council, and the hall of the Lords of the Night ... and having had several discussions with master-craftsmen who in matters of this sort are well-trained ... advise that the hall ... should be constructed over the hall of the Lords of the Night in the following way: it is to be made as long as is the hall of the Lords of the Night ... and as wide as the existing gallery over the columns looking towards the canal. But although the said masters claimed that the hall will be stable without placing columns over[33] the hall of the Lords of the Night, the advisers recommend that for greater stability as many columns as will be deemed necessary should be placed over the hall of the Lords of the Night ... And that a long, open stairway should be built from the head of the new hall, looking east, to the embankment, as wide as the gallery that is over the piazza ... For the construction work, the advisers consider about L 950 to be necessary, not including the cost of gilding and painting, which could be L 200.

---

31 Who policed public order at night.
32 *savi.*
33 *super.*

22 January 1344

As the upper prisons, because of work on the new hall of the Great Council, will have to come down, and it will be necessary to rehouse the prisoners, because the inmates of the upper and lower prisons amount to so many that they cannot be placed together owing to the confined space, and also because those using the stairs which are to be built up to the hall will smell the full stench of the prison, it is proposed to elect three advisers to find and examine places where the prisoners can be held and housed in the future.

5 July 1348

Because, as times change, so there are changes of custom, according to what is recognised to be the common good, and as knowing and understanding the time and acting according to prevailing conditions is always judged most beneficial ... the advisers have decided that, as the commune of Venice is more greatly burdened in expenses than in income, provision is to be made for the good of the commune and the conservation of the *status* of the city ... And ... as the work at present on the Hall of the Great Council is at such a point that it can easily enough be suspended for the moment, and as for this work L 50 are put in deposit every month, which can be of much use in other projects, they unanimously advise that ... the other side of the Hall, towards San Georgio, be wholly roofed, if there remains part to be covered ... with as much haste and speed as possible, finishing the office of the Lords of the Night and other rooms of the doge's staff, which require little expenditure. And that, once these are completed, the deposit of L 50 should cease ... and that, once all the walls around the Hall are cemented, all the scaffolding, poles,[34] masonry, wood and everything else around the Palace should be wholly removed, such that the piazza remains clear, and that all officials, notaries and workers involved in this should cease work.

24 February 1350

At the time of the plague it was decided to suspend work on the Hall of the Great Council because, owing to the apparent reduction and paucity of people, the hall was not thought necessary to contemporary times. But now the blessed Lord has repaired our *statum* to a better condition than was hoped, and the number of our nobles is so recovered and multiplied that what did not seem necessary during the

34 *tabanelle* and *antenelle*.

plague is now clearly recognised as opportune. So it is proposed, both for the aforesaid reasons, and because it does not seem honourable to abandon such magnificent work unfinished ... and because much wood and other materials which had been bought and prepared for the hall are being ruined by delay ... that the work on the hall should proceed to completion ...

16 December 1366

That the image of ser Marino Falier located in the new Hall of the Great Council be totally removed, and a vacant space, coloured azure, be left, with written in white letters 'This was the place of ser Marino Falier, beheaded for treason', taking down his [coat of] arms. [Motion carried]

That the image ... be altered in the following way: that the head should hang down, cut off at the neck, and it should be written that he was beheaded for treason. [Motion not carried][35]

22 July 1400

Because it is the honour of our doge and council that such an important work as the new Hall of the Great Council, in that part which can easily be finished, should be completed, and as all clearly see the place in which it was planned to put a balcony looking towards San Giorgio remains empty, greatly deforming the hall ... the motion is carried that this balcony should be made in the form in which it was long ago depicted and drawn ...

25 May 1409

As the upper hall of our Great Council is much ruined in paintings, it is proposed that our Salt and Rialto Officials should have the pictures repaired ... at the smallest possible cost, not exceeding the sum of 200 ducats.

35 Doge Marin Falier was deposed and executed in 1355, allegedly for plotting with the Venetian *popolo* against the nobles – to liberate Venice of 'patrician pestilence' and the 'o'ergrown aristocratic Hydra', in Byron's phrase – but in fact for his continued adherence to a policy of war against Genoa beyond the point when it could be afforded (G. Pillinini, 'Marino Falier e la crisi economica e politica della metà del '300 a Venezia', *Archivio veneto*, 5th ser., 84 (1968)). Part of the repression that followed his execution was the removal of his image from the series of doge-portraits in the Hall of the Greater Council. It is significant that the decision goes in favour of effacing the portrait rather than transforming it into *pittura infamante*.

21 September 1415

As among other magnificent works built in our city the new Hall of the Palace is wonderful and remarkable, and this is evident from the fact that all the lords and notables who come to our city desire greatly to see it because of the fame of its exceeding beauty ... And if this is the truth considering its size and decoration, nevertheless the same cannot be said of either the access or the approach to the Hall, because the route via the stairs is most unsightly, covered and dark, such that, when any distinguished person wishes to see it, he or she is led through the Quarantia and the small door, rather than through the main doorway. And to complete such beauty, and for the repute and honour of our city, it is necessary for access to the Hall to be in a different form, as our government has already had it investigated, such that it will greatly please everyone, when the work is done of building a stone staircase ... with its foot by the church of San Niccolò ... and it will be an open and uncovered route up to the balcony, to the great enlightenment and embellishment of the Palace, in which work there will be less expense than many perhaps think. So, it is proposed ... that the work can proceed ...

9 July 1422

Having had careful consideration for the suitable and useful conservation of the new Hall of the Great Council, because, as is well known, the paintings of the Hall are daily falling down causing great deformity, some definite provision needs to be made for the perpetual fame of such solemn work and for the honour of our government and city, to keep this Hall in a proper and honourable condition, such that any damage to the pictures be quickly repaired. It is therefore proposed that the Procurators of St Mark, in order to have the paintings repaired and kept constantly in good order, be instructed to engage and keep a suitable and appropriate master-painter ... spending on his salary 100 ducats per year, from the money collected in rent from the shops under the palace.

7 Making space for sermons: Florence, 1296

The guild responsible for the cathedral building project proposes moving a hospital.

G. Pampaloni, *Firenze al tempo di Dante: Documenti sull'urbanistica fiorentina* (Rome, 1973), pp. 57–8.

6 June 1296

Before you, lord Priors of the Guilds and Standardbearer of Justice of
the Florentine *popolo*, whom it becomes, out of duty of office, to
provide for and procure the beauty and honour of the city of Florence,
especially as regards the greater honour of the Florentine Duomo, it
is expounded on behalf of the consuls of the Calimala guild and of the
members of the Opera [Board of Works] of Santa Reparata, as follows.
The piazza of the Church of St John the Baptist and Santa Reparata is
narrow and can hold few people, such that when sermons are being
given there by the bishop or other prelates or friars, and when festival
ceremonies are held there, people cannot easily be accommodated or
stay there to hear the word of God. It is therefore petitioned that you
see fit to approve the enlargement ... of the said piazza in the
following way, namely, that a certain hospital of St John, which is to
one side of the piazza, in which little hospitality is provided, be
removed from there (which can easily and reasonably be done, as it is
said to be there at the pleasure of the bishop and the commune), and
eventually be relocated and established just outside the gate of the
new road of the swordmakers, on land belonging to the commune ...
or in some other place in which it will seem appropriate to build the
hospital. And this as the protection of this hospital belongs to the
commune of Florence. Also once the hospital is removed, the men
whose houses will have aspect onto the piazza (and will therefore rise
in value and price) are to be compelled, in whatever manner will be
thought best, to pay a sum of money for each house, as declared by a
decision of good men chosen by the lord Priors and the Standardbearer ...

All of these things are to be implemented by the officials deputed
to recovering the rights and properties of the commune, to whose
office belongs the creation and laying of roads and squares ... Item, it
is ordained that the tombs that are around the church of St John be
raised, removed and placed elsewhere.

8 Commune and new cathedral: Perugia, 1300

Though the Italian communes developed strongly the secular architecture of
town halls and civic squares, they also devoted much attention and expense
to their main civic churches, starting with the cathedral.[36]

36 Jones, *City-State*, pp. 292, 440–7.

M. R. Silvestrelli, 'L'edilizia pubblica del comune di Perugia: dal "Palatium communis" al "Palatium novum populi"', in *Società e istituzioni dell'Italia comunale: l'esempio di Perugia (secoli XII–XIV)* (Perugia, 1988), pp. 590–1.

22 March 1300

The following was established and ordained in a general assembly of the artisans of all the guilds of the city and suburbs of Perugia, convened in the usual fashion in the cloister of the Franciscan friars of Perugia:

As the commune of Perugia has attended carefully to the beauty of its city, both of the palaces of the *popolo* and commune and of the piazza, it is appropriate that this commune, which among other communities of Italy has shone forth in the serenity of its faith, should adorn its cathedral church where divine offices are continuously celebrated. Therefore we declare as law that the Perugian cathedral church is to be built wholly and anew on behalf of the commune of Perugia, in praise of God's name and of the glorious martyrs Lorenzo and Ercolano, to whom the said church is dedicated. This rebuilding is to be done as will be decided by the consuls of the guilds, the experts whom they call on, and the masters. The supervisor of all the necessary rebuilding work is to be fra Bevignate of the Benedictine Order, who is expeditious and experienced in such projects. The guild consuls are to elect two good men ... into whose hands all the revenues of the new church and its Opera [Board of Works] are to pass: they are to make all the expenditures necessary to the Opera, and are to render account of all income and expenditure to the Captain of the *popolo* and the consuls every two months for as long as the work lasts, and a notary appointed by the consuls is to register these revenues and expenses. Fra Bevignate, however, is to be maintained in food and drink at the expense of the lord bishop and the canons of Perugia. The consuls are to set as they please the salary of the Operai and the notary, and the [money for] fra Bevignate's clothing ...

In aid of this expenditure, we order that all the church's offerings during this work and all the revenues of the canons are to be assigned to the Opera, reserving to the canons and their chaplains and servants the costs of a moderate diet, as decided by the bishop.

9 Granary and oratory: Orsanmichele, Florence

Giovanni Villani, *Nuova Cronica*, ed. G. Porta (Parma, 1991), vol. 3, pp. 150–1 (XII.67).

1337: On the 29th of July work began on erecting the piers of the loggia of Orsanmichele, in large and well-formed stones of ashlar, whereas before they had been thin, of brick and badly supported. Present at this commencement were the priors, the podestà and the captain, with all the members of the Florentine government in great formality. And they planned that above should be built a large, magnificent palace with two vaults, for storing and administering the annual grain-supply for the people. And the building project was assigned to the guild of Por Santa Maria, and the gabelles of the piazza and grain market, and some other gabelles giving a small revenue, were earmarked for the project, so that it could be finished more quickly. And it was ordered that each guild of Florence should take one column and on it have an image of the saint of that guild, and that each year on the feast of their saint the guild consuls and the craftsmen should make an offering, which should be dispensed to the poor by the Society of Santa Maria of Orsanmichele.

10 Concealing a butchery: Pisa, 1382

E. Cristiani, '*Decus edificiorum pisane civitatis* (1381)', *Bollettino storico pisano*, 47 (1978), 183–4.

27 November 1382

The lords Anziani of the Pisan popolo have provided for the beauty of buildings in the city of Pisa, attending especially to planning the city more honourably to the advantage of its citizens and inhabitants, and decorating it with a more handsome kind of building ... and ... they have ordained, giving an example of better construction to other citizens ... that Giovanni di Neri Berrettini, spicer and citizen of Pisa, wishing to enlarge the living quarters of his house or tower, situated in Pisa in the district of San Michele in Borgo, on the corner towards the Torre di Brachio, which has one frontage on the borgo, the other in the city butchery, and one side on land belonging to Giovanni, the other on the public street that leads to the butchery, may and is licensed to take in and occupy from the public roadway that runs from the *borgo* to the butchery where beasts are slaughtered ... as much as the length of one brick or tile only, and on this space ... he may freely, legally and with impunity build and construct some stone stairs by which there may be access and ascent into the tower or house ... as, from this licence the beauty of the *borgo* is especially increased, on account of the concealment of the butchery ... by the stairs, and this site is made to look more attractive to passers-by ...

11 New church building: Bologna, 1390–2

A taste for *grands projets* did not fade in the second half of the fourteenth century, as shown in the building of a new church in Bologna: 'a huge urbanistic operation ... without parallel in terms of scale until the twentieth century', involving the demolition of existing churches, houses, towers and streets. The resulting church, which progressed in the fifteenth century but was never finished, came to supplant the cathedral itself (dedicated to St Peter) in terms of site (on the main square) and functions. San Petronio, whose tomb lay in the church of Santo Stefano, had been adopted as a patron of the city in the thirteenth century, but this association strengthened in the fourteenth century, with official processions, miracles [31], and a two-week fair around his feast-day (4 October). Although the chronicles stress the combination of civic elements (the foundation stone) with religious (funding through indulgences), in fact the project represented an attempt by the urban government to appropriate the cult of San Petronio: the government chose the site and assigned funds to the project (draining other pious causes in the process), no clerics were on the Board of Works, and the chapels were allocated to government magistracies, guilds and prominent families.[37]

Matthaei de Griffonibus Memoriale historicum de rebus bononiensium, ed. L. Frati and A. Sorbelli, *RIS*, vol. 18, pt. 2, p. 83; *Corpus chronicorum bononiensium*, ed. A. Sorbelli, in *RIS*, vol. 18, pt. 1 (4 vols), vol. 3, pp. 403, 413, 439, 440.

1390: The houses opposite the *Ospedale della Morte* were demolished in order to start building the church of San Petronio. Supervisors of the work were the notary Andrea di Giuliano and the wool merchant Georgio de' Bonsignori.

The tower which was opposite the *Ospedale della Morte* fell down, but it fell because it was undermined, pinned, and then set fire to, and it was brought to the ground because it was impeding work on San Petronio. This was on Saturday 9 April.

On Wednesday morning, 7 June, the first stone was laid in the foundations of San Petronio ... This stone was brought from [the

37 M. Fanti, 'La Basilica di San Petronio nella storia religiosa e civile della città', in *La Basilica di San Petronio in Bologna* (2 vols, Bologna, 1983), vol. 1, pp. 9–30.

cathedral of] San Pietro and was consecrated there, and was carried by two Standardbearers of the *popolo* ... accompanied by the *Anziani* and colleges and all the clergy of Bologna. And the bells rang out when the stone was laid, and the shops were kept shut until terce. On this block were sculpted the arms of the commune of Bologna.

1392, 4 October: A chapel was built at San Petronio ... and there mass was said on San Petronio's day by the abbot of San Felice, the newly elected bishop of Bologna. And this was the first Mass ever said in San Petronio.

1392: In the name of God, his mother and all the saints of heaven, here below I shall make record of how, on 25 November, were read out the privileges brought back to Bologna by its ambassadors to Pope Boniface in Rome. The bells of all the churches rang out and the pardons granted us by the Holy Father were read out. And they were these: he granted 'the jubilee' [indulgence] to the commune of Bologna and to the country-dwellers, to all the territory held by the commune ... starting next Christmas and lasting until the following Easter. And he wanted the following conditions to be followed: the bishop of Bologna is to appoint twenty confessors, who are to hear confessions and to give penances; everyone who wants this indulgence has to visit nine churches, namely San Pietro maggiore, San Sigismondo, San Giacomo, Santo Stefano, San Domenico, San Procolo, Santa Maria in monte, San Petronio and San Francesco; everyone who wants this indulgence should place on the altar of San Petronio half of what one person would have spent in going to Rome for eight days, and this money is to be used for work on the church and in buying books and vestments that are needed there; also, each person who comes to visit the feast of San Petronio may have the same pardon as is available at Ascensiontide in Venice or at San Francesco in Assisi, that is of the sin and the punishment.

＊

12 The rise and fall of urban towers

'The definitive decline of the tower as a noble symbol was signalled by the opening of shops at its base and the construction of external stairs, things unthinkable in the classic structure which was that of a stronghold, as isolated as possible and connected to the outside only by a narrow, raised little door served by a retractable wooden ladder'.[38]

38 Balestracci and Picinni, *Siena nel Trecento*, p. 100; and in general see Jones, *City-State*, pp. 211–12, 316, 320–1, and below, p. 142.

a. *Statutum lucani communis an. MCCCVIII* (Lucca, 1867, repr. 1991), p. 287.

If during my term of office any person of the city or suburbs of Lucca builds or causes to be built a tower, whose height exceeds the tower of the sons of Paganello, Baratella and Boccella ... or that of the sons and grandsons of Bongioro as it now is, I [the podestà], having measured them, shall absolutely prohibit it from exceeding that measure. And I shall not permit towers already made and begun ... to be raised or built above the measure of those towers. And within one month ... I shall have all the towers in the city inspected by good and worthy masters, and those that I find taller than the said towers I shall have destroyed within two months at the expense of their owners ...

b. *Statuti della città di Roma*, ed. C. Re (Rome, 1880), pp. 114–15 [1360s].

If from any tower or house taller than five *palariae* are thrown stones in any battle, fight or affray, the tower or house is to be confiscated to the city fisc, except that, if the owner wishes, he may redeem the tower or house for L 50 ... but if stones are thrown from a house jointly owned among several kinsmen in a battle or affray of one or more of the kinsmen, he in whose cause the stones were thrown is required to redeem and to pay the said penalties ...

c. *Statuta communis Parmae* (Parma, 1855–6), p. 472.

So that the men of Porta Nova wishing to come to the communal piazza to assist the commune and to maintain the podestà and the honour of the city, may come safely and without any impediment, and lest anyone might obstruct them, as has often been done by enemies of the commune and of the Guelf party[39] ... the podestà is to have the whole tower and arch of the Ildizoni [family] destroyed to its foundations, and is to have the road opened up in a straight line going from the Porta Nova along the communal canal to the communal piazza ... and this at the expense of the men of Porta Nova, whether of the city or territory ... [1266]

d. *Matthaei de Griffonibus Memoriale historicum de rebus bononiensium*, ed. L. Frati and A. Sorbelli, in *RIS*, vol. 18, pt. 2, p. 82.

1389: The tower of the Rodaldi family, which was opposite the houses of the Bianchi family, fell to the ground and destroyed four houses,

39 *pars Ecclesiae.*

two belonging to the sons of fra Bagarotto de' Bianchi, one to a merchant, Giorgino Cospi, and one to Enrico da Ferro. Giorgino later bought the site and built on it a most beautiful residence.

e. *Statuti di Perugia* (1342), vol. 2, p. 363.

As cities, castles and fortresses acquire great beauty and sometimes benefit from towers, and to knock them down in any way seems a disfigurement of the city, we decree and ordain in perpetuity that no one in the city and *contado* of Perugia ... may sell, donate, bequeath or give in any other way any tower in the city and suburbs to be demolished or destroyed ... and if he contravenes, he is to be punished with a fine of L 200. And from henceforth, no one is to dare or presume to demolish or destroy any tower in the city or suburbs, on pain of L 1,000, for each tower ... And from henceforth no one is to dare or presume to undermine ... insert windows in or do any alteration to any tower as a result of which it might fall down or be in danger of collapse ...

13 On the magnificence of his buildings: Azzone Visconti

Galvano Fiamma (1283–c. 1344) was a Dominican of the convent of Sant' Eustorgio, Milan, which he entered in 1298 and where he rose to become lector in moral philosophy. Staunchly pro-Milanese, he wrote extensive works of history and hagiography. He became the confessor of the lord of Milan, Lucchino Visconti, and chaplain of Archbishop Giovanni Visconti. He has suffered from a bad reputation as an apologist for 'tyranny' or as a 'nasty plagiarist' (Hyde).

Gualvanei de la Flamma, *Opusculum de rebus gestis ab Azone, Luchino et Johanne Vicecomitibus*, ed. C. Castiglioni, in *RIS*, vol. 12, pt. 4 (Bologna, 1938), pp. 15–16. There is a translation of this passage in L. Green, 'Galvano Fiamma, Azzone Visconti and the revival of the classical theory of magnificence', *Journal of the Warburg and Courtauld Institutes*, 53 (1990), 101–3.

Azzone Visconti, seeing that he was now at peace with the church and freed from all his enemies, turned his heart to making his house glorious, for, as Aristotle says, it is a magnificent work to prepare a dignified house. For the people, seeing marvellous residences, stand dumbfounded out of admiration ... and believe the prince to be of such power that he cannot be attacked ... Moreover, it is necessary for the magnificent prince to build magnificent churches, whence Artistole says ... that honourable expenditure, that which the magnificent prince makes, pertains to God. Therefore, Azzo Visconti began to build two magnificent structures: first ... the marvellous chapel in honour of the Blessed Virgin Mary, and then magnificent palaces suitable for his residence.

The chapel of the Blessed Virgin Mary is within high walls and arched over three vaults. There are marvellous images of gold and blue, of wonderful workmanship. In the principal chapel, where the main altar is, there are grills of metal and gems, images from the life of the Virgin Mary, and wonderful windows ... The choir is paved in ivory ... There are two pulpits of ivory in the middle of the choir, very lofty and tall, the sight of which is stupendous. There are many altars with ornaments in gold and silver, and other such things that cannot easily be written or spoken of. There are chalices of great weight, vessels of porphyry with silver details for offering holy water. There are relics of many saints ... Among other things, there is a small cross decorated with precious pearls, on which is the sign of the holy cross; when thrown into the fire, this cross sprang back intact, and when brought out in rainstorms or tempests it drives away all harm.[40] To the side of the chapel is a round bell-tower of brick, decorated from the top down with little marble columns, which is a great delight to see. On the summit is an angel, made of metal, holding a flag with a viper.[41] And though at the top of the bell-tower there are many bells, there is one admirable clock, for it is a very large bell that strikes twenty-four times according to the twenty-four hours of the day and night ... which is highly necessary for all conditions of men.

No one can adequately describe his palace buildings. Among other things, there is a great tower with several floors having rooms, chambers, galleries, washrooms, gardens and much else, decorated with various paintings. At the foot of the tower, and all round it, are many furnished rooms with such marvellous painted decoration that the world hardly has more beautiful buildings. There are bedchambers with exceedingly noble furnishings, and doors within doors,[42] with trained doormen, lest easy entry be made to him without licence. In front of the door to his chamber is a large cage ... enclosed on each side with copper nets: here, there are all sorts of small birds, singing tunefully, which is not only beautiful but wonderful to behold. In various cages are different kinds of animal: a lion, bears, monkeys, baboons, and many other such. Among birds, he has an ostrich, in

40 Cf. doc. 32.
41 The Visconti family emblem.
42 'succession of doors': Green.

whose belly over 200 eggs have been found. At the side of this large cage, opposite the small birds, is a large hall, exceedingly glorious ... where are painted Vainglory ... and illustrious pagan princes of the world, such as Aeneas, Atilla, Hector, Hercules and many others. Among them is only one Christian, Charlemagne, along with Azzo Visconti himself. These figures are decorated in gold, azure and enamels, so beautifully and with such fine workmanship as would not be found in all the world.

In addition, there are two quick-flowing fountains, supplied by conduits, which through various channels spread water within the walls of a courtyard. In the middle [of the courtyard] is a column, at the top of which is an angel holding a banner bearing a viper, and under whose feet are four lions' mouths, and from there the water flows down. In the basin of the fountain are various kinds of fish. On one side of the fountain projects the beautiful cloister, where there are images of ships and other figures depicting the Punic War; on the other side is an exceedingly pleasant garden, with flowers and leaves, where there are lake- and seabirds never seen here before. Rising up over this garden is a tall palace, at the base of which is a store-room, with rooms for servants above ... At the other side of the fountain is the chapel already described.

14 The Sienese Opera in financial difficulties, 1299–1310

Siena was 'a city in which civic pride was unable to come to terms with economic reality'.[43]

G. Milanesi, *Documenti per la storia dell'arte senese* (3 vols, Siena, 1854), pp. 163–4, 166–7, 170–1, 175–6.

11 February 1299

To you, lords of the Nine, governors and defenders of the commune and popolo of Siena, the Supervisor[44] of the Board of Works[45] of Santa Maria, Siena, proposes and says that in the Opera he has no money to carry out any further work, and therefore, if it please you to provide so that the Opera can work as before, such that the *maestri* do not take on other work, which would cause the Opera to fail in its duty, and if

43 Balestracci and Picinni, *Siena nel Trecento*, p. 112; and see Jones, *City-State*, p. 247.
44 *Operaio*.
45 *Opera*.

it please you to provide ... for the Opera to continue its work, so that the work is not abandoned, which would not bring honour to the commune.

15–16 March 1299

The council of the Nine: having seen the petition to them on behalf of ... the Supervisor, and considering that it was decided by the Council of the Bell ... that the Nine should provide for the Opera from communal funds ... up to the feast of Saint Mary next August ... for these two months of March and April an order should be made to the treasurer of the commune ... to pay to the Supervisor ... L 200 to be spent in the said work ... Item, it is ... decided that the Supervisor carry out a review of the masters working for the Opera and ... all those who are not competent should be dismissed, such that the expenses of the Opera are reduced ...

28 November 1310

Let it be known to all that, as it pertains to the office of the Nine to have care, concern and love for the Opera of the Blessed Virgin Mary ... and regarding the ending of unnecessary expenditure which burdens the Opera, while accepting necessary expenditure ... having heard and carefully inspected the provision taken by those elected and deputed specifically to provide for the benefit and advantage of the Opera ... the Nine have decided, considering the Opera's income, resources and expenses, that it should proceed with all care and promptness in making and having made the mosaic work which is started, and in the work of the new, large panel of the Blessed Mary the ever-glorious Virgin, such that they are completed as quickly as possible, and that to do and complete all the works there should remain only ten masters, of the best and most useful, and no more, and that all the other masters should be dismissed and removed from the said works, as the income, resources and revenue of the Opera are not sufficient to sustain so many intolerable expenses ...

Cronache senesi, p. 313

1311: The Sienese had a beautiful and rich panel made for the main altar of the cathedral, and the painting of it was finished at this time. It was painted by master Duccio di Niccolò of Siena, one of the ablest painters of his day ... And the Sienese conveyed the panel to the cathedral on Wednesday 9 June, with great devotions and processions, with the bishop of Siena ... all the cathedral clergy, the monks, the *Signori,* civic officials, the podestà, Captain and all the worthiest citizens in order, with lighted candles in their hands, and, after them, the women and children. They all walked in devout procession around the Campo, while the bells were ringing out a gloria. And all this day the shops remained shut, and throughout Siena many alms were given to the poor, accompanied by prayers and orisons to God and his mother, the ever-virgin Madonna Mary, that, as the city's advocate and protectress, she might aid, preserve and increase Siena in peace and good state, and avert every danger and evil against it. And so the panel was placed on the main altar in the cathedral. The back of the panel is painted with part of the Old Testament and the Passion of Christ, and the front with the Virgin Mary with her son at her neck and many saints at her side, and all is adorned with fine gold. It cost 3,000 florins.

15 *Pittura infamante*

An anonymous Florentine chronicler gives one of the few descriptions of defamatory painting. The victim's response to this insult is then developed into a story by the contemporary *novella*-writer Franco Sacchetti.

a. *Diario d'anonimo fiorentino,* in *Cronache dei secoli XIII e XIV,* ed. C. Minutoli (Florence, 1876), p. 340.

Today, 13 October 1377, work was begun on plastering the façade of the podestà's palace and on painting the head and body of the traitor Messer Ridolfo da Camerino, traitor to Holy Mother Church, to the *popolo* and commune of Florence and to all its allies. Likewise he was painted on the façade of the Army Pay Office. He is depicted upside down on the gallows, suspended by the left foot, at the top. By his left side he has a siren, by his right a basilisk. At the bottom, on his head, he has a large mitre. He is tied at the neck by a devil. And he has parted both his arms and is giving two fingers to the Church and to the commune of Florence, as he betrayed the Pope and Florence.

b. Franco Sacchetti, *Il Trecentonovelle,* no. 41, in F. Sacchetti, *Opere,* ed. A. Borlenghi (Milan, 1957), pp. 159–61.

Ridolfo da Camerino was painted in Florence, to shame him, when he fell into disgrace with the commune. When he was told this, he said, 'Saints are painted: so, I've become a saint' ...

After a time, some Florentine ambassadors were sent to him, and to them he did two things. First, having invited them to dinner in

July, he had lit behind them in the hearth a great fire, as if it were January. The ambassadors, feeling through the summer heat the painful effect of the fire on their backs, asked Messer Ridolfo why he kept a fire lit by the table in July. Messer Ridolfo replied that he did this because, when the Florentines painted him, they had him depicted without stockings on his legs, as a result of which his legs had got so cold that never since then had he been able to warm them up, and so he had to keep a fire lit nearby. The ambassadors smiled a little, but were almost struck dumb.

Following the meats came boiled capon and lasagna, and Messer Ridolfo [secretly] ordered that his own bowl should be prepared so far in advance as to be lukewarm, while those of the ambassadors should be brought to table scalding hot. So, when the bowls were brought to the table, Messer Ridolfo confidently began to take whole spoonfuls. The ambassadors, seeing him do this, were led to think that they could do likewise, and as a result the first mouthful burned their palates, such that one began to cry, and the other to look at the ceiling and sigh.

Messer Ridolfo said, 'What are you looking at?'

'I'm looking at this ceiling – it's so well made. Who did it?

'Maestro Blow-on-Your-Food did it. Don't you know him?'

The ambassadors got the message and let their lasagna cool off. Later they said to themselves, 'Haven't we done well: we rush to paint lords as if they were porters, and he has really shown us what we deserve'.

And so, mocked, they returned to Florence where, when the story was told, Messer Ridolfo was thought to have given as good as he got.

16 Saintly gates

Paintings on city gates served several functions at once, asserting the city's identity, encouraging respectful public behaviour, honouring the city's patron.

a. *Statuti di Verona del 1327*, ed. S. A. Bianchi and R. Granuzzo (Rome, 1992), p. 593.

We issue as law that on all the gates of the commune of Verona, of the city and its suburbs, whether open now or opened up in the future, there shall be painted in the name of God and of the blessed Virgin Mother, a picture or pictures of the glorious Virgin Mary, with her merciful son in her arms, and of Saints Christopher, Zeno our city's protector, and Peter with the keys in his hands. And the same thing should be understood as to be done on towers built over the city ditches.

b. F. Filippini and G. Zucchini, *Miniatori e pittori a Bologna: Documenti dei secoli XIII e XIV* (Florence, 1944), p. 169.

24 April 1389

We order you ... general depositary of the money and resources of the commune [of Bologna], to pay L 2 10s from the commune's funds to Michele di Giovanni from France, painter, who yesterday at the request of the syndic of the commune ... painted on the façade of a house situated outside the gate of the Strada Santo Stefano ... the arms of the commune, with two lions and the banner of the commune.

17 Symbols of communal strength: lions

Many communes kept lions in captivity. These were living symbols. In Venice they symbolized St Mark, that city's patron; in Florence and Perugia they symbolised the Guelf party (the Angevin/papal alliance) to which those cities adhered; and everywhere they symbolised near-regal status.[46] The cities took pride in their lions, appointing paid officials for their upkeep, housing them close to the seat of power, identifying their breeding with the success of the city, publicizing their fertility, and using pups as diplomatic gifts to foreign powers, carefully recording their pedigree and origin. But whereas an individual city might have one or two lions, lords like Azzone Visconti had a whole menagerie of exotic beasts [13].

a. Giovanni Villani, *Nuova cronica*, XII.67 (p. 150).

At the end of June 1337, six lion cubs were born in Florence to the old lioness and to her two young daughters. This, according to ancient pagan augury, was a sign of the great magnificence of our city of Florence; and certainly around this time, it was at a peak of its power ... The commune made gifts of these lions, when they had grown somewhat, to friendly lords and cities.

b. Matteo Villani, *Cronica*, ed. G. Porta (Parma, 1995), vol. I, p. 691 (V.68).

3 August 1355: Four lions were born in Florence, two males and two females. One of the males was given to the duke of Austria, who asked the commune for it, the other to the lord of Padua.

46 Jones, *City-State*, pp. 356–7.

c. G. B. Lorenzi, *Monumenti per servire alla storia del palazzo ducale di Venezia* (Venice, 1868), no. 33, pp. 10–11.

15 September 1316

To the eternal memory of persons living now and in the future, and in order that it become known to all: in this year, in the dogeship of doge Giovanni Soranzo ... in the courtyard of the ducal palace, under the portico ... a male lion and a lioness were living together in an enclosure or cage ... These animals had been sent to the doge, when small, by Frederick, king of Sicily. The lion carnally knew the lioness and impregnated her, in the usual fashion of animals to mount each other ... and this was seen by many people. The pregnant lioness carried for about three months ... and early on 12 September ... when it was almost day, she gave birth, naturally as animals do, to three lion cubs, alive and furry, who, immediately they were born, began to move and run around their mother in the enclosure, as was seen by the doge and almost all Venetians and people from elsewhere who were in Venice on that day, who ran up to see this near-miracle. And one of the animals is male, the other two are female.

d. J. P. Grundman, *The Popolo at Perugia 1139–1309* (Perugia, 1992), p. 444.

[1299] Wishing to keep the lion, which the commune of Perugia has, uninjured, and lest those who injure it escape without punishment, we establish and ordain that if anyone kills the lion in any manner, he is to be punished and fined by the commune L 500 ...; if he attacks the lion in some other way, causing bloodshed, he is to be punished and fined L 100.

18 Symbols of communal strength: *carrocci*

The identity and power of cities was also asserted through mobile structures. Many cities, especially in Lombardy, Emilia and Tuscany, had *carrocci*: these were massive painted wagons, drawn by several pairs of oxen and bearing a tall mast on which the communal banner was raised.[47] The *carroccio* had both practical and symbolic functions. In warfare it provided a focus: it led armies on the march, and, when drawn up in a protected, eminent position in sieges and battles, it intimidated the enemy and acted as a rallying or reference point for troops. But more important were its functions as a symbol of the city's strength and unity, and strength *in* unity. The *carroccio*, it is argued,

47 H. Zug Tucci, 'Il carroccio nella vita comunale italiana', *Quellen und Forschungen aus italienischen Archiven und Bibliotheken*, 65 (1985).

precisely because it was not a chivalric banner held and paraded by knights on horseback, enabled sentiments of common loyalty to overcome social divisions between the knightly and non-knightly classes. It was a symbol of the city, and of the city's just war: patron saints were depicted on the wagon (though not on the banner); it was kept in the cathedral between campaigns; and its departure was marked by prayers and processions. The *carroccio* embodied the authority of the commune, indeed personified it, as some *carrocci* were given names. For this reason, capture of the *carroccio* was a sign of defeat and dishonour, and the return of a captured one a sign of pacification. However, the *carroccio*'s fortune followed that of the independent city-state: its heyday was in the period from the late eleventh to the early fourteenth centuries, and thereafter it was used, if at all, only for ceremonial functions, for example, the reception of visiting dignitaries.

a. Salimbene de Adam, *Cronica*, ed. Scalia, pp. 84–5, 305; ed. Holder-Egger, pp. 60, 213.

1229: In August the Bolognese besieged the castle of San Cesario and captured it in the sight of the Modenese, Parmesans and Cremonese who were there with their armies. And one night there was a great fight between them and the Bolognese ... and there was a great slaughter of men, footsoldiers and knights, on both sides. The 'battle grew hot' [Judges, XX.34] against the Bolognese: wearied and exhausted, they turned their backs on the enemy and fled, leaving their *carroccio* and all their equipment in the field. The Modenese wanted to take the Bolognese *carroccio* with them back to Modena, but the Parmesans did not let them, saying that it was not good to do all the harm they could to their enemies, and that this would be an indelible affront and would provoke many evils. The Modenese believed the Parmesans, as friends and collaborators, and left the *carroccio* in Piumazzo, a Bolognese castle.

1247: [While ill from the cold in the infirmary of the friary at Sens, Salimbene is visited by some of the French friars of that convent who have heard by letter that Salimbene's home town of Parma had captured the Cremonese 'cart'] And they asked me what was the value of the 'cart'. I replied that the Lombards call this sort of cart their *carroccio*, and that if the *carroccio* of any city is captured in war, that city considers that a great affront has been done to it, just as, if the *oriflamme*[48] were captured in war, the French and their king would consider it a great affront.

b. *Chronicon estense*, ed. G. Bertoni and E. P. Vicini, in *RIS*, vol. 15, pt. 3 (Città di Castello, 1908–37), p. 45.

48 Sacred banner.

Saturday 6 September 1281: An exchange was made, amid great celebration, of captured *carrocci* between the communes of Parma and
Cremona, because peace had been made between them. Because of this,
the commune of Cremona began to act well, because they beautifully
prepared Parma's *carroccio*, which was called 'Biancardo', repainting it
and having a new banner made for it. And the Cremonese brought the
carroccio into Parma's territory, with three pairs of oxen covered in
purple and sendal, and at a place called Reginoldo gave it back to the
commune of Parma. And on the following Sunday, the Parmesans
took their *carroccio* to Parma with great celebration and rejoicing ...
And the Parmesans had the Cremonese *carroccio*, which was called
'Berta', painted and well-prepared, with a new banner, restored to a
better condition than when the Parmesans captured it in Victoria at
the time of Emperor Frederick.[49] The podestà of Parma, with the
knights and people of the city gave this *carroccio* back to Cremona at
Ragazzola, near a ditch on the border, along with three pairs of oxen
covered in scarlet and sindon.

19 *Nettezza urbana*: legislation

Statuti di Bologna dell'anno 1288, vol. 1, pp. 135, 136, 137–8, 139, 140–4, 147–
8, 149, 155, 165.

We order that no one throw or cause to be thrown into the piazza of
the commune of Bologna or in the crossroads at the Porta Ravennate,
any stinking or dead animals or rotten fish or shellfish or any filthy or
stinking thing or foodscraps, sweepings, dung or prison filth. Item,
that no butcher, or anyone else, is to slaughter ... any animal within
four houses of the piazza, nor to pour onto it the blood or intestines of
any animal ... And whoever contravenes any of the above ... is to be
fined 40s for each occasion ...

We establish that no one is to keep outside the columns or walls of
houses around the commune's courtyard any wood or barrel-hoops which
might obstruct passage through the courtyard ... and whoever contravenes is to be fined 100s ... The same penalty is to be incurred by
those who keep any straw, hay or rushes in houses within 25 perches[50]

---

49 Victoria was the name that Frederick II gave to a fortified encampment he built
   during his siege of Parma in 1248. The *carroccio* had thus been held in captivity for
   over thirty years.
50 The Bolognese linear perch was equal to 3.8 m.

of the communal piazza, except that innkeepers and taverners can keep enough hay in bundles as needed for their guests ...

We establish that no one is to have over the public thoroughfare a bucket, bowl, water conduit or spout or any other thing of any material that might fall into public space during the day and which might contain dirt ... and if anyone contravenes, he is to pay 100s... and to repair any damage done. And no one by day is to throw or pour water from the solar or balcony or house, and if any is thrown or poured, those who live in the house are to pay 20s. ... Item, that where there are latrines or water-conduits around the piazzas or streets in which there are sewers, they are to be channelled underground into those sewers, lest they leak onto the piazzas ... Item, that it is licit for anyone to channel water from the water-courses that flow through the city and suburbs for the purpose of cleaning house-drains and other filth at appropriate times. We also say that no one may have a water-conduit or rain-pipe unless he or she has at least half a foot of their own land beyond the spot where the water falls (this applies to those who are not on the roadway) ...

We establish that no one should throw lime or lime-water within the suburbs or elsewhere, except into the Aposa [river]. Item, that all water of dye-works or anything else pertaining to dying that contains filth ... or tanners' waste[51] ... is not to be disposed of in the city or suburbs except into the Aposa or Savena, when it flows, and then only at night ... Item, we prohibit the placing of skins for stripping or soaking in the public streets at any time between Easter and Michaelmas, except in the Savena, when it flows into the Aposa. Item, that no one is to beat skins during the day in the squares or porticoes in front of shops ...

We establish that every person who has an alley where there are latrines is to keep it walled in, in stone, lime or daub, up to the height of the house, or at least to 12 ft. And this is to apply in alleys which have houses on each side and walled-in sewers ... such that passersby receive no injury. Except that they can be opened at the time of cleaning, but once cleaning is done, they should be closed and kept closed. Item, we say that no wall or building is to be built cross-wise into any communal alley, so as to obstruct the flow of water or dirt, and if any is so built, it is to be removed. And anyone who contravenes in any of the above is to pay L 10 as penalty.

51 *multitium.*

We order that no person is to throw grape-skins or dung or horses, asses, dead meat or other filth along the walls or into the city ditches, and whoever does so must remove it and if he does not, he is to be punished [with a fine of] 20s, and is still required to remove it. The same penalty is to be incurred by anyone who takes a horse, mule, ass, dog, cat or other animal for skinning on the bridge of the Aposa or in the Aposa … and by whoever carries any of the said filth, or anything else, into the courtyard of any friars or religious persons.

We say that no one is to make gut strings in the city or suburbs, or within 1 mile of the suburbs, on pain of L 10.

Item, that no one is to break up tallow or fat in the city or suburbs, day or night …

Item, that no one is to bury any animal bones or to cook them to make dice or for other purposes, in the city or suburbs. And whoever contravenes will be fined for each occasion L 100. Also that no one is to have in the city any kiln in which gypsum is cooked, or to make paint in the city or suburbs … on pain of 100s … Also that no kiln or workshop or refinery is allowed in the city in which silver or other metal is refined …

Item, that no one presume to have a latrine near the city gates or over the city walls or near the walls and ditches that is visible from the side … and whoever contravenes is to be fined L 25 and is required to remove or close it …

Item, that no one is to obstruct the flow of rain water or other water that usually runs into sewers or alleys … Item, that drains that flow along a wall where there is a latrine are to be walled in, lest the filth, once it is on the ground, be seen from the public streets and squares … Item, we say that all alleys and latrines which are on the piazza may not be opened … so that material can come out, in the months from March to September. Item, we say that where several houses have latrines over an alley they are to have it cleaned and washed by the Savena once a year … Item, that any landlord of a house which has an alley or latrine which is open at the top of the alley or is badly walled, such that stench comes to passers-by or neighbours, is to be fined L 25 … Item, that no one with a latrine over an alley is to put in it any bath water or … refuse or food scraps, and whoever contravenes is to pay 20s … Item, that there may not be any latrines in any alley less than one foot wide and four feet long …

We establish that whoever has paving in front of their houses is to maintain it, and if it is broken, to redo it at their expense … on pain of 20*s*. Item, that if any paving is to be laid or repaired in front of houses built on land belonging to some other person, then this is to be done half at the expense of the landlord and half at the expense of the householder. And this is to apply to both clergy and laity, and if a cleric refuses to contribute, he is to be put outside the protection of the commune of Bologna ... And we say that paving is to be level and smooth, such that horses and pedestrians may cross it without danger ... Besides, if there remains any unpaved road in the city or suburbs, and a majority of the neighbours of that district wish to pave it, then it is to be paved and all the neighbours are to be compelled [to contribute] ...

We order that everyone must remove, from the street in front of his house mud, earth, grape-skins ... and all other dirt ...

We order that each district of the city and suburbs that has a neighbourhood well is to have it cleaned twice a year and is to keep by the well a water-container of stone or wood, a basin or cask, of at least 7 *corbe* capacity.[52] And each of these wells in or near the street is to have, at the expense of the neighbours, a windlass or wheel or frame with an iron chain and an iron-bound bucket fixed to the chain so that it cannot be removed.

We ordain that the Savena weir, and the branch of the Savena and the bridges through which water flows into the city, are to be maintained and repaired by the commune ... We give permission to the Franciscan and Dominican friars to take water from this channel as is customary, and to the nuns of Sant'Agnese ... And that this water is to flow into the city so that half goes to the quarters of Porta Stiera and San Procolo, and half to the other two quarters. Item, that this water is not to flow through the city from mid-May to mid-September without the consent of the podestà ... and Anziani of the *popolo*, except in the event of fire ... and except that from mid-September to mid-May it can flow once or several times a month to clean and wash the districts, as and where necessary. And that in these months no one can take water from the said channel to clean his alley except on only two days per month ... and at night only, not by day ..., saving that at all times some of this water is to flow along the Strada Castiglione for the honour and benefit of those exercising the craft of wool-manufacture and dyeing. And on Sundays and other solemn days, water is not to be channelled through the city ...

52 The Bolognese *corba* was equal to 78.5 lt.

We order that no innkeeper, male or female, keeping wine for sale, may have as a sign any fruitbearing tree or any banner or pennant of linen, silk or wool, and whoever contravenes is to be fined 100*s.*

20 *Nettezza urbana*: enforcement

The exceptionally rich Bolognese judicial sources allow us to follow the enforcement of hygiene regulations by special officials who toured the city looking for infractions.

Archivio di Stato, Bologna, Comune, Capitano del Popolo, busta 806, fols 18, 18v, 19, 20, 21.

1376

1 October: Bonino di Mengobrio, second-hand clothes-dealer of the Capella[53] of San Lorenzo, found by me Antonio, notary and official, selling wine at retail, and for an inn-sign having a branch of a fruit tree, contrary to the statutes.

8 October: Martino di Viano, inn-keeper of the Capella San Toma, found by me to have measured and sold three quarts of wine, and of each of them to have made bad measure [*assagium*], contrary to the statutes.

13 October: Domenico di Nanne da Viadagola and Filippo di Cavalino, inhabitants in the Capella SS Jacomo e Filippo, found by me to have a pipe over the public roadway from which water fell into public space, contrary to the statutes.

14 October: Catarina, wife of Cantino da Burgo, and Christina, wife of Rigo di Azzolino, of the Capella of San Felice ... found by me washing cloths in the Reno canal contrary to the statutes.

Mengo di Vitale, ploughman of the Capella of Santa Maria di Mascarella, found by me ... driving a cart through the city of Bologna and not holding his hand on the reins nor being next to the oxen, contrary to the statutes.

20 October: Giovanni di Dindolo, cooper of the Capella San Procolo, found to have barrels and buckets on the street that leads to the church of San Pietro, blocking passage, contrary to the statutes.

22 October: Viano di Bartolomeo, butcher of the Capella of Santa Caterina di Saragossa, found to have thrown a dead dog into the butchers' alley, contrary to the statutes.

53 City district.

21 Clean water: the Perugia Fountain

Water-supply, like grain-supply, was a vital task of government, indeed 'a symbol of the city, of urbanistic grandeur',[54] and one that attracted monumental building projects. The Perugian *Fontana maggiore*, which was protected by the criminal law from damage and misuse, has been described as a 'Perugian encyclopedia in stone', of unmatched 'importance in the history of late medieval secular iconography'.[55] Formed of two basins, each decorated with relief sculptures by Nicola and Giovanni Pisano, it both declared civic identity and symbolically organized central urban space. Its many figures – including images of the months, the zodiac, the liberal arts, and scenes from the Bible, myth and history – include the legendary founder of the city (Eulistes, a Trojan knight who came to Italy before Rome was founded) and its patron saint (Sant'Ercolano, the martyred bishop of the city who defended it against barbarian attack). These are placed among images of other founder-figures, lawgivers and announcers of new religion: Romulus and Remus, Moses, Solomon, John the Baptist. The rich correspondences between these figures proclaim Perugia's identity as the *'alter ego'* of Rome, the bearer of a tradition at once Roman and pre-Roman, and the purveyor of law and religion, of victory and abundance.

Statuti di Perugia (1342), vol. 2, pp. 263, 268.

So that the fountain of the piazza of the commune of Perugia be kept clean, we enact ... that outside or along the steps of the fountain five or seven stone basins or vases should be made, in which those taking water from the fountain are to wash the jugs and other vessels, and especially the bottoms of the vessels, before they go to the fountain. And if anyone takes water from the fountain in any other way, he is to pay 5*s* on each occasion. And around the spouts of the fountain, in the most appropriate places, are to be made thirteen watertight, copper vases which are to be fixed to the fountain by iron chains, with which water can be taken for the purpose of drinking or filling vessels. And whoever disfigures any of these vases will be punished with a fine of 100*s* and be obliged to repair the vases ... In addition, we wish that no man do any injury or violence to any woman going to collect water, while collecting water, or returning from doing so; and if anyone contravenes, he is to be punished in double the penalty incurred for such injury or violence committed elsewhere ... And no one should dare or presume to take to the fountain any barrels to collect water, nor ...

54 L. Riccetti, '"Per havere dell'acqua buona per bevere". Orvieto: città e cantieri del duomo, secoli XIV–XV', *Nuova rivista storica*, 78 (1994), 253.

55 J. White, 'The reconstruction of Nicola Pisano's Perugia fountain', *Journal of the Warburg and Courtauld Institutes*, 33 (1970), 70.

put barrels into the fountain or any other oiled, musty or dirty vessel, on pain of 100s. And no one is to take or send a horse, donkey, ass or any other animal from the steps towards the fountain, on pain of 100s. And no man may take water from the fountain for mixing mortar, slaking lime, making walls ... or paper ... [for filling] water-tanks or for washing clothes, on pain of 20s. We also order that no one dare or presume to get into the fountain, or bathe in it, or wash their feet, legs or head or ... face or hands in it, and who contravenes shall be punished in L 50 for getting in and bathing ... 10s for washing face or hands ...

And to have greater abundance of water in the city and suburbs of Perugia, we order that at each gate of the city be placed two cisterns, one inside the city, and one in the suburb, as large as possible, at the expense of the commune, in those places that the Priors, with experts and master-craftsmen think best ...

22 Public health: salaried doctors, supervised hospitals

From an early stage, Italian communes began to make interventions in the area of public health,[56] but whereas the cities of the north and centre appointed their own public physicians and inspected their own hospitals, towns in the south had to ask for permission.

a. *Statuti di Perugia* (1342), vol. 1, p. 280.

We are led to enact that the Priors ... are to establish, for the commune of Perugia, a good and sufficient foreign physician, expert in the setting of broken bones, for a fixed period and at a suitable salary ...

b. *Statutum lucani communis an. MCCCVIII* (Lucca, 1867, repr. 1991), p. 327.

We establish that a physician is to be appointed by the treasurers of the commune of Lucca ... who knows how to mend broken arms ... and other limbs, of poor people of the city ... without fee, and who is to have whatever benefit, remuneration or exemption that the treasurers decide to give or assign him.

c. *Codice diplomatico brindisino*, ed. A. De Leo and G. M. Monti (2 vols, Trani, 1940–64), vol. 2, pp. 284–5.

17 September 1381

To your royal majesty, [from] the community of your faithful men of

56 Jones, *City-State*, p. 447.

your city of Brindisi, convened by the town crier at the order of the *baiulo*[57] and judge before the cathedral in the customary fashion ... We need a physician learned in surgical science to heal wounds and to achieve results in the practice of his profession. We have no physician except maestro Piero di maestro Ivano [Giovanni], who practises in both medical sciences (physical and surgical), nor can he easily attend to all the diseased bodies when they need to be treated. There is, though, among us maestro Ivano, son of maestro Jacutio di maestro Ivano, deceased, who was a capable doctor, experienced in surgery, and this maestro Ivano, as one who grew up under his tutelage and expertise in medical science, is experienced in the practice and conduct of surgery. He is a freeman of your domain of the city of Brindisi, is personally bound or obliged to no one except your majesty, was born in legitimate wedlock, is of legal age and was born in this city to a loyal family of good repute and behaviour, but because of poverty and certain bodily defects from which he suffers cannot easily come to your Majesty's sight or to your feet ... We are therefore led to petition for him ... that your Majesty might deign to grant him licence to practise in the profession of surgery, and might commit examination of him and the reception of his oath to the said maestro Piero or to whomever else your Majesty appoints.

d. *Statuti di Perugia* (1342) vol. 1, pp. 174–5; vol. 2, pp. 446–7.

The podestà, Captain and priors are obliged to maintain all the goods and properties of the lepers of the Hospital of Colle, and of the Hospital itself, and to conserve them for the benefit of the hospital, especially that property given to the hospital by the commune of Perugia ... And if they find any leper in the city, suburbs or *contado*, according to the judgement of medics whom the podestà and Captain are obliged to consult, the podestà and Captain are to compel such a leper to leave the city and go to live at the said hospital ... Moreover, the podestà and Captain, before the end of May [each year] are obliged to ensure that the prior of the hospital elects an almoner there, one of the hospital's servants, the most suitable they can find, and the prior of the hospital is to distribute the alms among the lepers and the healthy as he thinks fit. And the almoner and prior must render account of the office twice each year to the priors of the city of Perugia ...

The consuls of the merchants of the city of Perugia are obliged in good faith ... to maintain in good state the goods and property of the

57 The chief royal official.

hospital of the Sant'Angelo gate ... And each month all the consuls, or at least two of them, are to go to the hospital, to visit it, to inquire of the lives of the carers and to give advice and assistance, as they see is required ... and they are to give to the poor of the hospital a jug of oil out of the revenues of the Mercanzia ... And whoever is prior of the hospital must reside there continuously and every year give account to the consuls of the merchants. And if the prior has been good, then he should be confirmed; and if he has not been found good, then he should be dismissed ...

23 Public subvention of education: Lucca, 1348–79

In the mid-fourteenth century Lucca provided communal funds for all levels of education, elementary, secondary and university (though the latter were subject to cutbacks).

P. Barsanti, *Il pubblico insegnamento in Lucca dal secolo XIV alla fine del secolo XVIII* (Lucca, 1905), pp. 195, 196–7, 200–1, 202–4.

14 August 1348

To you, lords *Anziani* of the commune of Lucca, is reverently expounded by Master Filippo, teacher of boys, that he, who has long been in the service of the Lucchese in teaching their children, because of the misfortune of the current hard times, has been reduced to great poverty. Nevertheless, he does not want to cease teaching boys, but because of the poverty of the city and the paucity of boys, he cannot live from the boys' fees alone ... Therefore he petitions that, out of your accustomed goodness and benevolence, you might order that some provision be paid annually to him from the commune, on which he might live and continue in teaching.

On this Bonannus Cianfognini said and advised that Master Filippo should have from the commune every month L 3 ...

Having put this motion to a ballot among us, as is usual, and finding no one against, we establish and provide that Master Filippo, for a term to last at our pleasure, should have from the commune L 3 ... as, because of the plague occurring this year, almost all the teachers of boys are dead, and lest the boys go wandering like vagabonds here and there and, from the lengthy absence of teachers, become ignorant in reading and writing ... and having considered the loyalty and praiseworthy life of Master Filippo ...

15 February 1353

In the said council, it was reported by the *Anziani*, that the following petition had been delivered to them:

To you, lords *Anziani* ... is expounded with reverence by Nello Specchielli from Florence, abacus teacher ... humbly requesting that some provision from communal funds be made to him, as pleases you ... And the said Nello offers to hold a school in the city of Lucca and to teach boys, and others who wish to learn, and to welcome any person. And in so far as some assistance is given to him, he will shortly invite enrolments from pupils and will stay to hold a school in Lucca. If he does not receive any benefit, because of the small number of pupils who are at present placed under him, he would not be able to stay and would have to leave for other parts ...

Ser Niccolò da Ghivizzano, citizen of Lucca, one of the members of the council, rose and advised ... that the *Anziani* should enquire into the quality and condition of Master Nello, and, if they found him competent and able to teach this skill, then they could assign him a grant from communal funds of L 5 per month for two years ...

Having held a secret ballot of the whole council, as is usual, the motion was carried by 44 ballots found in the parti-coloured 'Yes' box, as against the 6 found in the yellow 'No' box.

27 January 1379

To the lords *Anziani* and Standardbearer of Justice of the *popolo* and commune of Lucca, Giacomo di maestro Giovanni, Giacomo di Piero, Masseo di Aitante and ser Niccolò da Decimo, all citizens of Lucca, humbly expound ... that their sons and others, who have been accustomed to learn the teachings and science of logic in the church and *studio* of Sant'Agostino, cannot reach perfection in this science because the teacher, Maestro Giovanni, has given up teaching, apparently because the commune of Lucca no longer wishes to pay him his customary salary or provision. For this reason, these young men cannot reach perfection in this science, which is the illumination of all others ... Therefore, they humbly have recourse to you, given that the said Maestro Giovanni will be content with any salary appointed by you to give his usual lecture ... So, as much for the honour of the city as for that of your citizens, lest they have to go elsewhere to hear this science, may it please you to provide Maestro Giovanni with some salary ... especially as no loss will result to the commune of Lucca, as from the gabelles on food and clothing, which they would not pay if they went elsewhere to study, the commune receives more than it pays out in the master's salary.

17 September 1347

We, the college of *Anziani* ... wishing that the city of Lucca fill with virtuous men, especially in the liberal arts, of which it is denuded at present because of the poverty of the citizens and because of other setbacks which militate against the wellbeing of the city, we ... provide that from this day forward all Lucchese citizens, and even *contadini* ... who wish to study civil or canon law or medicine at Bologna are to have from the commune of Lucca ... from its revenues each year for the next five years, starting on 1 October, 10 florins for each student ... Assurance must first be given from trustworthy people that they ... will persevere in their studies ... for the whole of this period ...

4 November 1379

The *Anziani* ... considering the number and size of expenses burdening the city of Lucca, and wishing ... to provide lest the state is led into ruin through intolerable expenses, and seeking rather to relieve such burdens as far as possible, by omitting useless expenditure ... considering the statute in which it is ordered that an annual subsidy from communal funds be paid to students at a general *studio*[58] ... as a result of which much money ... has been paid to many students, both citizens and *contadini*, of Lucca, and this statute is recognised as being much more damaging to the commune than beneficial ... the said statute, wherever it is to be found in the volumes of the communal statutes, is rescinded, annulled and abolished ... And because many payments were perhaps less cautiously made under this statute and not according to the letter of the law, they order that the *Anziani* and Standardbearer are to review the payments made up to now to all persons and ... when they find that they were not done according to the law, they are to be withdrawn ... and repaid to the commune ...

58 Institution of higher education

24 Pistoia head-hunts a grammar teacher, 1377

A. Zanelli, *Del pubblico insegnamento in Pistoia dal XIV al XVI secolo* (Rome, 1900), pp. 121–3.

25 September 1377

By decision of the General Council of the popolo on 2 September ... authority was given to the current *Anziani* and Standardbearer of Justice of the *popolo* and commune of Pistoia to elect and nominate a grammar teacher for the period of three years at a maximum salary of L 300 per annum ... They have made diligent search and inquiry through all the neighbouring cities and places for such a teacher. According to a report made by ser Filippo di ser Corradi, who was sent to search for a teacher, there has been found, among others, a suitable and willing teacher of grammar and rhetoric whose name, it is said, is Maestro Pietro da Forlì, at present living in the city of Volterra. Asked by ser Filippo on behalf of the commune of Pistoia if he might want to come to Pistoia to teach grammar and rhetoric, he replied, as ser Filippo claims, yes, but at the salary, terms and conditions as set out in his letter to the *Anziani* ... the tenor of which follows ...

> It has been proposed to me on your behalf by ser Filippo that you need a grammar teacher for the pupils in your city, and were wanting to appoint me at a salary of L 300. Not happy at the size of the salary, I replied that if the appointment that he promised me be modified to 80 ducats per year without any deductions and a suitable house for my duties and my residence, I would accept very willingly indeed, and this to start from St Luke's day 1378 for 23 months ... And I moreover ask for exemption from all material and personal burdens of your commune for the duration of this term. I advised ser Filippo that he should leave Volterra lest rumour, already begun, should spread among the citizens here ... Volterra, 22 September.

Considering the reputation and learning of this master, and the profit, honour and benefit that would accrue to the commune of Pistoia from his arrival and hiring, and that the salary, terms and conditions specified in his letter ... cannot be agreed to by the *Anziani* alone, and that all his requests in their view should be granted except the exemption from gabelles, they have decided to propose the matter to the present council, as without its decision the said master cannot be hired on those terms. What therefore does the Council wish to decide?

Bartolomeo di ser Sofredo advised that the said master be hired ... on the terms in his letter, except that he should in no way be exempt from gabelles. And that the *Anziani* and Standardbearer may hire at the commune's expense a house suitable for the residence of master and pupils ... provided that they do not spend more than L 50 per annum on rent.

[Proposal approved by 89 votes to 27]

25 A teaching monopoly: Bassano, 1259

An unusual, and unusually early, communal intervention in the education 'market' was made by the small north-eastern town of Bassano.

Statuti del comune di Bassano dell'anno 1259 e dell'anno 1295, ed. G. Fasoli (Venice, 1940), pp. 95–6.

Item, we establish and ordain that no one should dare to hold schools in Bassano except the master who will be elected by the podestà and council of Bassano, and if anyone contravenes, he is to pay 5s each day to the commune as penalty. Item ... that the master who is to hold grammar schools in Bassano and the scholars from Bassano or elsewhere who enter the schools of this master to hear him and do so for eight days are required to pay the master for the whole month even if they do not want to hear him for longer. And the grammar pupils hearing Cato[59] and above are each to pay 40d per month, but if they board with the master 5s per month ... And pupils hearing Donatus and below are to pay 2s per month. And if a pupil remains in school for one month, he is to pay the fee for the whole year, although he does not want to hear the said master ... And the said master is not required to pay any public levy or impost.

It is added in 1267 that all men of Bassano wanting to send their sons to school have to send them to the school of the master elected by the commune of Bassano, except for two small boys who can go to the priests for the purpose of carrying crosses and censer.

---

59 'Cato' and 'Donatus' were two of the basic texts of the elementary curriculum: Cato was a collection of moral sayings, Donatus a grammar book. Grendler, *Schooling*, pp. 111–12.

II: CIVIC RELIGION

Civic religion is a term much used, though also debated, in the context of late-medieval Italy. Though it is obvious that not all religion in towns was 'civic' and that the impact of 'civic religion' over the countryside could be marginal, the term is still useful for a group of religious practices that gave prominence to the role of the laity and that asserted or protected civic identity. As Vauchez has defined it, the essence of civic religion is 'the appropriation of values of the religious life by urban powers for the purposes of legitimation, celebration and public well-being'.[1] First of all comes the role of the patron saint – or rather, saints, for although cities might have one major patron, they also had a broader group of saint-protectors (for example, at Perugia eight with civic associations, and a further 107 with cults of varying degrees of activity and appeal).[2] The festivals of the patron, as well as other key feast days, were 'adopted as community festivals', when 'the whole social body' processed in honour of the saint, and games and horse races were organised.[3] Enshrined in urban statutes were laws ordering full candlelit processions in which all the components of political society – government officials, guilds, neighbourhoods, confraternities – were to parade and make offerings to the patron saint. On these days all other activity – particularly trading – was to cease; and as cities expanded, first into the *contado* and then in some cases to control other cities, the obligation to make annual offerings was extended to the city's rural subjects and its subject cities.

A second feature of civic Christianity are the lay confraternities that were common in towns in north and central Italy (less so in the south where the growth of such collective bodies was restricted). The number of confraternities was striking: a hundred in fourteenth-century Florence; fourteen even in a small town of San Sepolcro's size (pre-

---

1 A. Vauchez, 'Introduction', in *La religion civique à l'époque médiévale et moderne* (Rome, 1995), p. 1.

2 G. Dickson, 'The 115 cults of the saints in later medieval and Renaissance Perugia: a demographic overview of a civic pantheon', *Renaissance Studies*, 12 (1998).

3 G. Chittolini, 'Civic religion and the countryside in late medieval Italy', in *City and Countryside in Late-Medieval and Renaissance Italy: Essays presented to Philip Jones*, ed. T. Dean and C. Wickham (London, 1990), pp. 69–71.

plague population of perhaps 5,000). Equally striking are membership numbers: at San Sepolcro the confraternity of San Bartolomeo seems to have had about a thousand members at any time, divided roughly between men and women, and including all social groups (clerics, noblemen, merchants, craftsmen, servants, even peasants).[4] The counterpart to, and explanation of, this strong growth was the apparent weakness of parish organisation in Italian towns. Not that confraternities developed in opposition to the church: they were supported by local clerics, especially the mendicants. But confraternities did serve two functions that might otherwise have been associated with the parish clergy: poor relief and burial/commemoration of the dead.

Communes also gave assistance in various forms — tax concessions, regular gifts of money, building materials — to groups of friars, nuns, and hermits, and promoted the cults of local holy people, providing money for tombs and chapels, solemnizing their feastdays by the attendance of communal officials. Individual families were present in the day-to-day life of church: possessing rights of patronage to benefices, collecting tithes, congregating their burial chapels around the new churches of the mendicant orders. The maintenance and decoration of important churches might be entrusted to major guilds. Churchmen and church spaces were also pressed into service of the commune: friars and monks were called on to officiate at elections or to serve as communal treasurers; their monasteries or convents were used as places in which to stow documents or treasure in safe keeping, while the cathedral was often used as a meeting place for communal councils.

On the other hand, though church and commune clearly collaborated, they also quarrelled, while the ruling class also dominated church offices and properties. The commune's attempts to extend its jurisdictions and, especially, to tax the clergy, ran up against local ecclesiastical opposition and against fierce papal protection of so-called 'ecclesiastical liberties'. From the late twelfth century onwards, disputes occurred over a great variety of issues: the episcopal courts, the control of hospitals, tithe, episcopal lands and jurisdictions in the countryside, the use of ecclesiastical properties in town, the tax status of the church and its dependants. Meanwhile, canonries were largely dominated by local noble families, in some places (Siena) the bishopric too; nobles put pressure on monasteries at times of abbatial elections and dominated, to the point of expropriation, ecclesiastical landholdings.

4 J. R. Banker, *Death in the Community: Memorialisation and Confraternities in an Italian Commune in the Late Middle Ages* (Athens, Georgia, and London, 1988), pp. 51–64.

Civic Christianity also included charity. Hospitals and poor relief are mentioned with pride in descriptions of Italian cities: Bonvesin da la Riva mentions ten hospitals in Milan, singling out Santo Stefano in Brolo as the principal hospital, caring for hundreds of adults and infants. He also mentions the secondment to the hospital of surgeons, paid from public funds. Giovanni Villani reckoned that there were over thirty hospitals in Florence in the 1330s, with over 1,000 beds. An anonymous Genoese poet boasted that charities in that city attracted the poor from all over Lombardy. Hospitals were an institution of which some cities were rightfully proud: in 1399 the duke of Milan wanted a commission appointed to study a project for a poor hospital on the model of Siena's; and in 1414 Emperor Sigismund, impressed by reports of the buildings, endowments, food and medical equipment of Siena's hospital, asked the government of Siena for a painting of it clearly detailing the rooms, refectories, dormitories and other buildings.[5] Many thirteenth-century communes assumed supervision of hospitals and had 'surgeons' (who were more than mere bone-setters and wound-patchers) on the civic payroll. Communal governments and guilds took rights (of inspection, control) over hospitals, in return for the responsibility of material support [22].

However, despite early interventions of this sort in welfare, the general picture of assistance in the thirteenth and early fourteenth centuries was marked by three features. First the fragmentation of assistance: relief of the sick and poor was provided by a great variety of institutions and charitable practices, public and private, municipal and ecclesiastical, and including governments, monasteries, parish clergy, confraternities, guilds and neighbours. Second, there was little specialisation: charitable societies, like the Consorzio of the Holy Spirit in Piacenza, took on all the biblical categories: feeding the hungry, clothing the poor, nursing the sick, helping prisoners, burying the dead, as well as supporting widows and orphans. Their model, it has been said, was 'charity in all its aspects',[6] though in practice charities might come over time to prioritise certain categories. Third, the

---

5 G. Soldi Rondinini, 'Gli interventi dei Visconti', in *La carità a Milano nei secoli XII–XV*, ed. M. P. Alberzoni and O. Grassi (Milan, 1989), p. 130; G. Gaye, *Carteggio inedito d'artisti dei secoli XIV, XV, XVI* (3 vols, Florence, 1839), vol. 1, p. 92. And in general: K. Park and J. Henderson, '"The first hospital among Christians": The Ospedale di Santa Maria Nuova in early sixteenth-century Florence', *Medical History*, 35 (1991), 164–9.

6 G. Albini, 'L'assistenza all'infanzia delle città dell'Italia padana (secoli XII–XV)', in *Città e servizi sociali nell'Italia dei secoli XII–XV* (Pistoia, 1990), p. 117.

extent of government intervention and control varied from city to city and from time to time. There were after all church laws regulating hospitals (especially insisting that the carers, often lay brothers, adopt semi-monastic conventions of life, wearing a habit, taking vows, having their own internal rule), and communes sometimes deferred to these and to episcopal overview. Santo Stefano in Brolo, for example, was run first by deacons and friars, then from 1260 by the Humiliati.

This picture changed during the fourteenth century, largely it seems as a result of the effects of demographic crisis and economic change on the nuclear family. Infants, according to Albini, 'paid the price' for the chronic poverty of the labouring classes: the abandonment of children increased, widows with children to support were in more manifest difficulties, and fathers had insufficient means to provide daughters with dowries. Such circumstances brought two developments to poor relief and hospital provision: first, the growth of specialisation, in hospitals for foundlings and charities that concentrated on the shame-faced poor, that is those who had fallen on hard times; and second, the amalgamation of hospitals, already evident in the late fourteenth century (Santa Maria Nuova in Reggio Emilia, 1374), though the most significant examples of this trend came about later in the fifteenth century (the Ospedale maggiore in Milan, etc.). Along with these developments went the growth of lay presence and control: as at Santa Maria Nuova in Reggio, or the Consorzio della Misericordia in Milan (1368), the founder's family and groups or corporations of notaries or merchants were now in control. This limitation of the role of clerics in the management of charities was accompanied by greater priority given to the distribution of food and clothing to the poor. In Florence, the alms distributed by Orsanmichele came during the fourteenth century to focus increasingly on support of the nuclear family, in a period of subsistence crises, economic depression and epidemic disease. In the same city, the Company of Roast Chestnuts in the parish of San Frediano redirected its charity after the Black Death: away from the burial of dead members and the poor, towards assistance to living women.[7]

This growth of lay control was accompanied, and partly motivated, by revelations of mismanagement and corruption. At Monza, visitations of hospitals in the mid-fourteenth century suggested persistent

---

7 J. Henderson, *Piety and Charity in Late-Medieval Florence* (Oxford, 1994), pp. 214–26; 'The parish and the poor in Florence at the time of the Black Death: the case of San Frediano', *Continuity and Change*, 3 (1988), 253–65.

problems in maintaining the fabric, in ensuring adequate spiritual life of the *conversi* or adequate physical conditions for the patients. At Milan in the early fifteenth scandals of bad management and careless administration left hospitals indebted, with their properties signed away or usurped.[8] Perhaps the most spectacular of the scandals was that which hit the great Florentine company of Orsanmichele, the city's wealthiest charity, in 1353, when the governors' fraudulent holding of government bonds was discovered. This lost Orsanmichele much public support and began its long-term decline [43].

Religion is not wholly captured by a study of institutions, of course, and there were both episodic religious movements which 'overcame and humiliated institutions'[9] and a proliferation after 1300 of visionaries, prophets and mystics from outside the institutional hierarchy of the church: those with what Vauchez has termed 'pouvoirs informels'. Several of these themes are illustrated here. First the two great episodic movements of the period were the flagellants of 1260 and the Bianchi of 1399. The greater and more influential movement was that of 1260: it was 'the most far-reaching and long-lasting of the ... popular orthodox movements of the thirteenth century'.[10] Though it started in Perugia, it spread first to central and north Italy, then crossed the Alps to southern Germany, Hungary and Poland. In Italy it gave rise to the foundation of countless confraternities, as the devout sought to perpetuate the sense of solidarity and fervour that the movement had created. The origins of this collective, public flagellation were multiple: it was a generalization of monastic practice or of penitential punishment imposed by the ecclesiastical courts; it fused flagellation with penitential processions at times of political danger or natural disaster; it manifested a widespread sense of sin across society that needed expiation.[11] The ritual was christocentric, recalling Christ's flagellation before his crucifixion. It has also been read, by Dickson, as a mobilisation of the Christian faithful against

8 G. Albini, 'Continuità e innovazione: la carità a Milano nel Quattrocento fra tensioni private e strategie pubbliche', in *Carità a Milano*, pp. 140–2; in the same volume, R. Mambretti, 'L'Ospedale di S. Gerardo nei secoli XII e XIV'.

9 G. Cracco, 'Aspetti della religiosità italiana del tre-quattrocento: costanti e mutamenti', in *Italia 1350–1450: tra crisi, trasformazione, sviluppo* (Pistoia, 1993), pp. 365–8.

10 G. Dickson, 'The flagellants of 1260 and the crusades', *Journal of Medieval History*, 15 (1989), 235.

11 J. Henderson, 'The flagellant movement and flagellant confraternities in central Italy, 1260–1400', *Studies in Church History*, 15 (1978); J. P. Grundman, *The Popolo at Perugia, 1139–1309* (Perugia, 1992), pp. 126–9.

heresy and against Ghibelline rulers, hostile to the papacy, who were often accused of heresy or of harbouring heretics. One such ruler, Uberto da Pallavicino in Cremona, certainly saw the flagellants as a political threat (according to a hostile Franciscan source: Salimbene de Adam) [39].

The Bianchi was a mass movement, sanctioned and led by local bishops, in which nine days of fasting, processions and peacemaking were kept by crowds of the faithful dressed in simple white robes, with the devotion passing in relay fashion from one city to another. Bornstein has carefully insisted on the differences between the flagellants of 1260 and the Bianchi of 1399: in the absence chiefly of flagellation, but also of new forms of devotion;[12] while Diana Webb has argued for the more markedly rural nature of the Bianchi. However, the Bianchi did share some characteristics with the flagellants of 1260: both originated in visions of the Virgin Mary, who urged penitential processions to placate Christ's decision to destroy the world for its sins; both were socially inclusive mass movements, going from town to town; both had an emphasis on peacemaking and penitence. Yet, as in 1260, there were those who kept their distance from the movement, though more for personal than political reasons, it seems, as well as others who fraudulently sought to take advantage of it [40].

Heresy

If the emphasis in civic religion was increasingly on religion in the service of the city, and on lay domination of the church, the church's long and eventually victorious struggle against heresy reveals the successful imposition of orthodoxy, often to popular opposition. Significant communities of heretics were present in Italian cities from the late twelfth century.[13] There were several phases in their growth and many groups under different names – over twenty-five have been counted – but chief among these in the thirteenth century were the Cathars and the 'Patarenes' (an ambiguous term that changed meaning several times, for a while coinciding with 'Cathar', but later shifting to denote 'materialists' or so-called 'Epicureans'). Especially important were the heretical groups in Milan, Verona, Florence and Orvieto, but

12 D. E. Bornstein, *The Bianchi of 1399: Popular Devotion in Late-Medieval Italy* (Ithaca and London, 1993), pp. 36–41, 45–7.

13 Jones, *City-State*, pp. 295–6.

there were active groups in many other centres (Vicenza, Treviso, Ferrara, Cremona, Piacenza, Rimini, Viterbo). The presence of Cathar heretics in the first half of the thirteenth century was favoured by local political conflict, which weakened communal government, and by an influx of refugee heretics from southern France. The ideal of apostolic poverty also inspired a popular religious reaction against the local church for its close association with the aristocracy: most cathedral canons came from families of the urban elite; tithes were held as fiefs by laymen; the great monasteries were enriched by lay gifts and dominated more by aristocratic members and aristocratic property interests. The local clergy showed no appetite for reform, wearing fine clothes, playing dice, carrying weapons, being more devoted to monetary gain than cure of souls. Nor were the church's weapons against heresy always dependable: the Humiliati, who combined prayer and work in a humble life of cloth-making, though generally orthodox, experienced some heretical moments; the mendicants quickly became attached to the aristocracy; and repression through the despatch of inquisitors could run into difficulty, as inquisitors sometimes faced physical violence or failed to receive co-operation from secular governments. Campaigns against heresy were also made difficult by disputes between communes and their local churches over other matters: when the bishop and clergy left the city imposing an interdict (suspension of divine services) this allowed heretics unchallenged opportunity to spread their ideas. Communal governments had no will to repress and were slow to ratify the papal and imperial decrees against heretics. In Milan, the pope alleged, 'anything that can be shown to disagree with the catholic faith is accepted as religion'.[14]

Turning points in the long papal battle against heresy in Italy came in the 1250s and 1260s: the activity, and then the assassination, of fra Pietro da Verona (St Peter Martyr, canonised 1253) created a favourable climate for an anti-heretical campaign, marked by an extension of the powers and effectiveness of the inquisition, and by the launching of crusades against heretics and their Ghibelline protectors. In 1260 came the flagellant movement − 'by its very nature anti-Cathar'[15] − with its stimulus to confraternities, which both attracted people away from heresy and acted as agitators and organisers of

14 D. Webb, 'The pope and the cities: anticlericalism and heresy in Innocent III's Italy', in *The Church and Sovereignty, c. 590–1918: Essays in honour of Michael Wilks*, ed. D. Wood (Oxford, 1991), p. 150; and, for the foregoing, P. Racine, *Plaisance du Xème à la fin du XIIIème siècle* (Lille, 1979–80), pp. 798–887.

15 M. Lambert, *The Cathars* (Oxford, 1998), p. 179.

local anti-heretical action. In the 1260s the Angevin/Guelf victories against the Ghibellines in southern Italy weakened Ghibelline regimes throughout Italy, which, with their anti-clerical attitudes, had sheltered heretics in the past. In Orvieto in 1268–9, a wide-ranging inquisition 'smashed Catharism' there,[16] and in northern Italy the persecution of heretics was given solid support by the emergent *signori*: Alberto della Scala, lord of Verona, earned papal praise for his support of a military campaign against a community of heretics at Sirmione in 1276, as a result of which 166 men and women were captured and later burned in the Arena at Verona. In Ferrara the Este lords protected the inquisitor from popular violence following the sentence against a local heretic, considered a saint. Thus, by the 1280s in Verona the inquisitor was pronouncing sentences against deceased heretics, ordering their bones to be disinterred and burned, which is arguably a sign of an absence of living heretics (though also arguably a sign that the war was now being carried to the dead as well as the living).

The inquisition operated in a climate of tension and uncertainty, and this is well illustrated in the episode of Armanno Pungilupo of Ferrara. The Pungilupo inquiry in the 1270s and 1280s seems to show the great difficulty lay people and churchmen had in distinguishing between orthodox and heretical holy men: recording the miracles performed at his tomb was the first stage in consolidating his cult for possible canonisation. But at another level, it also reveals the tensions between friars and the regular clergy of the cathedral: as Salimbene (though himself a friar) notes, the bishop of Ferrara's support for the cult derived from the earnings the cathedral made from it, whereas it was friars and their ex-heretic informers who attested against Pungilupo. Steven Wessley noted that 'some contemporaries suspected that inquisitorial investigation of putative saints supported by older orders served mendicant interests', and cited a case at Brescia in which the populace demanded the death of the friars for their desire to burn a 'saint'.[17]

From the early fourteenth century, the inquisitors turned their attention to other targets: Beguines and *fraticelli*, astrologers and sorcerers, and, as John Stevens showed for Florence, it was in this period, when heresy itself was no longer 'organised and continuous', that the inquisition acquired 'notoriety' for pursuing the inquisitors'

16 *Ibid.*, p. 274.

17 S. E. Wessley, 'The thirteenth-century Guglielmites: salvation through women', in *Medieval Women*, ed. D. Baker (Oxford, 1978), p. 302.

own financial profit through various forms of extortion. This led the government to intervene in order to restrict the inquisitor's activities.[18] Similar accusations, of abuse and extortion, had earlier been made of the inquisitor in Padua (1302).[19] Another target of inquisitors in the fourteenth century was those who expressed any sort of materialist disbelief in the various supernatural aspects of orthodox doctrine and practice: those who, in summary, believed that 'there was no other world but this one', declaring that the gospels were fictions, that 'whoever has goods in the world does not need the grace of God', that money was better than religion, denying the possibility of resurrection, the existence of heaven and hell, the authenticity of relics or the sacrality of the Host.[20]

Inadequate belief of this sort was very different from the excessive or misapplied belief investigated by inquisitors in other cases, for example the Guglielmites in Milan, an extraordinary, if 'eccentric',[21] episode in late thirteenth-century religious history, in which a largely female group of devotees of Guglielma venerated her memory as that of a female Christ and looked forward to the appointment of women as pope and cardinals. The incomplete inquisition record (which consists only in depositions, without record of sentence), does seem to have resulted in a condemnation, if a report from Colmar may be associated with this case. As with Pungilupo, initial support was given to the cult of 'Saint' Guglielma by elements of the ecclesiastical establishment: the important monastery of Chiaravalle, just outside Milan, obtained her body, had an altar erected and a fresco painted, and supported her feast day with food and sermons. But Chiaravalle seems extraneous to the direction that the cult took under the influence of its leaders, Andrea Saramita and Suor Manfreda of the Humiliati. Nevertheless, Wessley has shown how the ideas of the Guglielmites derived from three strong elements of thirteenth-century religious enthusiasm pushed to their extremes: the Joachimite idea of the birth of a new age (of the Holy Spirit); the idea of imitating Christ; and the model of the apostolic life.

18 J. N. Stephens, 'Heresy in medieval and Renaissance Florence', *Past and Present*, (1972), 33–4.

19 A. Rigon, 'Francescanesimo e società a Padova nel Duecento', in *Minoritismo e centri veneti nel Duecento*, ed. G. Cracco (Trent, 1983), p. 30.

20 A. Murrary, 'The Epicureans', in *Intellectuals and Writers in Fourteenth-century Europe*, ed. P. Boitani and A. Torti (Tübingen and Cambridge, 1986).

21 Larner, *Italy in the Age of Dante and Petrarch* p. 233.

26 Paradise on earth: the feast-day of St John the Baptist, Florence

The feast-day of John the Baptist (24 June) – here described by the early fifteenth-century writer Goro Dati[22] – was the chief civic festival in Florence, significant in economic and social terms as well as political and religious. The *palio*, which has given its name to the race, was actually the first prize, made out of some rich fabric. Such races were run in many cities on the important feast-days.

C. Guasti, *Le feste di San Giovanni Batista in Firenze descritte in prose e in rima da contemporanei* (Florence, 1884), pp. 4–8.

When springtime comes ... every Florentine begins to think of making a fine day of the feast of St John, which falls in mid-summer, and everyone in good time supplies themselves with garments, decorations and jewels. Whoever is planning a wedding banquet ... postpones it until then in order to honour the feast day. Two months ahead, making of the *palio* begins, and of the servants' garments, the pennants and trumpets, as well as the *palii* that the dependant territories bring as tribute, and the candles and other things that are to be offered. [And work is begun on] inviting people, ensuring supplies for banquets, getting horses to come from everywhere to run the *palio* race, and all the city is busy preparing for the feastday ... Once the eve of St John's day arrives, early in the morning all the guilds make a display, on the outside walls of their workshops, of all their rich things, ornaments and jewels. As many cloths of gold and silk are displayed as would adorn ten kingdoms, and as many gold and silver jewels, rich hangings, painted panels and marvellous carvings, and things pertaining to feats of arms ... Then at around the hour of terce, a solemn procession is made by all the clerics, priests, monks and friars ... with so many relics of saints, that it is a thing of immeasurable devotion ... With them are many companies of secular men ... dressed as angels, sounding musical instruments of many sorts, singing marvellously, and enacting the stories of those saints that each company honours ... Then in the afternoon, at around the hour of vespers, when the heat has fallen somewhat, all the citizens assemble behind the banner of their local district. There are sixteen of these, and they march one behind the other, with the citizens two by two, the worthiest and eldest at the front and so on down to the boys

22 For discussion, see R. C. Trexler, *Public Life in Renaissance Florence* (New Haven and London, 1980), ch. 8.

at the back. They march to the church of San Giovanni, each to make his offering of a 1 lb wax candle ... The streets they pass along are all decorated, the walls and seating with hangings, *spalliere* and bench-covers, covered in sendal. And all the streets are full of young women and girls dressed in silk, and adorned with precious jewels and pearls. And this offering lasts until sunset. Once the offering has been made, every citizen and woman returns home to make arrangements for the following morning.

On the morning of St John, whoever goes to see the Piazza dei Signori will see something magnificent, marvellous and 'triumphal' ... Around the piazza are one hundred towers, which seem to be of gold, some of them borne on carts, some by porters ... These are made of wood, paper and wax, and decorated with gold, and colours and drawn figures; they are empty inside, so that men can stand inside them, and continuously make the figures go round and round. The figures are of men on horseback jousting, or of foot soldiers running with lances and shields, or young girls round-dancing ... Around the rostrum of the Palazzo there are one hundred *palii* or more, fixed on their poles with iron rings. The first are those of the principal cities who pay tribute to the commune of Florence, such as Pisa, Arezzo, Pistoia, Volterra, Cortona ... and of some of the lords of Poppi and Piombino who are allies[23] of the commune. They are made of double velvet, some of squirrel-fur and some of silkcloth; the others are all of velvet or other fabric ...

The first offering to be made in the morning is that of the Captains of the Guelf Party, with all the knights, and with foreign lords and ambassadors, and a large number of the most honourable citizens of Florence. Ahead of them the banner of the Guelf Party is carried by one of their squires on a big palfrey covered in a white cloth, bearing the arms of the Party and reaching to the ground. Then follow the other *palii*, carried one by one by a man on horseback ... and they go to offer these to the church of San Giovanni. And these *palii* are given as tribute by cities acquired by Florence ... from a certain date. The wax candles, like gilded towers, however, are renders from the old territories controlled by Florence, and they proceed in order of rank, one behind the other, to offer to San Giovanni. The following day the *palii* are hung up around the inside of the church, and they remain there all year, until the next St John's day, when they are taken down, and they are either used to make altar covers or are auctioned off.

23 *raccomandati.*

After this, a marvellous and countless quantity of large candles are offered, some of 100 lb, some of 50 lb, some more, some less, down to 10 lb. They are carried, lit, by the peasants of the villages who offer them. After them the Officials of the Mint make their offering, a magnificent candle carried on a richly-adorned cart pulled by a pair of oxen covered with a caparison bearing the arms of the Mint. They are accompanied by about four hundred worshipful men, members or dependants[24] of the Calimala and Cambio Guilds, each with 1 lb wax torches in their hands. Then come the Priors and their Colleges, accompanied by the judges, the podestà, captain and executor [of the Ordinances of Justice], and with such display, servants, and the sounding of trumpets and pipes that all the world seems to resonate.

When the Priors return, all the riders who have come to race for the *palio* make their offerings, and after them all the Flemings and Brabantines, weavers of woollen cloth in Florence. And then twelve prisoners are offered, who have been released from jail out of mercy and to honour St John; and these are destitute people, imprisoned for any reason.

When the offerings are complete, everyone returns home to dine. And, as I have said, throughout the city on this day weddings and banquets are held, with so much music and singing, dancing, rejoicing and celebration that the city seems to be paradise.

After dinner, when people have had some rest ... all the women and girls go and stand along the course of the *palio* race: the course passes straight through the middle of the city, where there are a good many homes and fine houses of the good citizens, more than in any other district. And from one end of the city to another, along this route, filled with flowers, are all the women, and all the jewels and rich decorations of the city. And there are always many foreign lords and knights who come from neighbouring cities to see the beauty and magnificence of the feastday ... The horses are readied for the off and, at the sound of three tolls of the big bell of the Palazzo dei Signori, they begin to race. And at the top of the tower are boys whose support for this or that horse can be seen from their gestures. The most superior Barbary horses in the world come from all over Italy. And the one that first reaches the *palio*, wins it, and is borne on a triumphal four-wheeled cart, decorated with four carved lions that seem alive, one on each corner, and drawn by two horses ... the *palio* is very large and rich, of fine scarlet velvet, in two parts joined by

24 *sottoposti.*

gold trimming as wide as a man's palm, lined with squirrel belly and edged with ermine, fringed with silk and gold, and it costs in total 300 florins or more ...

27 The *palio* race in Bologna, 1288

Statuti di Bologna dell'anno 1288, vol. 2, pp. 220–1.

We establish that every June on the feast-day of St Peter[25] the commune of Bologna is to buy 8 *braccia*[26] of scarlet [cloth] and a pole on which the cloth is to be fixed, and also a cock, for running to the prize or *palio*, such that no more than L 20 are to be spent on these. In this *palio* all stallions that wish to run may do so, but no mares. A proclamation to this effect is to be made three days before St Peter's feast day. And the race is to be run from the Reno bridge to the enclosure at the Porta Stiera ... And the horse that reaches the prize ahead of the other horses is to have the scarlet cloth, and the second is to have the cock. Similarly, on the feast of San Bartolomeo in August, the commune of Bologna is to buy a roncey, a sparrowhawk, a pair of gauntlets and a pig, on which L 20 is to be spent (and the pig must be roasted if the feast of San Bartolomeo falls on a day when meat may be eaten, otherwise it is to be alive). The roncey and the sparrowhawk are to be awarded to the horse reaching the prize ahead of the others, the pig to the second horse. The course is to run from the Ponte Maggiore to the crossroads at Porta Ravegnate, and all that wish to race may do so ... And we say that all the householders along the said courses are required, two days before the race is to be run, to clear the streets in front of their premises of all wood, stones, dung and other rubbish, on pain of 40s ... And that no one is to put themselves in the path of any horse or its rider, or to place any obstruction or inflict any injury, on pain of L 25 ... And that all the horses that are to run in these races are to be registered by one of the podestà's notaries, and no other horses may run except those registered.

25 To whom the cathedral church was dedicated; only later was St Peter overtaken by San Petronio as a patron.

26 About 6 yards.

28 The costs of a feast-day in Pistoia, 1252

As Goro Dati's description makes clear, preparations for the major feast-day were extensive. The costs to the local church are revealed in an account from Pistoia for the feast of St James (25 July). The account was prepared by the supervisors (*operai*) of the Board of Works (*Opera*).

P. Bacci, *Documenti toscani per la storia dell'arte* (2 vols, Florence, 1910–12), vol. 2, pp. 31–3.

1252: These are the expenses for the month of August made by Ranuccino and Rainelmo *operai* of San Giacomo, on behalf of the Opera:

To Salvo Rodolfino, messenger, for two days on which he helped erect and set up the pavilion and curtain on the feast day of San Giacomo; and for three days on which he worked as manual labourer on the campanile with master-craftsmen to repair the bells; and for three days on which he was with the *operai* helping to sell candles for the feast day of San Giacomo; and for guarding the candles in the church of San Giacomo for one night on the feast of San Giacomo	12*s.*
To Onesto, for sweeping the piazza	30*s.*
To Franco da Paciano, for the cost of two beams for supporting the bells	11*s.* 6*d.*
To Lunardo di Uliverio, for making 4,000 candles	15*s.*
To master Giovanni, painter, for painting a panel of San Giacomo	20*s.*
To Lunardo di Uliverio, for making 108 lb of candles	4*s.* 4*d.*
To don Alberto, priest of the chapel of San Giacomo, for giving them to the priests of the city of Pistoia in the procession on the eve of San Giacomo's day ...	10*s.*
To Bonagiunta di Benesano, money which he gave to the man who brought myrtle on and after the feast day ...	8*s.*
Total	114*s.* 6*d.*

29 Regulation of holy days: Perugia, 1342

Cities regulated saints' days by statute, in order to limit the number of official holidays, to enforce prohibitions of work and trade, and to prevent violence. *Statuti di Perugia* (1342), vol. 2, pp. 62–5, 93–4, 244, 376.

So that it be known what are the non-working days in the criminal court, we establish that these are: all Sundays, Christmas day and the two preceding days, the feast of St Stephen in December and its octave, the feasts of St John the Evangelist, the Holy Innocents, the Circumcision, Epiphany, the Conversion of St Paul, the Conception, Nativity, Purification, Annunciation and Assumption of the Virgin Mary, the Enthronement of St Peter, all the feast-days of all the apostles and evangelists, the feasts of Sant'Ercolano in March and November, of San Lorenzo, of San Francesco in October, of San Domenico, San Benedetto, Sant'Agostino, the whole of Holy Week, Easter Sunday and the whole of the following week, Ascension Day, Pentecost and the two following days, Corpus Christi, the feasts of St Louis [of Toulouse], John the Baptist, Mary Magdalen, St Peter *in vincula*, the Beheading of John the Baptist, All Saints, St Martin, Holy Cross, St Michael Archangel, San Bevignate,[27] San Martino IV Pope, Santa Lucia, San Costanzo bishop of Perugia, San Niccolò of Bari, the first day of Lent and the two days of indulgence at San Domenico and St Stephen in August, the feasts of St Catherine, San Silvestro, St Thomas Aquinas, and every Friday, out of reverence for the Suffering of Our Lord ... And we establish that criminal trials should have holidays on no other days ... And we order that on each and every of these days ... no artisan is to dare or presume to work, open his shop or perform his craft. And whoever contravenes will be punished 100s ... but this does not apply to butchers, spicers, bakers, innkeepers and smiths (for shoeing animals).

Every Friday of March is to be kept, out of reverence of God and of the Crucifixion, and no craft or work is to be done by artisans, except that this does not apply to food and drink necessary for living ...

To prevent all pestilence and harmful water, commonly called hail, we ordain that the feast and octave of Santo Stefano the protomartyr at Christmas is to be kept by all men and women of the city and *contado*

27 Not a saint officially recognised by the church, but an example of 'civic canoni-ation': Dickson, 'The 115 cults of the saints in later medieval and Renaissance Perugia', pp. 14–16.

of Perugia, with all due reverence, such that everyone is to abstain from all work. And the podestà and captain, a fortnight before the feast, are to have it proclaimed on each Saturday, such that no one fall foul of the edict, imposing a penalty of 100s on every transgressor.

As it often happens that, during candle-lit processions on the eve and feast-day of Sant'Ercolano, on the eve of the Assumption of the Virgin Mary, on the eve of San Costanzo, on the eve of the translation of Santo Stefano, and on the day of the procession to San Domenico, there are shouts, noise, affrays and assaults, we ordain and enact that no one is to dare or presume on these or other days of procession as established by the commune of Perugia, or on the following day, to carry forbidden weapons or to make any shout, affray, noise, assault or crime. And whoever contravenes will pay four times the penalty due if these things were done at any other time ... But if anyone henceforth assaults anyone in Holy Week or on Easter Day, if he kills, he is to be punished and condemned to beheading without mitigation and to the confiscation of all his property to the commune; and if he assaults at these times with any type of weapon, causing bloodshed, his right hand is to be amputated. And this out of reverence of the Passion and Resurrection of our lord Jesus Christ.

On the eve of the feast of Sant'Ercolano in March, and on the day of the feast itself, no one is to play games on horseback through the city or suburbs of Perugia, or through the streets and squares, on pain of L 50.

As on the night of Christmas and in Holy Week and on the night of Carnival it is customary for great damage to be done, we declare as law that the staff of the podestà and captain are to mount diligent guard on the nights of Holy Thursday, Good Friday, Holy Saturday and Carnival, such that on none of these nights is any damage done on the piazza of the commune of Perugia or in any other place in the city and suburbs to the stalls of moneychangers, merchants or artisans ...

30 A popular 'saint': Alberto of Cremona

In his chronicle, the Franciscan friar Salimbene 'shows us every side of his age, clothed all round in living flesh, and answering in every part to the dry bones we find scattered elsewhere'.[28] In the following passage, Salimbene ridicules enthusiasm for unapproved (and working-class) 'saints'.[29]

Salimbene de Adam, *Cronica*, ed. Scalia, pp. 733–6; ed. Holder-Egger, pp. 501–3.

1279: In this year there appeared the false miracles of one Alberto, who had lived in Cremona and had been a wine-carrier, as well as a wine-drinker and a sinner. After his death, as was claimed, God performed many miracles in Cremona, Parma and Reggio ... In Parma, at the church of San Pietro by the Piazza nuova, all the wine-porters of the city gathered, and blessed was the man who could touch them or give them something. Women did the same. And companies were formed in the city neighbourhoods, which marched out to the streets and squares, so that they could all come together in procession to the church of San Pietro, where the relics of this Alberto were kept. And they carried crosses and banners, and sang as they marched, and they gave purple cloth, samite, baldachinos and much money to the church. Later, [however,] the porters divided all these things among themselves and kept them. Seeing this devotion, the parish priests arranged for Alberto to be depicted in their churches, so as to obtain more offerings from the populace. At this time, his image was painted not only in churches, but also on many walls and porticoes of cities, villages and castles. This is expressly contrary to church law, because no one's relics are to be held in reverence unless they are first approved by the Roman Church and inscribed in the register of saints, nor is anyone's image to be painted in the manner of a saint unless his canonisation has first been announced by the church ... When a man from Cremona came to Parma, claiming to have with him a relic of Sant'Alberto (that is, the small toe from his right foot) all the Parmesans gathered together, the great and small, men and women, 'young men and maidens, old men and children' [Psalms 148.12], laymen, clerics and monks, and in a great, singing procession, they bore the toe to the cathedral, which is the church of the Glorious Virgin. When the toe was placed on the main altar, lord Anselmo da San Vitale, a canon of the cathedral and vicar of the bishop, arrived

28 G. G. Coulton, *From St Francis to Dante* (London, 1906), p. 10.
29 Jones, *City-State*, p. 323.

and kissed it; but when he caught the smell of garlic, and told this to the other clerics, they saw and realised that they had all been deceived and tricked, as they found that the 'toe' was nothing but a clove of garlic. And so the Parmesans were duped and ridiculed, because 'they have walked after vanity and are become vain' [Jer. 2.5].

In Cremona, in the church in which Alberto was buried, the Cremonese sought to show that God performed infinite miracles through him, and so, many sick men came from Pavia and other parts of Lombardy 'that they might be delivered of their infirmities' [Acts, 5.15]. Many noble ladies also came to Cremona from Pavia, with their daughters, some out of devotion, others in the hope of gaining full bodily health ...

Take note and consider carefully that, just as the Cremonese, Parmesans and Reggians have made fools of themselves now over Alberto the porter, so the Paduans did over Antonio Peregrino and the Ferrarese over Armanno Pungilupo ...[30]

This devotion to 'saint' Alberto came about for many reasons: on the part of the sick, because they sought healing; on the part of the curious, because they wanted to see something new; on the part of the clergy, because of the envy that they have towards the new religious orders; on the part of bishops and canons, because of the earnings that followed, as is also evident in the case of the bishop and canons of Ferrara who earned much on account of Armanno Pungilupo.

31 Miracles in Mantua and Bologna, c. 1300

Urban chronicles often record miraculous cures that took place in city churches – a sign of civic monopoly of the sacred – and often these were associated with the tombs and relics of local saints, but the relic of the Holy Blood of Christ in Mantua was different: allegedly brought to Mantua by Longinus, and twice lost and rediscovered, the relic enjoyed a revived cult from the late thirteenth century onwards under the combined impulse of the Grail legend, eucharistic miracles, the restoration of the monastery of Sant'Andrea and the construction of the Bonacolsi family lordship.[31]

a. *Annales mantuani*, in *MGH*, ed. G. H. Pertz (Hannover 1866, Leipzig, 1925), vol. 19, p. 31.

30 See [**33**].

31 R. Capuzzo, 'Note sulla tradizione e sul culto del sangue di Cristo nella Mantova medievale', in *Storia e arte religiosa a Mantova* (Mantova, 1991).

1298: On the feast of the Ascension, miracles of the blood of Christ began in the church of Sant'Andrea in Mantua. On that day fra Alberto from Trent was cured: he was arthritic and paralysed such that he could not move without sticks, and walked badly even with them. And in the following days, many paralysed men and women, lame, blind, mute and hunchbacked were released from their disabilities and pains by virtue of the precious blood of Christ.

b. *Corpus chronicorum bononiensium*, vol. 2, p. 282.

1307: San Petronio, father of Bologna, began to perform miracles on the day of Pentecost, that is, the 4th of May; and he did many miracles, healing the disabled of many afflictions, such as the deaf, the hunchbacked, the dumb, and the crippled in hands, arms and feet who could not move their limbs. These miracles were done with the water of the well that is beneath the altar of San Petronio [in the church of Santo Stefano], that is, the sick washed their bodies with this water. And sick people came from all over Italy to receive these miracles.

32 Rainmaking in Florence and Bergamo

The cult of 'Our Lady of Impruneta' – a miraculous image of the Virgin Mary held in the suburban church at Impruneta – was 'the most remarkable and durable' of Florentine saint cults.[32] The chronicler Matteo Villani gives the first description of the use of this image to control the weather – a practice soon copied elsewhere.[33]

a. Matteo Villani, *Cronica*, ed. G. Porta (Parma, 1995), vol. 1, pp. 480–1 (IV.7).

1354: For over three months this year, at the time when the crops had greatest need of rain, there was continuous drought, due to the influence of the constellations and signs occurring in the sky. As a result, the crops throughout Tuscany were already dry and dying, auguring sterility and hunger. The Florentines, afraid of losing their harvest, turned to divine aid, having prayers said, and continuous processions through the city and *contado*. But the more processions were held, the clearer the sky became, day and night. The citizens, seeing that this was not working, with great devotion and hope turned to the aid of

---

32 R. C. Trexler, 'Florentine religious experience: the sacred image', *Studies in the Renaissance*, 19 (1972).

33 The Madonna di San Luca, Bologna: *Corpus chronicorum bononiensium*, vol. 4, pp. 63–4.

Our Lady, and arranged for the old image of Our Lady of Impruneta, painted on a panel, to be brought out. The commune prepared many candles, and on the 9th of May, almost all the people, men, women and children, along with the clergy and all the religious, with the arm of San Filippo, the venerable head of San Zanobi and many other holy relics, with the Priors and other members of the government, went to meet the panel outside the gate of San Piero Gattolino, while the bells of the commune and churches rang out in praise of God. The panel was watched over and carried reverently by members of the Buondelmonti family, patrons of the church of Impruneta, along with the men of the parish. When the bishop and the procession, with the relics and the people, met the holy image, they escorted it, with great reverence and formality, to San Giovanni and from there to San Miniato al Monte, and then it was taken back to its home in Santa Maria Impruneta. And it happened that, on the same day, during the procession, the sky filled with clouds. On the second day, the cloud cover continued, whereas on previous occasions it had been burned off by the heat. On the third day, it began to drizzle a little. On the fourth day, it rained hard, and then followed seven consecutive days of fine, quiet rain, which enriched the soil, in clear and singular benefit, bringing what was needed to restore the crops and fruits. And this steady and beneficial kind of rain was no less a marvellous gift of grace than rain itself. So, whereas great sterility had been expected following the harvest, instead there was an abundance of all the goods that the earth produces.

b. *Chronicon bergomense guelpho-ghibellinum*, ed. C. Capasso, *RIS*, vol. 16, pt. 2 (Bologna, 1926–40), p. 103.

1401, Sunday 24 July: In the morning in the church of Sant'Andrea, a tomb was opened under the main altar by all the clergy of Bergamo. In this tomb were found the bodies of three martyrs: namely Domno of Bergamo and his nephews Domneone and Eusebio, as appeared by some writing on a square stone found in the tomb. And I saw the bodies and read the writing. This tomb was opened in order that it might rain, because there was at that time a great drought, such that trees, vines and crops were desiccated; and after a few days it rained. And on 1 August the tomb was closed.

33 Saint or heretic?: Armanno Pungilupo of Ferrara

'For some twenty odd years, Armanno Pungilupo of Ferrara led a double life', as a Cathar believer and perfect and as a Catholic of conspicuous devotion, whose death inspired a miraculous cult at his tomb in Ferrara cathedral. 'He was a much better and more interesting man than the other well-known crypto-Cathar, Pierre Clergue of Montaillou'.[34]

L. A. Muratori, *Antiquitates italicae medii aevi* (6 vols, Milan, 1738–42), vol. 5, coll. 98–101, 118–39.

a) Examination of twenty-two miracles which were claimed to have been performed at the tomb of Armanno of Ferrara.

In the name of our lord Jesus Christ, Amen. In the year of his birth 1269 on 16 December. The man of God, the blessed Armanno of Ferrara, having persevered for a long time before God and men in praiseworthy penitence, in vigils, fasts and speeches ... faithful, chaste, humble, patient, merciful, benign and simple ... devoted to God and the glorious Virgin ... was miraculously called to Him and ended his days. In the briefest space of time, his contented death ... became known to the Ferrarese people, and crowds of men and women immediately flocked to the cathedral, where his lifeless body was laid out. When this worthy body had been reverently taken to its tomb with funeral ceremonies ... the Almighty King soon began to make this man of God, Armanno, famous with miracles, as is declared below.

19 December: Madonna Nova, daughter of Mainardino da Maderio, and wife of Giovannino da Achille, of the *contrada*[35] of Santa Maria in Vado, Ferrara, swore in the presence of ... lord Alberto ... bishop of Ferrara, and of ... lords Federico, archpriest, Ferrarino, canon, and the noblemen Aldigerio Fontana, Petrocino Menabuoi, his son Pietro and many others, to tell the truth regarding her infirmity and cure, confirming under oath ... that she had suffered for about nine years in her right eye and that from about eight days ago the swelling and pain in that eye grew stronger, such that she could not see out of it. And today she came in person to the cathedral, where the body of Armanno, the man of god, lay, and three times with devotion she kneeled before his tomb, devoutly beseeching God the Father that, through the merits of this man of God, Armanno, he would cure her of this infirmity and restore her sight. Having said which, she made an

34 Lambert, *The Cathars*, pp. 281–2.
35 City district.

offering and soon the swelling vanished from her eye and she recovered her sight.

On the same day, in the presence of the above witnesses, Gisla, widow of Castellano, of the *contrada* of Santa Maria in Vado, a sworn witness, said on oath that she had known Nova for seven years, and had seen the affliction in her eye, until today ...

20 December: Gisla, formerly of Lendinara, wife of Stefano da Villanova, who lives in the *contrada* of Borgonuovo, swore in the presence of the lord bishop ... of lords Federico archpriest, Amedeo and Ferrarino canons, the chaplain Alberto and the mansionary Cossa ... and on oath said that for eighteen years she had been crippled in her right arm, until today, and had not been able to raise it to her mouth, nor hold anything in it. And yesterday ... she vowed to God and the blessed Armanno that she would offer at his tomb a waxen arm and hand and a candle in the shape of an old woman, as she is, and that on his vigil she would always for the rest of her life fast on bread and water, and would watch at his tomb that night. And, having formally made this vow, she came to the tomb of the blessed Armanno and watched there throughout the night in pure devotion and reverence. And this morning, while the body of Christ was being elevated by the priest in the cathedral, Gisla, who was still there, stood up out of reverence ... and raised both her arms up high and was freed from the infirmity in her arm.

On the same day, Stefano, Gisla's husband, attested, having first given oath ... that his wife Gisla up to today suffered in her right arm, as stated above, but he does not know how she recovered health in it ...

20 December: Gerardo, a porter of Borgonuovo, sworn in the presence of the above lords, said on oath that his daughter Marchesina, a girl of eight years, there present, from the time of her birth had limped on both sides. And last Wednesday this girl, at the hour of vespers, asked him in tears to take her to the tomb of the blessed Armanno, because she hoped that he would make her upright. And so he took her up in his arms and carried her to the tomb of the blessed Armanno, and placed her reverently on the box in which the body lay. And when the girl had been there for an hour, he asked her how she felt, and she replied: 'Well'. And then he lifted her down into the church, and, in the sight of all the onlookers, she began to walk upright. The girl, present, said that, when she was released, she felt her pains pass like pins and needles ...

28 December: Marinello, shoemaker of Boccacanale, swore in the presence of the lord bishop and lords Federico archpriest, and Ferrarino and Amedeo canons, and said on oath that for eighteen months he was immobile with gout, from his groin to his feet, until Christmas eve just passed. And he had hardly been able to turn over in bed, and was strongly tormented in his legs and hips, and he had no relief day or night. And on Christmas eve, before daybreak, he came to the tomb of the blessed Armanno, and stayed there in supplication and devotion all day until Nones, praying to god to release him from this gout through the merits of the blessed Armanno. And when the bell rang out, he felt free of the usual pain in his hips and legs, and he began to walk about freely and without a stick, which previously he had not been able to do ...

4 January 1270: Madonna Candiana, wife of Petrocino di Mazzo of the *contrada* of San Romano, Ferrara, in the presence of the lord bishop and many others, clerical and lay, swore to tell the truth regarding the infirmity and liberation of her daughter Tommasina aged two years, whom she showed to the lord bishop. On oath she confirmed that her daughter was for four months afflicted with the disease of multiple ulcers on both sides of her hips, such that she was in despair of release. And thus she remained afflicted until Christmas eve just passed. At which time Candiana vowed her girl to God and the blessed Armanno, that if he liberated her, she would bring her to his tomb and offer a waxen image in her likeness. Having made this vow ... on Christmas day Tommasina was liberated, the ulcerations having healed. And she showed the ulcerations, which appeared totally healed, to the bishop and to a great number of people.

On the same day, Master Enoch, medical doctor and citizen of Ferrara, as a sworn witness, asserted on oath that he had had this girl, Candiana's daughter, who was there present, in his care, and had done much over a month and more to liberate and treat her. And he knew for certain that she had been afflicted with terrible pain from the ulcers on her hips. And when he saw that her infirmity was incurable, he had discharged and left her. And he had told the girl's mother to bind her and do the best she could for her. And this was just before Christmas just passed.

b) Examination of witnesses against Armanno Pungilupo, Ferrarese heretic, 1270–1288.

[Among the twenty-six general charges were the following:]

1. that he was a heretic …

4. that he said that there was no salvation in the Roman church, but only in the heretics

5. that he spoke ill of the body of Christ

6. that he gave and received the *consolamentum*[36] to and from heretics according to their rite

7. that he had friendship, familiarity, acquaintance and conversation with heretics

8. that he said heretical things, speaking ill of ministers of the Church, calling them demons and wolves because they persecuted the 'good men', that is, the heretics …

10. that he relapsed into heresy after he had sworn to obey the inquisition …

11. that he abjured heresy before the inquisition in 1254 …

13. that he was a messenger for heretics, taking them bread blessed by heretics …

16. that heretics came to him and revered him after his death.

Master Ferrarino da Lignamine, on 8 August 1270, said on oath that Pungilupo was a believer of the heretics and loved them. And he saw him with Martino da Campitello, who was a heretic.

Fra Tebaldino, on 4 November 1270, said on oath that he heard it said many times and from many persons that Pungilupo was a believer of the heretics and that he said words against the Catholic faith …

Fra Bonfadino of the Dominican order, on 28 November 1270, said on oath that before he entered the Order, he knew Pungilupo and that he was reputed a believer of heretics.

Madonna Veneria, who was a believer of the heretics, on 29 November 1284, said on oath that Pungilupo was a believer, receiver and familiar of heretics … the reasons for her saying this are that two years or so before his death Pungilupo knowingly took heretics to her house; and that she saw him make reverence to a female heretic; and that she saw him give the *consolamentum* to a woman; and that Pungilupo often said heretical things to her …

Madonna Bengepare, who was a believer of the heretics, on 10 November 1274, said on oath that Pungilupo was a believer of the heretics

36 The Cathar rite of consecration, 'the sole rite of salvation': Lambert, *The Cathars*, p. 189f.

of the sect of Bagnolo. And she said that she heard the Cathars do many tricks and say derisory things of the Roman church, including 'How, after this, will those of the Roman church say that we are bad men, when they make one of us a saint?'

Gavino da Satta, who was with lord Menabò of Ferrara who kept heretics in his house, said on oath that he heard heretics say 'Whatever friars or others of the Roman church might say, Pungilupo was one of our people and was our believer'. And that this was common knowledge among them.

Lord Jacobino, a judge, on 5 July 1270, said on oath that he believed Pungilupo to be a believer of the heretics. Asked why, he replied, because he only rarely went to church, because he did not take advice from any wise churchmen, and because he said many bad things about clerics.

Rengarda of Verona, on 26 April 1285, said on oath that eighteen or twenty years ago, roughly, she saw Armanno of Ferrara ... in Verona. And, as a believer and friend of the heretics, he came to the house of the witness to visit her mother, for she was a believer of the heretics and received him, and he stayed there ...

Albertino, who was a heretic, on 3 August 1273, said on oath that Pungilupo was a 'consoled' Cathar. And he said that Pungilupo did him reverence in his own house and many times elsewhere. And that Pungilupo came to Verona about six years ago, on account, so he said, of a prisoner who had fled there. And there Pungilupo received the laying on of hands in the house of the Cathars ... from Alberto bishop of the sect of Bagnolo and from Albertino himself, who was ... an elder son[37] and visitor of their sect in Lombardy ...

Lord Enrico, who was a Cathar-catcher and officer of the inquisition, on 28 November 1270, said on oath that he heard say and it was common knowledge that Pungilupo was a believer of the heretics. And he had heard say that he thought ill of the body of Christ. So, when he found Pungilupo on the piazza of Ferrara, he said to him, 'I have heard of you, Pungilupo, that you think ill of the body of Christ. I have the office of arresting heretics. I arrest you'. And Pungilupo replied, 'What do you believe?'. To which he replied, 'I believe that it is truly the body of Christ, after it is consecrated by the priest' ... and Pungilupo said, 'And I, for love of you, will so believe from now on'.

37 *filius major*: a sort of Cathar bishop-in-waiting: *ibid.*, p. 158.

Fra Bonfadino ... on 28 November 1270, said on oath that after he entered the Order, he heard Pungilupo say many times, 'If the body of our lord Jesus Christ were as big as a mountain, it would all have been eaten up by now'. And he said that Pungilupo refused to pray towards the east, but prayed towards the west, saying publicly that he did not want to pray in the same direction as the fat, plundering clergy ...

Grazio da Bergamo, who lives in Ferrara, on 12 December 1270, said on oath that, at the time of Pungilupo's death, some men from Bergamo came and lodged in his house. Among them were some heretics, one of whom pretended to be dumb and then to have been cured, though the witness knows well that he was not dumb before, nor had he used to be. And he said that many heretical believers from Bergamo, whom he knew well, came to Ferrara in order to see Pungilupo's deeds and they did him great reverence.

Fra Atasio da Bergamo, of the Dominican order, on 12 January 1270 said on oath that while he was in the convent in Ferrara he saw many heretical believers, who had never been used to going to church, coming to the body of Pungilupo, carrying votive offerings and glorying in him, that one of their own had been made a saint.

34 'Saint' Guglielma and her followers: Milan, 1300

It is often claimed that heresy was attractive to women because it allowed them a greater role in religious practices, but here the Guglielmites look forward to women taking control of the Catholic church itself.

a. F. Tocco, 'Il processo dei guglielmiti', *Rendiconti dell'Accademia dei Lincei. Classe di scienze morali, storiche e filologiche*, 5th ser., 8 (1899), 310–26, 331–3.

In the name of our Lord, Amen, 1300. As, by notoriety and clamour, the accusation has reached us, fra Guido 'de Cochenate' and fra Raynerio da Pirovano of the Dominican order, inquisitors into heretical misdeeds in Lombardy ... that some people, men and women, who had been summoned on suspicion of heresy on previous occasions by various inquisitors, and had abjured all heresy, for a long time after held secret conventicles and gatherings of many people, male and female, and also made preachings, we, wishing to see whether they have indeed acted as clamour reports, have begun to hold an inquisition against them, as is contained below.

20 July 1300, in Milan in the house of the Dominicans, in the room where the office of the inquisitor is exercised.

Andrea di Gerardo Saramita, of the city of Milan ... appeared ... abjured all heresy ... and swore to tell the truth about himself and others, living or dead, whom he knows to have sinned in heresy ... and to name, reveal and accuse them ... to the inquisitor ... Asked by fra Guido ... if he had ever had familiarity, acquaintance or friendship with any heretic of any sect old or new, he replied no. Asked if any of his family, on his father's or mother's side, was a heretic, he replied no ... Asked if, in her lifetime, he knew Guglielma, who is buried at the Monastery of Chiaravalle, he replied yes. Asked if he knew or heard where Guglielma was from, he replied yes, that she was the daughter of a king of Bohemia, as was said. Asked if he inquired into the truth of this, he replied yes, that he went to the king of Bohemia, found the dead king, and found that it was so. Asked why he went to inquire into this, he replied that he went to inform the king that Guglielma was dead and [to see] if he, Andrea, could obtain anything from the king because of the honour he had paid to Guglielma. Asked if he went to the said king in order to procure, with the king, that Guglielma be canonised by the Church, he replied not then, but he did indeed say this at other times ... Asked what life Guglielma led, he replied that she led a common life in her food, drink and dress. Asked if he knew or heard that Guglielma had performed any miracle in her lifetime, he replied yes, specifically in Master Beltrame da Ferno, of a mark that he had in his eye, and in Albertone da Novate, of a fistula that he had. Asked if he knew or heard that Guglielma had performed any miracles after her death, he replied that he heard from some women, who vowed to Saint Guglielma and by her prayers obtained what they asked for ... Asked if he ever heard that Guglielma said that she was the Holy Spirit, he replied no. Asked if he knew or heard that anyone said or believed in Guglielma's lifetime or after her death that she was the Holy Spirit, that is the third person in the Trinity, he replied that he indeed heard this from Suor Manfreda da Pirovano and Suor Megliore de' Saramiti, his sister, and from Ricadona his mother, which these women believed ... Asked if he believed that this belief is heretical, he replied that indeed, it is great heresy ...

26 July in the Dominican church of Sant'Eustorgio, Milan.

Bellacara, wife of Bonadeo Karentani, of the city of Milan ... appeared, abjured all heresy and swore to tell the truth ... Asked if she ever had acquaintance or familiarity with any heretic of any sect, she replied not to her knowledge. Asked if she knew or heard that any of her family, male or female, was a heretic, she replied that her father was given the sign of the cross by fra Anselmo, at that time the inquisitor. Asked about her [previous] statement, made to fra Manfredo da Dovaria, the inquisitor, that she believed that Guglielma was the Holy Spirit, and asked by whom she was taught this, she replied that she, Flordebella, daughter of Andrea Saramita, Megliore Andrea's sister, Suor Jacoba da Nova and Andrea were all taught this by Suor Manfreda da Pirovano, and that they were summoned about this by fra Manfredo and appeared before him in the house of the Humiliati in Monza ... and he absolved them, beating them on the shoulders with a stick. And from that time on she has not believed this ... Asked if she ever heard or believed or was taught that Guglielma was to rise from the dead before the general resurrection ... she replied no. Asked if she ever believed or heard from anyone who believed that Guglielma was the one through whom the Jews and infidels would be saved, she replied that she never heard or believed this ... Asked if she ever ate any hosts that Suor Manfreda gave or sent her, she said no, but she, Bellacara, did indeed buy hosts which she caused to be carried to and placed on Guglielma's tomb, and that out of devotion to Saint Guglielma she ate some of these hosts ... Asked what feast-days are held during the year in honour of Guglielma, she replied two, one on St Bartholomew's day, the other on All Saints, and no more. Asked if she heard that garments were made for Guglielma at the time of her death, and that she was to rise from the dead, she replied that she indeed heard that garments were made, but not because Saint Guglielma was to rise from the dead, but because she was to be taken to Bohemia. Asked if she was ever with other men and women when Manfreda preached or spoke words in the form of a sermon, she replied yes, many times, in the house of the sisters of Blassono, in the oratory, where many people gathered, such that the oratory was nearly full. And Suor Manfreda sometimes expounded the gospels, and sometimes spoke about St Catherine and other saints, but since Manfreda left the house of Blassono, she has not heard her preach ...

26 July, in Sant'Eustorgio.

Master Giacomo da Ferno, of the city of Milan ... Asked if a book, that the inquisitor held in his hand, and in which are written litanies, belonged to him, Master Giacomo, he replied yes. Asked from whom he got this book, he replied that he got it either from Suor Manfreda da Pirovano or from her lady Saint Guglielma. Asked how long he had had the book, replied that he had had it for ten years. Asked if, reading the book, he found in it anything which he believed to be an error, he replied no ... Asked if he ever heard say that a woman called Taria was to be made a cardinal, he replied that indeed he heard this, but does not know from whom, but for this he had great abhorrence. Asked if he heard that any of the followers of Saint Guglielma and Suor Manfreda were to be pope, he replied that indeed he heard this, but does not know from whom ...

30 July, in the Dominican house, in the large cell of fra Guido.

Don Mirano, priest of the church of San Fermo, of the city of Milan, who was for a long time one of the followers of Guglielma ... and who after her death went with Andrea Saramita to the king of Bohemia, and who was a special confidant of Suor Manfreda and of Andrea Saramita ... appeared and swore to tell the truth ... Asked ... to tell all that he knew ... of Suor Manfreda and Andrea Saramita and of others whom he knew or believed to be followers of Saint Guglielma ... he said that he many times heard from Andrea, Suor Manfreda and others ... that Saint Guglielma was the Holy Spirit, the third person in the Trinity, and that she was to rise from the dead and ascend into heaven, in the sight of her followers, and that they persuaded and taught many male and female followers of Guglielma to believe this, and that he knows this because he was sometimes present when Andrea and Suor Manfreda said these things to others ... perhaps ten or twelve years ago ... Item, he said that he heard from Andrea and Suor Manfreda that, just as Christ suffered in the form of a man, so Guglielma was to suffer in the form of a woman for the sins of false Christians and of those who had crucified Christ. Item, he said that he heard from Andrea and Manfreda that after Guglielma rose from the dead and ascended into heaven, she would send the Holy Spirit to her disciples at Pentecost. Item, he heard from Andrea and Manfreda that they were to change the laws and to make new gospels and to create cardinals and religious orders ... Item, that he firmly knows that some of Saint Guglielma's followers had her image painted under the name of Saint Catherine, and he knows this because he himself with his own hands painted her in the churches of Santa Maria Minore and Sant'Eufemia in Milan, and elsewhere, and this was before he became a priest ... Item, he said that he heard ... from many ... that one of the disciples would betray them to the friars, just as Judas betrayed Christ to the Jews ... Item, he said that Andrea and Manfreda say that those who visit the tomb of Saint Guglielma at Chiaravalle enjoy the same indulgence as those who go to the Holy Land. Item, that Andrea and Manfreda say that they have seen Saint Guglielma and that she blessed their table and spoke to them ... Item, he said that, when Guglielma died, Andrea had made a cloak of purple, with a silver buckle, worth about L 50 ... and a garment of purple and two gilded shoes for Saint Guglielma when she rose from the dead. And he saw this with his own eyes twelve years ago. Item, that he heard from Andrea and Manfreda that pilgrims would come from all parts of the world to the Monastery of Chiaravalle to visit the body of Saint Guglielma. Item, that when the followers of Saint Guglielma went to Suor Manfreda and when they departed from her, she made the sign of the cross and gave them her blessing ...

Tuesday 2 August in the church of the brothers of the Humiliati house of Marliano.

Suor Manfreda, of the order of the Humiliati, daughter of lord Morando da Pirovano ... asked if she wrote some litanies of the Holy Spirit, which the inquisitor showed her, she said that indeed she wrote them, and some poems, which she has not seen since she abjured in the hands of the former inquisitor, fra Manfredo da Dovaria ... Asked if she had acquaintance and familiarity with Guglielma in her lifetime, she replied yes, but not great or secret. Asked who was the greatest follower of Guglielma, she replied that Andrea was a greater follower than anyone else she knows. Asked who caused to be painted the cloth which is over the altar in the Humiliati house of Blassono in Milan, on which cloth are depicted three people, of whom two, to the left and the right, are seen releasing prisoners from jail, she replied that either herself or Andrea or the sisters of the house of Blassono, but she does not remember which. And she said that these pictures were made before she and Andrea and the others were summoned by fra Manfredo, because she then believed that Saint Guglielma was the third person of the Trinity, and that through her the Jews and Saracens were to be saved, and they are those who are depicted on the left-hand side ... Asked if in the last six to eight years, after she abjured, any people gathered to her, she replied yes, in the house of the sisters of Blassono, sometimes in the parlour, sometimes in the infirmary, and sometimes under the portico, and there she recited miracles of the gospels and letters of the apostles ... Asked if she was ever reproved by the sisters of the house of Blassono for these ... gatherings, she replied yes, many times ... Asked if she had any of the water, with which Saint Guglielma was washed when she was dead, she replied that indeed she did, but she does not know who collected it, nor does she give any of it to anyone to release them from any ailment ... Asked if she ever throws any crusts or remains of bread into the fire, she replied no.

2 August, in Sant'Eustorgio.

Sibilia, widow of lord Beltrame Malcolzati, of the city of Milan ...
appeared and swore ... to tell the truth ... Asked if she ever heard,
especially from Andrea Saramita or Suor Manfreda, or believed that
Saint Guglielma ... is the Holy Spirit, she replied no ... Asked how
many feast-days are held in the year in honour and devotion to Guglielma by her followers, she replied two, one on St Bartholomew's day,
the other in October when her body was carried or translated from
the cemetery of San Pietro *ad ortum* to the Monastery of Chiaravalle.
Asked how long it is since she first had acquaintance of Suor Manfreda, she replied that it could be eight years or so, and she had
acquaintance through her sister, Maria, wife of the lawyer, Manfredo
da Oreppa. Asked if since she has known Suor Manfreda she knew or
heard of any congregation of people anywhere, she replied yes,
especially in the house of the sisters of Blassono, and sometimes there
were ten or twelve people gathered there and no more. Asked if she
ever heard from Suor Manfreda or Andrea or another that Guglielma
had five wounds, as Jesus Christ had, she replied no. Asked if she ever
had or received any hosts from Suor Manfreda, she replied yes, once,
when she was suffering from a fever, Suor Manfreda sent her three
hosts ... and that Suor Manfreda gave hosts to others, but never gave
or communicated any host to her, Sibilia, with her own hands. Asked
if she knew or heard that Suor Manfreda persuaded or encouraged
any people to ... make vows to Guglielma, she replied no, except that
she, Sibilia, once vowed to Guglielma for an ailment, from which she
was released. Asked if she was ever at any feast given by the followers
of Guglielma in the house of the sisters of Blassono ... she replied yes,
she used to eat sometimes in the house of the sisters, with many other
women, especially on the feast of St Catherine ...

Saturday 6 August, in the church of the Humiliati friars of Marliano.

Suor Manfreda ... appeared again ... saying that she had spoken badly
... in her earlier statement ... but now she promised ... to tell the
whole truth ... Asked if, after she abjured in the hands of fra Manfredo
... she heard and was taught that Guglielma ... was ... the true God
and true man in the female sex, just as Christ was the true God and
true man in the male sex, and that as Christ suffered, died and was
buried as a man, so Guglielma, who was the Holy Spirit, was dead
according to human nature but not according to divine nature ... she
replied that all the above she heard from Andrea Saramita, and was
taught it all by him. Asked if she heard and was taught that just as

Christ rose again in the flesh, and ascended into heaven in the sight of his disciples, and on Pentecost sent them the Holy Spirit in tongues of fire, so Saint Guglielma would appear in the flesh ... and ascend into heaven in the sight of her disciples ... and was to send them the Holy Spirit in the form of tongues of fire, she replied that all this she was taught by Andrea ... Asked if she heard and was taught that just as Christ left his apostle Peter as his vicar on earth and entrusted him with his church and gave him the keys of heaven, so Guglielma ... was to leave Suor Manfreda as her vicar, she replied that when this was said to her by Andrea, she laughed, though she did believe that these things were to happen, but sometimes doubted it. Asked if she heard and was taught that just as the apostle Peter celebrated mass and preached in Jerusalem, so she was to celebrate mass at the tomb of the Holy Spirit, that is Guglielma, and after to celebrate mass ... and to preach in the church of Santa Maria Maggiore in Milan, she replied that she was indeed taught this by Andrea, though sometimes she believed it and sometimes not. Asked if she heard and was taught by Andrea that just as the disciples of Christ wrote gospels, letters and prophecies, she and he ... were to write gospels, letters and prophecies, changing their titles, thus: 'At this time, the Holy Spirit said to her disciples, etc.', and 'The letters of Sibilia to the Novarese', and 'The prophecies of Carmeo to such-and-such cities or peoples', she replied that she heard this from Andrea, but did not believe it ...

b. 'Annales colmarienses', in *MGH*, Scriptores, vol. 17 (Hannover, 1861; Leipzig, 1925), p. 226.

1301: In the previous year, an extremely beautiful and equally eloquent maiden came from England, saying she was the Holy Spirit made flesh for the redemption of women, and she baptised women in the name of the Father, the Son and herself. When she died, her body was taken to Milan and burned.

35 A corrupt inquisitor: Florence, 1346

Use of the powers of the inquisition to collect business debts draws a harsh reaction from the government of Florence.

Giovanni Villani, *Nuova cronica*, ed. G. Porta (Parma, 1990–91), vol. 3, pp. 429–32 (XIII.58).

In March this year [1346], the inquisitor into heresy in Florence was one fra Piero dall'Aquila, a Franciscan friar, a proud and greedy man.

Out of personal interest he was made agent and collector for Messer Piero, cardinal of Spain, of the sum of 12,000 florins which he was owed by the bankrupt Acciaiuoli company. The Florentine government put him in possession of some properties belonging to this company and one of the company's guarantors was detained pending payment of the rest. The inquisitor then had some government agents and some of the podestà's staff arrest one of the partners of the Acciaiuoli company, Messer Salvestro Baroncelli, as he was coming out of the Palace of the Priors, despite the fact that he was accompanied, with the Priors' permission, by their servants. At this, an uproar arose in the piazza, and Messer Salvestro was released by other officers of the Priors and those of the Captain of the Popolo. The agents and the podestà's staff were arrested. By order of the Priors, the former had their hands amputated and they were banished from Florence for ten years, for their presumption and audacity in contravening the Priors' immunity and authority. The podestà and his servants came before the priors, excused their own ignorance, asked for mercy and offered to pay whatever fine the Priors decided; after much pleading, the podestà's servants were released. The inquisitor, angered at this incident, but also fearful, left Florence for Siena, excommunicating the Priors and the Captain and interdicting the city (unless Salvestro Baroncelli was returned to him within six days). Florence appealed the interdict and excommunication to the pope, and sent a grand body of envoys to the papal curia ... with a full mandate. And they took with them the commune's legal arguments, along with 5,000 florins to pay part of the Acciaiuoli debt, and 7,000 florins-worth of promises-to-pay for the Acciaiuoli in annual instalments. They also took a written list of all the inquisitor's frauds and trickeries – he was said to have collected over 7,000 florins in two years from many of our citizens, mostly unjustly, on the pretext of heresy. And whoever reads this in times to come should not believe that there were in our day so many heretics in Florence as were fined by the inquisitor: it never had fewer, almost none. But to obtain money, for the smallest bit of loose talk against God, or for saying that usury is not a mortal sin, he fined people large sums of money, according to their wealth ... And the said ambassadors were well received by the pope and cardinals, and were honoured by the pope on their arrival, despite the fact that they disagreed among themselves, with most of them looking more to their own interests than to the good of the commune, such that they returned with little honourable or beneficial outcome for the commune; and they cost the city more than 2,200 florins.

For this reason, the commune of Florence, to prevent frauds by inquisitors, passed a law similar to those of Perugia, the king of Spain and other lords and cities, that no inquisitor could interfere in anything outside his official remit, and could not fine any citizen (if any were proved heretics, they were to be condemned to death by burning). And the prison that the commune had given him to hold his prisoners was taken away and dismantled; in future those he arrested would have to be put in the communal gaol. And an order was issued that the podestà, Captain, Executor [of the Ordinances of Justice] or other judge should not lend their staff to make arrests at the request of the inquisitor or the bishop of Florence, without permission from the Priors ... And they ordered that the inquisitor could not keep more than six servants with offensive weapons, or grant licences to carry weapons ...

36 Bishop and *popolo* in conflict: Reggio, 1280

In their frequent and varied disputes with the local church, cities were often denied spiritual services through interdict. Here one city replies in kind by denying the clergy all material services, and achieves an extraordinary outcome.

Salimbene de Adam, *Cronica*, ed. Scalia, pp. 738–40; ed. Holder-Egger, pp. 504–6.

1280: In October there arose dispute between, on the one hand, Guglielmo, bishop of Reggio, and the clergy of the city and bishopric, and on the other hand, the Captain of the People (Dego Cancellieri of Pistoia) and the *popolo* of Reggio, on account of tithes, for the clergy seemed to want to collect too much from the men of the *popolo* and city. And so the Captain, with twenty-four 'Defenders of the *popolo*', issued some statutes against the laymen who collected these tithes. On account of this, the bishop excommunicated the Captain and the twenty-four Defenders and the whole general council of the *popolo*, and placed the whole city under interdict. Angered, the *popolo* elected another twenty-four of their number, among whom were seven judges, and they issued many improper statutes against the clergy: first that no one should pay them any tithe, or give them any advice, aid or favour, or go with them to eat, or live with them as servants, or sell them anything, or speak to them, or stay in their houses or on their farms, or give them food and drink, and many more such things – and in each case they imposed the highest penalties – or mill their flour, or bake their bread, or shave their beards, or do them any professional service. And these twenty-four advisors assumed the authority to say and decide whatever they wanted, at their will and discretion, regarding the above ... And on this account many millers were fined L 50 each, in that they had stayed in the mills of the clergy against these ordinances ... and many other people were fined ...

In November, a concord was made between the bishop and clergy, on the one hand, and the Captain of the People, the *popolo* and the commune of Reggio, on the other hand, regarding tithes, in this way: that no one should be compelled to pay tithe, except according to his conscience ...

37 Communal assistance to religious groups: Parma, 1261–2

Communal assistance to religious groups, especially mendicants and the informal groups they inspired, was extensive.

Statuta communis Parmae (Parma, 1855–6), pp. 434, 435, 446, 450, 461–2.

[1261] That the Humiliati friars of Parma are not to be compelled to pay taxes on the mills which they hold in direct management and which are not leased to any laymen for rent or other return.

[1261] That the *convertite* sisters, the friars of Martorano and the hospital of friar Baratino are to have from the commune ... in alms as much as the Franciscan and Dominican friars receive. And the hospital of Rodulfo and the hospital of the Holy Sepulchre are to have 20s each in alms from the commune ... It is added [1264] that the friars of the Sack, the friars who are called the 'Apostoli', the hospitals of San Bartolomeo and San Francesco, the Franciscan and Dominican sisters, the sisters of Cistello and 'Vigorculis' are to have from the commune ... the same as is assigned to others ...

[1262] That the Humiliati may export from the city and district the cloths and wool that they produce, without any need for a seal ...

[1262] To the honour of God, the glorious Virgin Mary and all the saints, and so that the city of Parma be forever preserved in peace, the podestà is to have paid and given from communal funds to each hermit, male or female, in hermitages within one mile of the city, or in enclosure in the city, 20s. at Christmas and 20s. at Easter.

38 Prison releases on holy days: Perugia, 1342

One of the canonical works of charity was releasing prisoners. This was often attached by governments to specific, important feast-days, with the released prisoners being considered part of the city's offering to the patron saint.

Statuti di Perugia (1342), vol. 1, pp. 211–14.

The minister of the friars of penitence of the city of Perugia, and those friars of his order whom he calls to assist him in this, and no other official ... are to have authority and power to remove prisoners and to have them released and liberated from the prison of the commune of Perugia ... on feast-days and other days, for the honour of God ... The minister ... is to take and release five prisoners on Good Friday, and two on Christmas day, and two on the feast of Sant'Ercolano, and two on Corpus Christi, and two female prisoners on each feast of the Virgin Mary, if there are any, otherwise one man instead of two women, provided that those released were detained for minor penalties ... and had been imprisoned for six months continuously ... but the women released need to have been in prison only one month. Except that no one convicted or detained for homicide, wounding to the face with scarring, breaking a peace-agreement, highway robbery, adultery, theft or forgery may be released from prison for this cause, nor can anyone detained or imprisoned for any crime or convicted to a fine of L 25 or more ... Moreover, no one is to be released from prison, convicted for whatever reason, unless he has made peace with the victim or his heirs ... The minister and friars are to offer these prisoners on the day of their release and liberation in the chapel of Sant'Ercolano in the church of San Lorenzo, before all the priors ...

39 Flagellants in northern Italy, 1260

Salimbene de Adam, *Cronica*, ed. Scalia, pp. 675–6, 689; ed. Holder-Egger, pp. 465–6, 474.

1260: The flagellants came throughout the whole world, and all men, great and small, noble and commoner, processed through the towns, naked and whipping themselves, led by bishops and friars. And men pacified quarrels, restored ill-gotten gains, and confessed their sins: so much so that the priests hardly had time to eat ... And they wrote holy songs in honour of God and the Virgin Mary which they sang as they marched along whipping themselves. On Monday, the feast of

All Saints, all the men of Modena, great and small, and all those from the Modenese *contado*, came to Reggio with their podestà and bishop, and with the banners of all their companies, and they whipped themselves all round the city. Then on Tuesday most of them went on to Parma. And on the next day all the Reggians made banners for each of their neighbourhoods, and made processions around the city; and the podestà too, Ubertino da Mandello from Milan, joined them, whipping himself ... There was no one, whether stern or old, who did not gladly whip himself. If anyone did not do so, he was regarded as worse than the devil, and everyone pointed at him with their fingers as a notorious and diabolical man; and, what is more, such men within a short time suffered some misfortune, either dying or falling seriously ill. Only Pallavicino, then lord in Cremona, and his Cremonese subjects, shunned this blessed devotion ... and he had gallows set up along the bank of the Po, in order that, if any flagellants passed through, they would perish on the scaffold. For he loved worldly goods more than the salvation of souls, and the glory of this world more than the glory of God ... [and he feared] losing his lordship if the devout flagellants came to Cremona.

40 The *Bianchi*, 1399

In the summer of 1399 the arrival in Genoa of a procession of white-clad men and women from nearby valleys sparked off series of similar processions, accompanied by fasting and peacemaking, almost throughout north and central Italy. Here, one observer, who was sceptical about claims of miracles, nevertheless attests to the 'transformative power' of the Bianchi.[38]

Cronaca del conte Francesco di Montemarte in *Ephemerides urbevetanae*, ed. L. Fiumi, *RIS*, vol. 15, pt. 5, pp. 266–8.

1399: In this year there began in Italy a devotion, which was said to have started first in northern Europe ... some saying that certain little children on their own had dressed up in white sheets and gone around shouting 'Mercy', and that they were subsequently followed by men and women in similar attire and fashion. Some have said that this attire was derived from a miracle that appeared in Scotland,[39] and

38 Bornstein, *The Bianchi*, p. 146.

39 The story, variously placed by chroniclers in Provence, England, Scotland or Spain, was a commonplace one in which the Virgin Mary appeared to a peasant and instructed him on how Christian society should act in order to avoid destruction from Christ angry at its sinfulness: *ibid.*, pp. 43–52.

a letter was shown from the king there giving notice of this miracle, but this letter in my opinion and that of others seemed insincere and bogus rather than true. However, the whole thing seemed to be truely approved by God. Those dressed in this manner came into Tuscany from Lombardy and came first to Sarzano ... and they were called the Bianchi. And as soon as they arrived in some place they pacified every enmity there and afterwards turned round and went back. In Sarzano everyone put on the white robes – men and women, rich and poor – and went to Pisa and Lucca, and there it seems God allowed them the grace to pacify, and to restore all the bandits, and to release all prisoners, and they said that for nine days no one should lie in bed or eat meat or eggs or put table-linen on the table, and should fast on bread and water on Saturdays and process with the crucifix, whipping themselves and visiting the churches, and that the priests should go around in shirts and surplice singing certain hymns of praise – the main one sung on visiting churches was the 'Stabat mater dolorosa'. Those from Pisa went to Siena, those from Lucca to Florence, and the Florentines immediately dressed likewise, and I heard that as many as 4,000 passed through. Those from Siena then went to Perugia. My son Ranuccio was there and he too adopted the attire, and was the first to come to Orvieto, along with many from Perugia, Città della Pieve, Cetona and elsewhere. From our lands alone 200 joined the Bianchi, men and women, and arrived in Orvieto on Tuesday 2 September. They immediately made the pacifications that were to be made, and Messer Paolo Orsini, in Orvieto with 400 papal cavalry, adopted the attire, and he and his troops went around barefoot, whipping themselves, with a cross before them, singing hymns with as much devotion as one could say. On Saturday 6th, all the Orvietans donned white robes, men and women, and on the following day set off for Rome. Ranuccio left on Thursday 4th, and went to Montefiascone and Viterbo, where everyone at once dressed in this way and God granted them grace to make peace and release prisoners – among them, at Vetralla, the prefect at their request freed Marco di Ianne di Messer Francesco di Viterbo, who had been in prison for thirty-nine years. The Orvietans went to Rome, where no one had yet adopted this attire, and 10,000 were reckoned to be dressed thus. And the following day the majority of the Romans adopted it. The pope displayed the Veronica and all the relics ...

Many claim that many miracles were seen, but God knows if this is true. I saw nothing that seemed to me miraculous, save seeing all Italy affected at the same moment, with people of all conditions – rich and poor, men and women – dressing in this way, doing these things, confessing with great devotion, making peace and forgiving any injury, even death ... and this indeed seemed to me a miraculous thing, and still does, for no lord, pope, emperor or king would have been able to make this emotional stir, but only God's will ...

It happened at this time that some men of evil life and condition, seeing all men well-disposed and desirous to see some miracle and to believe what people said, schemed on making money from a trick. In particular a Spaniard, who ... had 3,000 people following him, along with the bishop of Soana. He entered Orvieto preceded by twelve crosses ... and he sent some messengers on ahead for him to be lodged in the sacristy of Santa Maria. Almost all the city of Orvieto was keen to process to meet him. I was one of those who persuaded them not to go, on the grounds that we should first see what sort of man he was ... That evening the papal collector, who was lieutenant in Orvieto of the papal vicar and governor, with Messer Paolo Orsini and certain masters of theology, went into the sacristy to speak to him, and immediately from his speech and behaviour they realised that he was a wretch, because he showed pride and foolishness in reprimanding them, and soon guards were posted around him. He immediately began to fear, and in the morning, without any harm having been done to him, and without being asked anything, he began to say that he had bought his crucifix for 20s, and to ask for pardon, and he admitted that, by advice of a priest he had with him, he had mixed vermilion and oil so that it looked like blood.[40] Once the priest heard of this confession, he immediately fled on a nag, but was detained; and he was called master Giovanni. When he was taken, certain leather bags of his were searched, and there were found jars of ointment, sachets of powder and tools for healing wounds, of which he seemed to be embarrassed, and also knives for cutting purses, and many towels, sheets and other things he had taken from women, and silver buttons and other things of value. He said that he wanted to make with them a tabernacle for his silver crucifix. With all these things he was taken bound in the presence of all the people into the piazza Santa Maria and then to prison in great disgrace, as he deserved. And in this case it seems to me there was a miracle, because he had said, the day before, that his crucifix would do miracles on the

---

40 Another chronicle describes this as 'a trick crucifix, deceptively decorated with vermilion, which spouted blood': Cronaca di Luca di Domenico Manenti, *RIS*, vol. 15, pt. 5, p. 407; but note the comments of Bornstein regarding this episode (*The Bianchi*, p. 100).

day he arrived, and ignorantly he told the truth, because his ribaldry and wickedness were revealed.

41 A sermon on usury

Usury was considered a sin by the church because it was an exploitative, not an immediately productive, use of money, and because it offended against Christian charity.[41] This was not a welcome message in commercial cities, as Franco Sacchetti here playfully illustrates. Sacchetti (c. 1330–c. 1400) was a much-travelled Florentine, probably a merchant, who in later life served as podestà in various towns. His religious writings were marked by a sincere, devout faith, alive to ethical problems but opposed to corruption among the clergy and to irreverence and shallow faith among the laity. Similar themes are evident in his famous collection of novelle, stories apparently developed from anecdotes he observed or heard about.[42]

Franco Sacchetti, Il trecentonovelle, no. 32, in F. Sacchetti, Opere, ed. A. Borlenghi (Milan, 1957), pp. 128–32.

In one of the large cities of Tuscany, a Dominican friar, preaching in many places at Lent, as is usual, saw that many people went to the other preachers ... and that almost no one came to himself. So one Wednesday morning in the pulpit he announced: 'Gentlemen, it is a good while since I saw all the theologians and preachers in a great error, but they have preached that lending is usury and the greatest sin, and that all lenders will be damned. However, from what I can understand and have found out, I have seen that lending is not a sin. And so that you don't think I am joking, or that I'm making subtle arguments in logic, I tell you that the truth is the complete opposite of what they have always preached. And so that you don't think that I'm telling stories, and because the issue is a great one, if I have time, I shall preach on this on Sunday ... so that you will go away content and free of error.'

Hearing this the people muttered and murmured around. After the sermon, they left the church and the news spread. Everyone asked 'What is this one on about?' Lenders were pleased, borrowers were sad, and whoever had not lent money started to do so. Some said, 'This must be a very clever man'; others said that he must be an ignoramus, as this had never been heard before.

41 Jones, City-State, pp. 200–1, 216.
42 N. Sapegno, Il Trecento (Milan, 1934), pp. 423–36.

Soon all the town was looking forward to Sunday morning. When
Sunday arrived, as people are always eager for new things, they ran to
take up their places, and the other preachers were left to preach to
[empty] benches. This one previously had had so few listeners that
several yards separated each of them; now they were so tightly packed
that they were suffocating. And this was just what the preacher had
wanted. Getting up into the pulpit, and having said the Ave Maria, so
as not to spoil his sermon, he began with a reading from the Gospel
and said: 'I shall speak first of certain moral matters, then I shall tell
the story of the Gospel, and lastly I shall give some lessons for our
edification as appropriate, and afterwards I shall speak of usury, as
promised'. Preaching for a long time, this clever friar spent most time
on the lessons of the Gospel, and when he came to the matter of
usury, it was very late (already past terce) ... and he said, 'Gentlemen,
this Gospel has deceived me this morning, for it is of great substance
and its meaning is profound, as you have heard, and I have so over-
run that this morning I shan't have time to tell you what I promised.
But have patience: on other mornings, the sermon will not be so long,
and when I have time, I shall preach to you ... to remove you from
this error'.

And so he put them off from one day to the next, until next Sunday,
on which an even greater crowd than before gathered. He mounted
the pulpit, and having preached, he said: 'Gentlemen, I know why
such a great crowd is here: only to hear what I have several times told
you, that is, about lending. I have to excuse myself this morning, as I
am suffering a little from fever ... but come again on such-and-such a
day, and, if God grants me grace, I shall preach to you about it'.

And so, making one excuse after another, he drew the people to
him throughout Lent, keeping them in suspense until Palm Sunday.
Then he said: 'I have promised so many times to talk to you about this
that I do not wish this morning to pass without telling you what I
promised. You know, gentlemen, that charity is a virtue dear to our
Lord, as dear as any other, or more. And charity is nothing other than
helping your neighbour, and lending is a form of help. So I say that
you may lend, that lending is licit, and, what's more, whoever lends
earns merit. So where is the sin then? The sin lies in *collecting* your
debt. Lending without collecting is not a sin, but is a great mercy,
very dear to God. What's more, I say that collecting can be done in a
way that is not sinful, but charitable. For example, if one lends 100
florins to another, and collects no more than 100 florins when the
time is up, that is legal lending and collecting, and pleases God. It

would please him more if, out of love or charity, the money was not collected at all, but generously left to the debtor. So you have it: usury lies in collecting more than the principal sum, the sin of usury lies in the interest, and that little amount [of interest] destroys all the charity there was in the 100 florins and the good service that the lender does turns into something illicit … So to conclude, brothers, I tell you that lending is not a sin, but the great sin is collecting more than you lend. And with this you may go, and lend freely, for you may safely lend in the way I have described …'

And he then said the confession of the faith, which was neither heard nor listened to, because of the great muttering and gossiping. And some laughed out loud and said, 'This one has really taken us in: all through Lent we've been coming to hear this sermon, and this morning we got here before dawn. I hope he gets stabbed to death, the charlatan'.

42 A charitable confraternity: Piacenza, 1268

The membership, activities and revenue-raising methods of charitable confraternities are well illustrated in the statutes of this Piacentine 'consortium', an early example of charity being directed to the 'shame-faced poor'. Following the statutes there is a list of 800 members of this society (three-quarters of them women), including wives, widows, washerwomen and servants, along with nobles, artisans, traders and priests.

a. G. Tammi, *Il codice del Consorzio dello Spirito Santo in Piacenza (1268)* (Piacenza, 1957), pp. 11–14.

This is the Society (*Consortium*) of the Holy Spirit, whose alms are distributed every week in six pious works. In the name of our lord Jesus Christ, son of the living God, and of the glorious Virgin Mary, of the archangels, angels, prophets, apostles, martyrs, confessors, virgins and all the celestial court, which should come to our aid, amen, and keep this land in peace, repose, concord and goodwill. Amen.

The first teaching that our lord Jesus Christ taught said: Love the lord your God above all things. The second: and your neighbour as yourself. And elsewhere he says: Blessed are the poor in spirit for theirs is the kingdom of heaven … And we, reflecting on this, with the aid of the Holy Spirit, ordain … that the shamefaced poor, the widows and orphans, hermits, crippled and sick are to be visited with mercy, and all others who live in great need, as God will grant us his grace, and as will seem best to us. And he who inspired the apostles through the Holy Spirit, may he inspire all those who are or will be in this society, such that, out of his love, they can never be separated from him, amen.

In the name of our lord Jesus Christ and his mother the glorious Virgin:

First, we, brothers and sisters, servants and visitors of the poor of Christ, ordain that we shall come together in concord in a church in this city every Sunday after dinner, and there collect alms for Christ's poor, and deliver them to the poor and sick, according as God will give us his grace.

Item, that each of the brothers and sisters must say, once, on entering the church, Our Lord's prayer and salutation of the Blessed Virgin Mary, in order that they come to our aid.

Moreover, we ordain that each of the brothers and sisters should honour each other everywhere as brothers in Christ, in order that they shall be honoured in eternal life by the Lord.

Also, we ordain that each one of the brothers and sisters of the society is obliged to make known and declare to the treasurers of the poor of Christ the poor and sick of his or her neighbourhood who are in great necessity, and the treasurers are to provide for them as best they can.

Besides, we ordain that messengers who will give alms to the poor and sick should warn them to entreat God to hold this land by the hand and increase and confirm it in peace, concord and good will, amen.

Furthermore, we ordain that each of the brothers and sisters of the Society ... should each week give one penny, and more or less according to his or her wishes, with a pure conscience and good will, to the treasurers of the poor, and any who cannot is in no way obliged to do so, and should be a partaker of all the benefits which accrue to the society, amen.

Indeed, we ordain that if any brother or sister of the society cannot be in church on Sunday, he or she may, if they wish, send alms to the treasurers of the poor of Jesus Christ, in order that, in reward of alms, he deign to grant us his grace ... amen.

Moreover, we also ordain that if any of the brothers or sisters of the Society ... fall into need, they are to make this known to the treasurers, and the treasurers are to assist them, just as God will grant them his grace. And if any brother or sister becomes ill, he or she is to receive confession of sins as quickly as possible.

Moreover, we ordain that, when in church at Mass the body of Christ is elevated, each brother and sister, prostrate if they remember, should pray for the brothers and sisters who are not doing penance, that God might illuminate their hearts and bring them to penitence ...

Besides, we ordain that, if any brother or sister of the society comes to die, the other brothers and sisters, if they can, are to go and pay them honour, as God does to them, and if they cannot go, they are not obliged to do so. And if the deceased is so poor that he or she cannot afford a burial, the treasurers are to have him or her buried at the expense of the society. Also we charge that each of the brothers and sisters, if they please, should say for the deceased every day for seven days the paternoster seven times, and the treasurers are to have seven Masses said on the seven following days for his or her soul, and for those of other deceased members of our society.

Besides, we ordain that if any property is bequeathed or donated to the society over 20s, the treasurers are to distribute it to the poor of Christ within fifteen days; and if any property is adjudged to the society of less than 20s, the treasurers are not to fear any labour of dividing it among the poor of Christ within eight days, in order that our enemy the devil, who never rests, may not deceive us under hope of any monetary gain.

Again, we ordain that all who wish to join this society may be received, in order that God receive them into eternal life, and that we may reach the grace of the true light and obtain the eternal kingdom, amen ...

Item, that all the treasurers are not to do any money-collecting ... unless for the society.

Also we establish that the treasurers of the society are to attend to and observe all the above, and not to make any money or movable wealth, as God says 'Possess neither gold nor silver nor any money make'.

Moreover, we establish that, when the society meets, in the customary fashion, no one should presume to stand up and speak ... except for the notary reading out the ordinances, or the treasurer speaking of the needs of the poor, or a brother pronouncing the word of God.

b. *Johannis de Mussis Chronicon placentinum*, ed. L. A. Muratori, in *RIS*, vol. 16, coll. 569–70.

The brothers of the Society [*Consortium*] of the Holy Spirit, of the Augustinian order, have their buildings in the Santa Brigida district, next to the church and buildings of the Dominican friars ... where they have a church dedicated to the Holy Spirit. They have a duty to give alms to the shamefaced poor throughout the city and also in the *contado*. In their own arms they carry through the city bread, wine and cooked food, sometimes flour, sometimes meat, and especially around Christmas time. In winter they give out blankets for the beds of the poor; they also give money to newly-weds; and they have cloth made in large amounts and distributed through the city and *contado*. Sometimes they bail prisoners. Property is left to them in wills, and they also collect money every day in the city, and many things are given to them; and when they ask for bread and wine in the *contado*, they find them in great quantities. They always dress in coarse grey cloth, and wear beards. They do not live luxuriously, but well enough, for they work hard ... They have a hospital in the San Donnino district, which is named after the Magdalen and is next to the church of Santa Maria Magdalena. The Brothers of Prisoners are under the society of the Holy Spirit. They take care only of prisoners, and every day they take them bread, wine and cooked food, so that they can live properly ... They go begging only in the city. It is allowed that they dress in coarse white cloth and carry the sign of the cross, but they live in one house, eat at the same table and are under one minister. Both they and the brothers of the Society have to give account to the bishop of Piacenza of their revenues and expenses. The brothers of the Society have also set up many houses in other cities, such as Cremona, Soncino, Parma, Bologna and Faenza.

43 A charitable confraternity in trouble: Orsanmichele, Florence

The Black Death had a huge impact on the fortunes of Orsanmichele, but its resulting wealth also generated problems.

Matteo Villani, *Cronica*, ed. Porta, vol. 1, pp. 19–21.

In our city of Florence, in the year of the Black Death, a marvellous thing happened: out of faith which the citizens of Florence had in the manifest organization and experience in clear, good and well-regulated alms-giving long practised by the charitable society (*Compagnia*) of Santa Maria of Orsanmichele, it was found that citizens, without any human prompting, had left in their deathbed wills, over 350,000 florins to be distributed to the poor by the captains of this society. Seeing themselves dying, and their children and relatives too, citizens drew up their wills in such a way that, if their living heir died, then the society would inherit. And many who did not have any heir, out of devotion to the customary holy charity of the society, left what they had to the society to be distributed to the poor; many others, not wanting their property to pass by inheritance to their relatives, left all their property to the same society. For this reason, once the plague had passed, the society suddenly found itself with such a great treasure ... [Yet] poor beggars had almost all died, and every young woman was full and overflowing with things, so that they were not seeking alms. As this fact became known among citizens, many eagerly sought to become captains of the society in order to administer this treasure. The captains began to gather the goods and money together. The best of the fine furnishings, once belonging to great citizens and merchants, they wanted to have for themselves at a cheap price, while the less valuable stuff was auctioned in public; the money they kept, each one taking part for himself. And as there were no needy poor at that time, each captain made great alms to whomever he most wanted, which was hardly agreeable to God and the Virgin Mary. And because of this improper behaviour, much of the treasure was quickly dissipated ... And for these reasons, faith in the society among citizens and countrydwellers began greatly to fall off, poisoned by the excessive treasure and by its greedy administrators ...

III: THE URBAN ECONOMY

In Italy 'between 1050 and 1300, population, wealth and resources concentrated in cities and commercial activity to a degree without precedent in the ancient or medieval world'.[1] Philip Jones' essay of 1974 is one of the greatest celebrations of the secular achievements of the Italian medieval merchant class. The growth of Italian towns' economic power was, as he says, 'spectacular'. Population growth was so strong that before 1300 several cities had to limit immigration from the countryside. Guilds proliferated as specialised groups of producers came together. The use and stock of money expanded enormously as mints multiplied in number and issued new coins which became the standard units of international trade. Ports – Pisa, Venice, Genoa – developed their maritime trade, as well as their shipping. Industrial production for export grew strongly: textiles of all sorts (woollen, linen, cotton, silk) in centres such as Milan, Cremona, Florence and Lucca, metalwork (especially arms manufacture) in Milan, Brescia and Bergamo, and particular local products in many cities (some of them small). Cities competed to hire the best artisans. Alongside production there developed the techniques and skills of international trade and finance, particularly in Tuscany, and where these were combined with production, there was strong economic growth and enrichment. The results of all this were widespread and far-reaching. In education, business needs fostered the growth of both literacy and numeracy. In society, a new social classification was required to denote the rich mercantile and industrial class (the *popolo grasso*), large sections of urban population depended on industrial production (30,000 in wool manufacture in Florence in the 1330s, according to Villani), and all social groups, feudatories included, participated in commerce. In material culture, there was a new appetite for the display of wealth and power on the part both of individuals and families (through dress, servants, horses, furnishings, banquets, housing) and of cities (through public buildings, fountains, paving). There was a belief in the power of money, which mocked the doctrines of the church regarding the sinfulness of usury.

1 P. J. Jones, 'La storia economica. Dalla caduta dell'Impero romano al secolo XIV', in *Storia d'Italia*, Einaudi, vol. 2 (Turin, 1974), p. 1681.

All of this encountered a reaction from the devout, to be seen in the penitential movements, in the Franciscans (St Francis famously renounced the possessions of his father, a cloth merchant), in the heretics (in their fervour for apostolic poverty), in sumptuary law, which tried to restrain lavish spending on clothes, food and ceremonies, and in the idealisation of the past, with its corresponding belief in the decadence of the present (especially the decadence of chivalry, corrupted by comforts). Such moral tensions were countered, however, by 'praise of the present', by the pride taken in the size and, especially, the number of commercial and industrial enterprises (markets, workshops, ships), which even carried some clerical writers with it (such as Remigio de' Girolami). It was countered too by the growing influence in urban society of merchants and producers: by acquiring knighthood, property and marriage, merchants mingled with the feudal nobility; government itself became 'a condominium of commune and greater guilds', as guild membership became a requisite, as guilds were given civic responsibilites, and as government policies became dominated by commercial interests.

On the other hand, Jones points out in another important essay in 1980,[2] the cities where republican, anti-feudal politics were combined with capitalistic, 'bourgeois' economies did not consitute the whole of medieval Italy, and a 'balanced evaluation' is needed: 'urbanisation and commercialisation, though spectacular to medieval and later observers, did not produce a profound or lasting change in the economy, society or political organisation of Italy' as a whole. Jones then maps out the limits and weaknesses of what he calls the 'myth of the bourgeoisie'. His argument has three main elements. First, there were many areas that the 'commercial revolution' did not touch, except to make them economically weak or backward: the great cities achieved their high levels of urbanization and commercialization not only by pushing southern Italy into a colonial status as a supplier of primary products, but also by extending their economic predominance over their neighbours, controlling or eliminating their markets, and extracting commercial privileges and tax exemptions (as Venice did to Ferrara and Ravenna, or Milan to Pavia and Cremona). The unequivocal centres of the commercial revolution were small in number, and even in cities that did combine banking, trade and manufacturing, the

---

2 'Economia e società nell'Italia medievale: il mito della borghesia', in P. J. Jones, *Economia e società nell'Italia medievale* (Turin, 1980), p. 5, and, for what follows, pp. 4–75.

priorities of the trading system remained local. Second, 'in no city was trade or industry the only source of wealth, power or prestige'.[3] Rural immigrants retained landholdings, citizens aspired to buy land. Merchants were also landlords, owning fiefs, castles and lordships as well as farms, land being attractive for reasons of power and prestige, as well as for security and profit. Agriculture pervaded urban life: much trade was in agricultural produce, many towns had guilds of agricultural workers, the lawcourts closed for the harvest season, when many citizens left for the countryside. 'Agricultural wealth and the beauties of the *contado* rivalled the glories of commerce in urban panegyrics' (for example, Bonvesin da la Riva). Third, communal liberty did not advance the interests only of merchants. Though some nobles continued to live in the countryside, urban expansion expanded the number of nobles living in town. The towns' economic development did not in general weaken the aristocracy, despite some contemporary laments to the contrary. Nobles mostly kept their wealth, not by engaging in trade, but by increasing their income from land, government service or warfare, and by keeping their patrimonies intact. Even in the great republics, where nobles did engage in trade (though only in large-scale commerce or banking), there was a flourishing nobility endowed with inherited possessions, a sense of lineage and class disdain for commoners and parvenus. 'In the great mass of communes, including those like Florence, the majority of nobles ... remained chiefly a landed, even feudal, elite'.[4]

Jones' vision, in which the achievements of communes and merchants are restricted and ultimately undone by the persistent weight of the feudal nobility, is controversial. Italian historians were perplexed at the 'perturbing difference' between Jones in 1974 and Jones in 1980. Polica criticized him for not giving enough recognition to the anti-feudal, anti-noble achievements of the *popolo*, especially in Tuscany, Malanima for misconceiving the relation between economic development in the north and economic stagnation in the south, in such a way as to underplay the 'dissolving and revolutionary effects' on 'the feudal reality'.[5] Several critics have objected to his method of flattening,

3 *Ibid.*, p. 37.

4 *Ibid.*, pp. 74–5.

5 S. Polica, 'Basso Medioevo e Rinascimento: "rifeudalizzazione" e "transizione"', *Bolletttino dell'Istituto storico italiano*, 88 (1979); C. Mozzarelli, 'La questione della transizione e del potere: soluzioni e rimozioni', in *Società e storia*, 7 (1980); in the same volume, P. Malanima, 'L'economia italiana tra feudalesimo e capitalismo: un esempio di crescita sbilanciata'.

decontextualizing, and failing to differentiate, that led Jones to create classes that appear as 'immobile blocks able to span the centuries almost unchanged', with a bourgeoisie 'that never manages to grow but always falls back into feudalism' (Mozzarelli). It could, of course, be countered that flattening and decontextualizing are inevitable in any attempt to generalize, and that to complain of not giving enough recognition of mercantile achievement, when Jones in 1974 does precisely that, is to fail to see the need for balance between the cities where the commercial revolution achieved its greatest results and those that it barely touched.

Obviously in a volume of this scale, it would be impossible to illustrate all these themes, but many of them are touched on: the great demographic expansion of cities, requiring the building of new walls and new housing [5], or the restriction of immigration [56]; the proliferation of guilds [50]; the empowerment at both an individual and urban level brought by coinage [45–6]; pride in the port of Genoa and its shipping [3], sadness at Pisa's decline [64]; the careful listing of crafts and markets [1–2], the interpenetration of trade and politics as commerce colonised the town hall [2], and guild membership became a requisite for political participation [96]; the disbelief in the sinfulness of usury [41]; the moral tensions evident in sumptuary law [89]; the importance of the countryside to townsmen and the continuing strength of chivalry [60–1]. The volume also illustrates other economic problems, those caused by warfare and by 'bullion famine', but mostly those deriving from over-population, then depopulation by plague: the sequence of severe food shortages in the first half of the fourteenth century [69], the decline in population after 1348 (quickly recovered in some cities, not at all in others) [5–6], the enrichment of some sections of post-plague society [77, 79], the social tensions that resulted, and the attempts by governments to repopulate their cities [57].

44 Economic growth: good and evil

'Particularly expressive of encroaching worldly values were the works of … Remigio de' Girolami, who although one of the sharpest censors of the growing rage for riches dwelt at length … on the merits and benefits attributable to money.'[6] Remigio, a Dominican friar of early fourteenth-century Florence, was also a theorist of the city-state, proceeding on the Aristotelian premise

6 Jones, *City-State*, p. 219.

that man was naturally a 'city-dwelling animal': 'he who is not a citizen, is not a man', he wrote.[7]

C. T. Davis, 'An early Florentine political theorist: fra Remigio de' Girolami', *Proceedings of the American Philosophical Society*, 104 (1960), 668.

God bestowed on this city seven almost unique gifts. Man, if he uses them badly, as often happens, becomes blinded, but if he uses them properly, he is illumined. [The seven gifts are:] abundance of money, nobility of coinage, multitude of people, a civilized way of life, the wool industry, arms manufacture and 'prestige building'[8] in the *contado*.

As regards the first, it is to be noted that money, if used greedily, blinds the greedy man.

As regards the second gift, note that the nobility of the coinage is apparent in three aspects: its material, for whereas the gold of *tareni* coins is good, and that of *augustali* is better, that of florins is best;[9] its decoration, in that it has on one side John the Baptist ... and on the other the lily, which is a thing of great excellence, on account of which both Christ and his mother are compared to the lily in the Song of Solomon;[10] and third its currency, because it is current almost throughout the whole world, even among the Saracens. But the arrogant and the vainglorious are blinded by this nobility.

As regards the third gift, note that those confident in the size of the population are blinded by their confidence ...

As regards the fourth gift, note that civility blinds if it stoops to evil, such as lust, gluttony, plunder, homicide, perjury ...

As regards the fifth gift, it is to be noted that the wool industry blinds if it is used hypocritically, as it were, by men not wishing to make evil gains, by usury and suchlike, but under this veil committing perjury, fraud, and usury ...

As regards the sixth gift, note that weaponry blinds if it is used against God, but illumines if used against God's enemies ...

As regards the seventh gift, note that house-building in the *contado* blinds the reckless man who places all or a large part of his wealth in such building, but illumines the prudent man who, though wealthy, takes his recreation elsewhere.

7 M. C. De Matteis, *La teologia politica comunale di Remigio de' Girolami* (Bologna, 1977), pp. cxxiv–xxx; Jones, *City-State*, p. 159.

8 *domificatio*: Jones, *City-State*, p. 216.

9 *Tareni* (or *tari*) and *augustali* were coins of southern Italy, the former being equivalent to one thirtieth of an ounce of gold, the latter to one quarter: P. Spufford, *Handbook of Medieval Exchange* (London, 1986), p. 59.

10 5.13: 'his lips like lilies, dropping sweet-smelling myrrh'.

45 The power of money: external relations

'The striking of fine gold coins in Genoa and Florence, 1252, ... was the most spectacular token of the economic gains accumulated by the Catholic world during the preceding two or three centuries'.[11]

Giovanni Villani, *Nuova cronica*, ed. Porta, pp. 345–7 (VII.53).

After its victories [against Pisa and Siena] ... Florence grew much in power, wealth and authority, and was at peace. For this reason the merchants of Florence, to honour the commune, arranged with the commune and the *popolo* for gold coins to be minted in Florence, whereas before silver coins had been minted worth 12*d* each. And so in November 1252 began the good gold coins called gold florins, of 24 carats fine and each worth 20*s* ... Eight of these florins weighed an ounce, and on one side was the figure of the lily, on the other St John. On account of this new coin, a nice story happened which is worth noting. The florins had begun to circulate through the world, and some were carried to Tunis, where they were brought to the attention of the king of Tunis, an able and wise lord. He liked them very much, had them assayed and, finding them to be of fine gold, praised them greatly. He had his interpreters translate the inscription on the coin, and found that it said 'Saint John the Baptist' and, on the lily side, 'Florenzia'. Seeing, therefore, that it was Christian money, he sent for the Pisan merchants who were then privileged and favoured by him ... and asked them what city this 'Florenza' was which had made the florins. Out of spite and envy, the Pisans replied 'They are our Arabs inland', meaning that they are mountain-dwellers. The king wisely replied, 'It does not seem to me the coinage of Arabs. You, Pisans, what gold coins do you have?' The Pisans, confounded, could make no reply. So the king asked if there was anyone there from 'Florenza', and he found a merchant ... called Pera Balducci ... and the king asked him of the power and condition of Florence ... Pera Balducci replied wisely, demonstrating the Florentines' power and magnificence, and how Pisa by comparison was not the half of Florence either in power or population, and had no gold coinage ... The Pisans were thus shamed, and the king, on account both of the florin and of our wise citizen's reply, gave the Florentines privileges ... like the Pisans'.

11 R. S. Lopez, 'Back to gold, 1252', *Economic History Review*, 2nd ser., 9 (1956), p. 219. And see P. Spufford, *Money and its Use in Medieval Europe* (Cambridge, 1988), pp. 176–7.

46 The power of money: internal relations

The main themes of the poetry of the Florentine Pieraccio Tedaldi (1290s–1350s) were women and spending, and though his approach was increasingly marked by remorse as he became blind, in this poem he celebrates the transformative power of money.[12] The effect he noted was rather different from that in Cecco Angioleri's poem 'When Nero Picciolino came back from France / he was so swell with all his florins / that everyone seemed like mice to him', and he could not bring himself to speak to his neighbours.[13]

Pieraccio Tedaldi, in *Poeti giocosi del tempo di Dante*, ed. M. Marti (Milan, 1956), p. 729.

Alas, I feel so bewildered,
when I have no money in my pocket.
Where people meet to exchange some news,
I almost fail in my courage to speak.
And if I speak, I am pointed at,
and I hear the words 'Look at that talker'.
I lose my courage like a little girl,
such that I become all dumbfounded.
But when I have coins in abundance
in my purse, pocket or haversack,
I am bold and brave enough to speak;
before me a circle, behind me a crowd
I have of many people, each hoping
that in some way I might assist them.

47 Wool production in Prato, 1397–8

The uniquely extensive records of the merchant Francesco Datini allow us to follow wool production through all its stages, from purchase of raw material to sale of finished product. These accounts show the fragmentation, decentralisation and dispersal of wool production: in the course of three years, over a thousand people were involved in producing some 220 pieces of cloth; some of the stages of production were carried out in town, others (mainly spinning) in the countryside; most of the workers, many of whom were migrant labourers, had no fixed associations with the Datini company.[14]

12 N. Sapegno, *Il Trecento* (Milan, 1934), pp. 95–7.

13 For other 'money poems', see Martines, *Power and Imagination*, pp. 79–83.

14 M. Cassandro, 'Commercio, manifatture e industria', in *Prato: storia di una città*, ed. G. Cherubini (Prato, 1991), pp. 406–13. In general, see H. Hoshino, *L'arte della lana in Firenze nel basso Medioevo* (Florence, 1980), and, for technical terms, F. Edler, *Glossary of Mediaeval Terms of Business: Italian Series 1200–1600* (Cambridge, MA, 1934), pp. 324–9.

F. Melis, *Documenti per la storia economica dei secoli XIII–XVI* (Florence, 1972), pp. 500–40 (omitting the details relating to other cloths produced in the same years).

1397: I bought four bails of white, yolky, 'French' wool
of the Cotswolds from Francesco di Marco and Stoldo
di Lorenzo of Florence [totalling], once beaten, 532½ lb ...
Of the said beaten wool we put 192 lb in three pale-blue
pieces of cloth, marked 45 ♛, @ 51s per lb ...　　　　　L 97 18s 5d

[1: Beating]

27 February: White French wool, marked ♛, to be beaten:

Meo d'Antonio di Bonconte, beater, returned on this day
12 lb of this wool, beaten, @ 8d per lb:　　　　　　　　　8s

13 March: The boys in the workshop returned 10 lb:　　　6s 8d

16 March: Luca di Gasparo, beater, returned 51 lb　　　L 1 14s

17 March: Gherardo di ser Braccio, beater returned 23 lb　15s 4d

17 March: Meo d'Antonio returned 33 lb　　　　　　　　L 1 2s

17 March: Andrea di Matteo, beater, returned 49¼ lb　　L 1 13s

17 March: Niccolò di Giovanni di Messer Mazingho, beater,
returned 40½ lb　　　　　　　　　　　　　　　　　　L 1 7s

...

This wool, beaten and returned, was 337 lb and cost to be beaten L 11 4s 8d *piccoli*.

[2: Dyeing]

Francesco di Marco and Niccolò di Piero, dyers in woad, of the Major Guild, are due, for the following work:

6 June: White French wool, marked 45 ♛, beaten, dyed pale blue in eight lots and measured: in total L 56 *piccoli*.

[3: Beating and Combing][15]

31¾ loads of pale-blue French wool, marked 45 ♛, to be beaten and combed:

15 At this stage, the long-fibred wool used for the warp was separated from the short-wool used for the weft.

7 July: Palmigiano di Berto da Pistoia, comber in the
workshop, returned 3 loads of this wool, beaten and
combed, @ 11s 6d per load   L 1 14s 6d

14 July: Palmigiano returned 6 loads   L 3 9s

21 July: Palmigiano returned 10 loads   L 5 15s

28 July: Palmigiano returned 7 loads   L 4 6d

4 August: Bonamico di Gualtieri from Florence, comber
in the workshop, returned 2½ loads   L 1 8s 9d

11 August: Palmigiano returned 3¼ loads   L 1 17s 4d

11 August: Palmigiano returned the short wool and the
wool waste @ 10s per cloth   L 1 10s

Meo di Guiduccio distaff-loader[16] returned the long-wool
of the above 31¾ loads, on a distaff   L 1 1s 2d

The boys of the workshop returned the short wool of
these 31¾ loads, clean and picked @ 8d per load   L 1 1s 2d

Total cost L 21 17s 4d *piccoli* which equals L 8 4s 9d in florins.

[4: Carding]

14 August: Pale-blue French short-wool, marked 45 👑,
for carding: Piero di Francesco da Orvieto, carder in the
workshop, returned 6 weights of the short-wool yarn,
carded. Each weight is 7½ lb. At 12s per weight   L 3 12s

18 August: Jacopo di Ventura da Siena, carder in the
workshop, returned 6 weights   L 3 12s

18 August: Piero di Francesco returned 2 weights   L 1 4s

2 August: Cecco da Orvieto, carder in the workshop,
returned 3 weights   L 1 16s

4 September: Cecco returned 3 weights   L 1 16s

6 September: Jacopo da Siena returned 6 weights   L 3 12s

15 September: Jacopo returned 13 lb @ 1s 7d per lb   L 1 1s 4d

Total amount carded: 208½ lb, at a cost of L16 13s 4d *piccoli* (equals
L 6 5s 7d in florins)

---

16 *apenechino.*

[5: Spinning]

30 July: Pale-blue, French long-wool, marked 45 👑, to be given for spinning:

Mona Nanna d'Orlandino, who lives at Porta a Corte,[17]
one bundle of 1lb 1oz. Was paid 12 October   7s

Mona Francesca di Guardino, in Roncolli, two bundles,
each of 1lb 1oz. Was paid 31 August   12s 8d

Mona Margherita di Tanbo, in Leccio, one bundle.
Was paid 31 August   5s

Mona Agnola di Necio, in Leccio, one bundle. Was paid
31 August   6s

Mona Domenica di Michele, in San Romolo,
Leccio, one bundle. Was paid 31 August   4s

Mona Tessa, from Santa Chiara, one bundle. Was paid
31 August   6s 4d

Suora Domenica di Priore, in the Monastery of Santa Chiara,
one bundle. Was paid 31 August   8s

Lorenzo di Nanni, grocer, in Ciereto Guidi, 9 bundles.
Was paid 31 August   58s

[and thirty-seven others]

4 August: Pale-blue, French short-wool, marked 45 👑, to be given for spinning:

Mona Lucia di Donato, in Padule, 7 lb. Was paid 31 August   17s

Mona Giovanna di Baldoccio, in Padule, 8 lb. Was paid
12 October   18s 8d

Mona Decha di Quatroasso, in Sommaia, 10 lb. Was paid
24 October   22s

Mona Simona di Ricordo, in Sommaia, 5 lb. Was paid
12 October   13s 10d

Mona Gemma di Nanni, in Sommaia 7½ lb. Was paid
24 October   20s

[and twenty others]

[71 lb 10 oz of yarn was given out for spinning] at a total cost of
L 20 10s *piccoli*

17 One of the gates in the old, twelfth-century circuit of walls.

[215½ lb of short wool was given out for spinning] at a total cost of
L 26 3s 8d piccoli

[6: Warping][18]

Pale-blue French long-wool, marked 45 👑, to be warped:

Mona Isabeta di Piero, warper, who lives in Porta a Corte,
had 25 lb 2 oz on 19 September. This cloth was returned,
warped, on 2 October, and she received   15s

Mona Stefana di Domenichino Orlandini, warper, at Porta
a Corte, had 24 lb 6 oz on 27 October, returned it on
29 October, and received   15s

Mona Isabetta, had 23 lb 9 oz on 22 January, returned it
on 24 January and received   12s

[7: Weaving]

Three pale-blue French cloths, marked 45 👑, to be woven:

27 October: Antonio di Giovanni, castellan of the Cassero nuovo, had
25 lb 2 oz, warped by Mona Isabetta [and] on 10 November, 15 lb 6
oz, on 17 November 14 lb 6 oz, on 23 November 18 lb 8 oz, 9 lb 6 oz
and 8 lb. He returned 5½ lb of wool.

22 December: He returned the woven piece [14 canne, 1 braccia][19] and
it weighed 97 lb. He received L 12 piccoli

29 November: Mona Domenica di Guglielmo, weaver in Olmo a
Gricigliano, had 24 lb 7 oz, warped by Mona Stefana,

[and]

on 4 January: 28 lb 8 oz, on 7 January 14 lb 7 oz, on 12 January 7 lb,
on 23 January 7 lb. She returned 4 lb of wool.

26 January: She returned the woven piece [13 canne, 2 braccia] and it
weighed 80 lb.

She received, in loan, on 22 December 30s, on 24 December 1 florin, on
5 January 29s, on 16 January 15s, and on 26 January 1398 2 fl. and L 4.

29 January: Antonio di Giovanni had 23 lb 11 oz, warped by Mona

18 The warp threads extend lengthwise in the loom, and warping consisted in
measuring these off: Edler, Glossary.

19 1 canna (ell or 2–3 yards) = 3–4 braccia.

Isabetta, [and] on 31 January 7 lb 6 oz, on 5 February 7 lb 2 oz, on 11 February 9 lb 6 oz, on 14 February 7 lb 6 oz, 10 lb, 8 lb 3 oz and 7 lb.

7 March: He returned the woven piece [14 *canne*, 1 *braccio*] and it weighed 86 lb. He received on 7 March L 12 *piccoli*.

[8. Finishing]

5 February 1397: Luca di Gasparo mender must have for
burling a pale-blue cloth marked 45 👑, @ 20*s* per cloth   L 1

8 March: Giovanni di Bartolomeo di Ghino mender must have
for burling a pale-blue cloth, marked 45 👑, @ 20*s* per cloth   L 1

13 March: ditto   L 1

[9. Scouring and Washing]

Franco di Simone, washer and scourer ... must have, for the following work, as follows

9 January: he returned one pale-blue cloth, of two,
marked 45 👑 cleaned   L 4

6 February: he returned one pale-blue cloth, of two,
marked 45 👑   L 4

[10. Stretching and Fulling]

Piero di Francesco, called Piero della Dagha, dresser, must have for the following cloths he dressed:

11 January: he returned one pale-blue cloth, marked 45 👑   L 3 10*s*

8 February: he returned one pale-blue cloth ...   L 3 10*s*

15 March: he returned one pale-blue cloth ...   L 3 10*s*

Niccolò di Giovanni, fuller at the Torricella fulling mill, must have for these cloths ...

11 February: he returned one pale-blue cloth

8 March: he returned one pale-blue cloth

30 March: he returned one pale-blue cloth

@ 10*s* per cloth

[11. Trimming]

Bartolomeo di Bonifazio and Antonio di Migliore, shearers, must have for these cloths, shorn ...:

14 February: returned one cloth marked 45 ♔, which they sheared @ 5s per cloth   5s

26 February: returned one cloth marked 45 ♔, which they sheared ... @ 16s   16s

[12. Dyeing]

Francesco di Marco and Niccolò di Piero, woad dyers of the Major Guild, must have for the following work ...

19 April: one pale-blue cloth marked 45 ♔, made elder-green   L 7

Sum of the cost of the above cloths: L 211 13s 6d in florins, from which is to be deducted, for surplus material, L 7 12s. Net cost: L 194 1s 6d.

[13. Sale]

20 July 1398: Block sale of two bails of cloth that I sent to Majorca via Lucca (to Tommaso di maestro Giovanni and co. in Pietrasanta, who sent them for me to Majorca, and to Francesco di Marco da Prato and co. who sold them for me) [including]

One pale-blue cloth, marked 45 ♔, 12 *channe*, 2 *braccia*

14 May 1398: Nanni di Bonacho da Pistoia must pay within six months for cloth bought from me ...

One pale-blue cloth, marked 45 ♔, 13 *canne* and 2 *braccia*,
@ L 5 6s per *canna*, amounts to   L 71 11s

One dark green cloth marked 45 ♔, 13 *canne* and 2 *braccia*,
@ L 5 10s per *canna*, amounts to   L 74 5s

48 The Mercato Vecchio, Florence

Antonio Pucci was 'one of the most individual and likeable figures of the fourteenth century' (Sapegno). In the course of a long life (c. 1310–1388), lived wholly in Florence, Pucci poured out popular poetry on all aspects of Florentine history from recipes and marriage to warfare and politics. In this poem he praises the Mercato Vecchio in Florence in his typical patriotic spirit.[20]

20 N. Sapegno, *Il Trecento* (Milan, 1934), pp. 404–15.

Antonio Pucci, 'Proprietà di Mercato Vecchio', in *Poeti minori del Trecento*, ed. N. Sapegno (Milan and Naples, 1952), pp. 403–7.

Truely I've seen many marketplaces
in various cities, but I wish to speak
of those nearby, leaving aside all others.
That in Perugia seems to me fine:
it is indeed full of many things,
and Florentines regard it as good.
But don't mention other cities:
even to save your life, you wouldn't find
anyone there to act as your witness.
The market in Siena, called the Campo,
seems a hollow: you expire there
of cold in winter, heat in summer.
But these and the others, if I see straight,
are as nothing for produce and beauty
and for that which sustains the people,
compared to the market that inspires me
to write these verses. For in the city
where I was born, it gives pleasure to all:
Florence, that is. And if report is true,
the Mercato Vecchio feeds the whole world
and takes the prize from all other markets.
So I have strengthened my intention
to describe to you quickly in words
the qualities I see in our market.
Briefly, then, they are these:
It has four churches at its four corners,
and at each corner two salient roads.
Around the market artisans and traders
of each and every kind: some of these, sirs,
I shall describe to you as we proceed.
It has medical doctors for all ailments,
and sellers of woollen cloth and linen,
grocers and traders in spices.
There are sellers of glasses and jars,
and those who give food, drink and lodging
to all sorts of miserable youths.
Great warehouses it has, of many sorts,
and the finest butchery you'll find,

in my opinion, selling good meat.
    And always great wheeling and dealing:
    the hustlers are in their element,
    for the market is full of their types,
that is, of moneylenders and ragmen,
exchange dealers and gambling houses,
and everything to ease their business.
    To another side are the poulterers,
    always supplied in all the seasons
    with hares, wild boar and venison,
with pheasants, partridge and capons
and other birds, hawks and falcons,
that would suit the Lord Spendthrift.
    There are always female costers of all sorts:
    I mean those who quarrel all day long
    over two dried chestnuts, swearing badly
and calling one another whores.
Their baskets of fruit are always full
to overflowing, according to season.
    Other women sell eggs and cheese
    for making vegetable pies and tarts
    or ravioli and other such things.
Close to these are the shrewd women traders
selling mustard and green vegetables
and all sorts of herb, both mild and strong.
    And countryfolk come here in the morning
    to give fresh supplies to their maidservants,
    everyone restocking her kitchen.
When the season for fresh fruit comes round,
young foreign girls turn up with their baskets
of figs and grapes and pears and peaches:
    If you joke with them, they'll gladly listen.
    ...
There never was so noble a garden
as the Mercato Vecchio at that time,
which feeds the Florentines' sight and tastes.
    It has no equal in the world, I think,
    as can be proved by winning reasons.
    ...
Every morning the street is filled
with cartloads of goods, and so great is the

throng that many stand waiting to pass.
    Noble men and ladies stand to one side
    and often see the costerwomen and
    the gambling hustlers come to blows.
And prostitutes there are, and their pimps,
and fools, bagmen and good-for-nothings,
and stingy, scabrous gentry-folk.
    And you can see whoever loses
    puffing with great blasphemies, hand to chest,
    giving and receiving many blows.
And sometimes they go to it with knives
and kill each other, altogether
disturbing the beauty of the piazza.
    And often people hang around and sing,
    because they come from all around,
    those who live hand-to-mouth by swindling.
And there are some so poor that in the cold
they crouch naked with their arse on their heels,
because they are totally without clothes.
    ...

    There are basket-makers and bakers,
    cleaners of wells and pruners of gardens,
    and carefree people of many sorts.
When the season comes, countryfolk bring here
many loads of *Calamagno* apples
from Poggibonsi and other places
    ...

    and dried figs and *Carvelle* pears,
    quinces and every similar fruit.
There is the seller of trenchers and bowls,
the make-up seller and the hosier,
who sells stockings and fine little hats,
    and the smith, ironmonger and key-man,
    and, again in season, peasant women
    in a crowd with their pitchers of milk
    ...

49 Enforcement of urban markets: Verona and Parma

Urban markets were not the product of the free choices of traders and customers, for cities legislated both to ensure an adequate flow of goods into the city and to prevent any outflow. Such legislation, it has recently been observed, 'impoverished the rural poor in an attempt to secure urban peace'.[21]

a. *Statuti di Verona del 1327*, ed. S. A. Bianchi and R. Granuzzo (Rome, 1992), pp. 546–7.

We issue as law that no person who transports or causes to be transported on their behalf any corn or vegetables to the city market in order to sell them should dare or presume to carry that grain or vegetables, or part of it, out of the market [until it is sold]. And anyone who contravenes this order will be punished with a fine of 20s each for each occasion, and will forfeit the grain. Except that, if any outsider from any foreign territory brings grain or vegetables to the said market in order to sell them, and is not able to sell them, either in whole or in part, then he may carry away what remains, to sell outside the market, provided he first obtains a licence from the lord or the podestà. Except, also, that anyone may carry away from the market unsold grain up to quantity of one *minale*.

b. *Statuta communis Parmae* (1855–6), pp. 44–5, 46, 60, 61, 178–80, 323, 325, 330, 412 (various dates in early to mid-thirteenth century).

The podestà is to compel merchandise of salt and other things going from Reggio to Brescello to come to the city, and is to ensure water-levels in the canal sufficient for ships to come to the city and suburbs at all times ... The podestà is to ensure that salt produced in the territory of Parma is brought for sale to the piazza in the city of Parma ... And the podestà ... is to have all the men of the salt wells come before him and swear to obey his orders, and to take from them guarantees that all their salt will come to the city and be sold there ... and will not in any way be exported out of the diocese ...

The podestà is to send his knight throughout the whole territory of the diocese of Parma to find grain ... after it is threshed, and to each owner he is to grant so much of his grain as suffices for his family and horses (if he has any), and for sowing, according to what he sees is needed, having made careful inquiry *ex officio*, and the rest of the grain he is to have brought into the city ... And this is to apply to clerics as well as laymen ...

21 C. B. Manning, in *Renaissance Quarterly*, 51 (1998), 207; and in general see Jones, *City-State*, pp. 160–3.

The podestà is to have the fair of Sant'Ercolano held in the gravel-bed of the river Parma ... to the west of the city ditch, such that draperies and other merchandise may be placed there [1227].

The podestà is to hold a fair, of cloth and livestock and other things, provided with stalls, on 1 May and San Siro's day [9 December] ... It is to last four days. And he is to announce this to [other] cities so that they come to this fair as they come to that of Sant'Ercolano. And the podestà is to ensure that Flemings and 'Frenchmen' come to the city of Parma and sell their cloth wholesale or retail, however they wish, in Parma ... [1226]

The podestà is to have those who sell oil retail swear a special oath that they will not have an arrangement by which no one can sell for a lower or higher price. And the same is to apply to all traders. And no citizen may compel anyone of his craft not to work or to sell, whenever they wish ... The furnacemen[22] are not to have any agreement by which they are not able to sell at a certain price, higher or lower ... nor any agreement among themselves that they cannot undertake any building work ... And the podestà is to ensure that all furnacemen work continuously, at appropriate hours ...

The podestà is to have men living within two miles of watercourses along which wood comes to the city, that is on each side of the Parma, Taro and Enza rivers, swear not to remove any of this wood ... And the podestà is to set up gallows in two suitable places, above Lisignano, and if anyone, male or female, is found stealing any of this wood, the podestà is to amputate one of their hands and hang it on the gallows, unless he or she redeems the hand at 100s, and if he or she redeems the hand, he or she must carry the wood around his or her neck through the city and be whipped ...

All the wood of the plain must not be exported from the diocese. And the podestà is to summon ... all the men who have woodland in the diocese of Parma and make them swear and order them on pain of L 100 not to export or allow to be exported any of the wood from their woodland ...

All people of the diocese of Parma must be compelled not to go to any market on a Saturday except in Parma, unless it is an annual fair. And the podestà is to place guards at the borders of the diocese to prohibit anyone of the diocese going to any Saturday market except in Parma.

1258: The podestà is to make all merchandise going through the diocese of Parma come to the city, wherever that merchandise comes from ...

22 Makers of bricks and tiles.

50 Proliferation of guilds: Perugia, 1342

In some cities guilds were formed in large numbers, a sign both of the successful organisation of collective business interests and of the use of 'divide and rule' tactics of the major traders and cloth-merchants, who had more weight in both business and government as a result.[23]

Statuti di Perugia (1342), vol. 1, pp. 123–6, corrected and interpreted according to the 1526 Latin printed version, and F. Agostini, 'Il volgare perugino negli "Statuti del 1342"', *Studi di filologia italiana*, 26 (1968).

So that it be known what guilds are included among the number of guilds, and what officials each guild should have, and how many, they are listed below, and the number of officials is declared[24] ... And first, the guild of the Mercanzia and of cloth, linen and 'mercery' is to have four consuls ... and forty-eight rectors to be distributed among the gates ... the guild of bankers ... the guild of shoemakers ... the guild of tailors ... the guild of second-hand cloth dealers ... the fish-mongers' guild ... the guild of smiths ... the guild of carpenters and masons ... the wool guild ... the guild of provisioners[25] ... the guild of butchers ... the guild of innkeepers, taverners and bakers ... the guild of iron- and crockery-mongers ... the guild of potters and pan-makers ... the guild of those who make hats and caps ... the guild of weavers and wool-carders ... the guild of hair, stuffing and mattresses ... the guild of bag-sellers[26] ... the guild of combers ... the guild of old shoe [sellers] ... the guild of clog-makers ... the guild of spicers ... the guild of swordmakers ... the guild of book- and paper-sellers ... the guild of painters ... the guild of barrelmakers ... the guild of stonemasons ... the guild of ropemakers and saddle-pack makers ... the guild of coppersmiths ... the guild of tilers and those who make bricks ... the guild of cowmen ... the guild of basket-makers ... the guild of furriers ... the guild of saddlers ... the guild of bakers ... the guild of barbers ... the guild of blanket-makers and dyers ... the guild of grocers ... the guild of goldsmiths ... the guild of shearers ... the guild of miniaturists ... the guild of makers of cotton cloth ...

No one can or should be elected prior or treasurer or rector except for that guild whose craft at the time of election he exercises or is accustomed to exercise ... notwithstanding that he appears to be enrolled in some other guild; but if anyone wishes to abandon his accustomed

23 Jones, *City-State*, pp. 228–30, 250–1; and see below, [96].
24 I have omitted the numbers of officials, after the *Mercanzia*.
25 *Procaciante.*
26 *merciare da le tasche.*

craft and to exercise another, he may be registered in that guild ...
provided that he is first removed and cancelled from the first guild ...
to which he may never return ... And as some men sometimes have
themselves secretly enrolled not only in one guild but in several, so
that the office of Prior, which they cannot receive from one guild, they
can receive from another, [we order] that no one henceforth dare to
have himself enrolled in more than one guild.

51 Statutes of a wool guild: Padua, 1384

The history of the wool guild in Padua illustrates a common development in
the economy of the late fourteenth century: cloth production had been weak
in Padua up to the mid century, whereas the trade in imported cloth had
flourished [2], but now cloth production expanded under the protection and
encouragement of the da Carrara lords of Padua, and the economic and
financial power of the guild masters over workers and lesser guilds increased.[27]

R. Cessi, 'Le corporazioni dei mercanti di panni e della lana in Padua sino a
tutto il secolo XIV', *Memorie dell'Istituto veneto di scienze, lettere e arti,* 28
(1908), 80, 105–41.

In the name of the Holy Trinity and of all the court of heaven, amen,
these are the statutes of the wool guild of the city of Padua, made,
reformed, compiled and approved by our magnificent and powerful
lord, Messer Francesco da Carrara ... by the grace of God lord of the
cities of Padua and Treviso ... in November 1384.

   1. That the guild is always to have a chest with two keys, the rectors
holding one, the treasurer the other, in which chest are to be [kept]
the names of all those members of the guild who have been elected as
possible stewards, assessors, advisors[28] and inspectors of the guild.
And eight or fifteen days before their terms of office expire, the rector and
stewards are to go and draw [their successor] stewards and officials ...

   2. In this chest are to be three boxes, one containing the [names
of] the major guildsmen, one the middling, and the third the minor
guildsmen, of those who have been elected as possible stewards, and
the rector and stewards must draw the names of the three [new]
stewards from these boxes. Likewise the assessors and advisors must
be drawn from these boxes. And the stewards' term of office is to be
six months ... And no one who has been steward or assessor can be so
again within one year ...

27 On this latter theme, see Jones, *City-State,* pp. 251–5.
28 *savi.*

3. From the said boxes ... three tickets must be drawn by the rector every month, and those named on them are obliged to inspect every member who belongs to the guild. And these inspectors can enter every shop, house and place to inspect on behalf of the guild, and anyone who prevents the inspector from entering ... incurs a penalty of L 10 ... And these inspectors are obliged to inspect the guild once every week ...

7. No one who does not know how to read and write can be steward or assessor ... except that each group of stewards may have one steward who cannot read, but he may not be the steward-treasurer ...

13. The rector and stewards are obliged, during the first month of their term of office, to convene a general chapter of all the members of the guild, in which nothing may be done but reading of the statutes of the guild ...

15. A chapter can be held by the rector and stewards and all those with name tickets, or a majority of them, whenever it seems necessary to them, in order to provide for all that is necessary and useful to the guild. And whatever is done by them (or the majority of them) will be binding, as if done in a general chapter, at the pleasure of our lord Francesco da Carrara ...

21. The rector and stewards have the authority to appoint one or more balers for the guild, as best seems to them, who are to seal all cloths made in the city and district of Padua with the lead seal of the guild, in the usual way. And the sealer is to write in a book the names of all the masters working in the city and district of Padua, with, after their names, the number of cloths which they make during the sealer's term of office, and he is to take 4d for every cloth ... And he is to consign to the treasurer of the guild 2d for every cloth sealed ...

22. The rector and stewards may and should hear and determine all disputes of the wool guild which arise between persons whether native or foreign of the city and district of Padua and settle claims regarding all cloth sold wholesale or retail in Padua and its district ...

24. No person, native or foreign, of whatever condition, is to dare or presume to buy in Padua or its district any wool produced in Padua or its district for the purpose of storing and reselling ...

26. So that the city of Padua may have abundance of wool, and to remove the possiblity or desire for anyone to take wool out of the district of Padua, we say that whoever wants to sell wool made in the district of Padua is obliged to bring it into the city and sell it in the city and not elsewhere ...

28. Everyone who wishes to work or to organise work in the city and district of Padua is obliged to enter and enrol in membership of the wool guild and to pay to the treasurer L 10 to enter ...

29. Every master or mistress or worker, of whatever condition, of the wool guild ... must obey the commands made to him or her by the rector and stewards ...

31. The rector and stewards are every six months to draw from the name tickets ... six names, who are to be the assessors for six months ... They are to value all wool (above one hundredweight) sold in the city of Padua, whether native or foreign ... and they may take as payment 2s per hundredweight (half to be paid by the purchaser, half by the vendor) ... and the valuers are obliged to write down all the valuations in a book and give it to the guild's notaries, who must copy them in order into the book of valuations, so that anyone can see them when he wants to ...

37. No master or mistress or factor of the wool guild, nor any other person for them ... is to dare or presume to go out of the city of Padua for the purpose of buying wool from the *contado* ... It is licit for all people of the city and district, who have wool to sell, to bring it to the communal piazza, and other usual places of sale in the city, and masters may go there to see and buy it ...

39. The wool guild is always to have available four large candles to carry by the corpses of those of the guild ... and each member of the guild who is at the funeral is obliged to remain in the church with one of the candles in his hands until the body is buried ...

43. No monastery of monks or nuns of the city or district of Padua may work in the wool craft unless it enrols in membership of the wool guild the names of those [monks or nuns], the monastery and the order to which it belongs ... and names good lay persons as guarantors of their observance of the statutes and orders of the wool guild ...

47. That no master or mistress or factor of the wool guild is to dare or presume to give anything to be worked to any worker or master who has been banned for theft of any wool in any city, village or castle, or who has a bad reputation as a stealer of wool ...

66. That no master or mistress or factor or others on their behalf is to dare or presume to have any wool ... transported for the purpose of having it spun within the suburban district on pain of 10s for every lb ... And everyone may send such wool outside the suburban district ...

72. If any dispute arises between a master or mistress of the guild and his or her workers over any sum of money received by the workers from the masters or mistresses, or for any work done by the workers

for the masters, or for any other reason ... the account book and sworn statement of the master or mistress are to be given credence ...

76. If any person who is currently enrolled as a master or mistress in the wool-guild's membership wishes at any time to go and work for any other person of the guild then he or she is to have his or her name cancelled from the list of members ...

82. That no person, native or foreign, of whatever condition, is to dare or presume to bring or cause to be brought into Padua or its district any spun or carded wool or warped cloth which has been spun outside the district of Padua, for the purpose of selling or working it in Padua or its district ...

92. That each master, mistress, factor or worker in the wool guild in the city of Padua is to keep and cause to be kept all the feast days that are written in the statutes of the wool guild,[29] except that weavers, dyers, fullers and stretchers are to keep all the principal feast days, as commanded by holy mother church, and those commanded by the guild, that is St Anthony, San Prosdocimo, Santa Giustina and San Daniele, on pain of 5s for every worker ...

104. That no worker in the wool guild, male or female, of whatever condition, who works for someone, may leave that person's employ ... during the week, until the next Saturday, without the permission of the master ... And that no master or mistress or factor ... of the guild is to dare or presume to receive in his or her workshop during the week any of these departed workers ...

105. That each master, mistress or factor ... of the wool guild ... who wishes to lend money to any worker of the guild, above 20s, is to have this written down by the notaries of the guild in the presence of the said worker ... And if any master wishes to take on any worker who wants a loan of 20s or more, the master is to go to the guild and see if he has a debt to any other master, and if he has, he may not take him on unless the worker settles with the first master ...

106. That no distaff-spinner or winder in the city or district of Padua is to dare or presume to take for spinning more than one ball of ... wool at one time from any master or mistress of the wool-guild, and is to spin this before she takes another ...

109. That no weaver or weaveress, of whatever condition, is to dare or presume to weave any cloth ... or piece of wool or wool mixture for any person who is not of the wool-guild, without permission from the rector and stewards ...

29 Clause 211 (pp. 164–5) lists 50 feast-days.

121. That no fuller, stretcher, dyer, teaseller or washer is to dare or presume to full, stretch, die, teasel or wash any cloth or remnant of cloth in the city or district of Padua for anyone except the masters who exercise the wool craft in the city and district of Padua.

August 1308

We establish and ordain that wool workers, wool beaters and generally all masters and workers of any guild who work on day rates are obliged to be at their work in the morning when the bell called the *Marangona* sounds, and to work continuously until terce, and to return to work when the bell sounds at the appropriate hour as decided by the podestà, and similarly at nones, and from then until the bell called the *Marangona* rings in the evening. And from every master or worker contravening this, the lord or patron may deduct one quarter of the pay promised them, at the hourly and daily rate.

And that day-labourers working at a fixed rate,[30] who may be called vagabonds since they stay a few days in one city and a few in another, are not to be compelled by any stewards to leave any work they have begun, for the purpose of paying their 19s 6d to enter their guilds, but each day labourer may legally work in any craft ... without being in any guild.

52 Derecognition of guilds: Ferrara, 1287

The rationale of this abolition of trade corporations is not clear: partly it seems a blow for the 'free market' against craft combinations, partly perhaps a dissolution of all unlicensed guilds (licensed guilds soon reappear in fourteenth-century Ferrara: see their role in celebratory spectacles, [105]).

Statuta Ferrariae anno MCCLXXXVII, ed. W. Montorsi (Ferrara, 1955), pp. 390–2.

29 June 1287

We establish and will to be inviolably observed that all colleges and guilds (*scuole*) of all kinds of craftsmen, merchants or traders, of whatever sort and however called ... are, by the authority of this present statute, abolished and invalidated, and are to be held as abolished and invalid from now on. And likewise their membership lists, statutes and ordinances ... agreements and oaths. Item, that henceforth no one should dare to hold any meeting or assembly about them, that is, to

30 *ad precium.*

reform, observe or create anew the said colleges, *scuole*, statutes and ordinances ... And if anything is done against this order ... in any way or form, the community, college or *scuola* is to be fined L 100 ... and the individual person ... L 10. From this we except the college of judges ... and assemblies and ordinances made, to the honour of God and veneration of the saints, in order to make offerings and funerals and to provide for members in time of need ... and which regard the liberties of the church and pious causes and works ... It is also excepted that the smiths may have an agent, appointed by themselves with the knowledge of the podestà, to buy coal and to distribute it among them, as practised by them up to now ... And for the implementation of this, they can assemble up to the number of four ... Item, we grant that the cobblers, as they have property in common, may gather once a year, with the consent and licence of the podestà, to elect and instal one or more syndics or administrators to administer their common property, leasing it and collecting the rents, spending and disbursing, as the cobblers instruct them. And we say the same of any college that has property in common requiring similar administration. Item, we allow that the criers may meet once or twice a year, as they are accustomed, but with the consent and licence of the podestà, to appoint two of their number to have command over the others, so that, when there is need for the business of the commune, they can choose those who have to stand at the stairs or doors of the palace ... However, under the general terms of this statute, we do not change the *scuola* and society of butchers, which was once before limited and curtailed by a deliberation of the Greater Council of Ferrara ... namely that their craft had to be exercised in certain places in the city and under certain conditions ... nor do we derogate from that deliberation. Adding that every artisan or worker of any craft or work, who is called or summoned by anyone to start any new work for him, or to remake, restore or repair any work from the beginning, middle or end, even if the work is begun or half-finished by anyone [else], is required as soon as he is asked, requested and summoned by the employer ... to hire, give and grant his labour at any working time ... to start any work not yet started, to continue any work begun by another, even with one or more other workers whose labour the employer has already received in the work ... and to complete half-finished work. Nor can he excuse himself under any pretext ... unless he is incapacitated by ill-health ... And that masters of any craft, and other workers, may not desist from any work begun by them on the pretext of any craftmaster or worker [being] requested by the

employer or sent by him to work with them ... And because the race
of boatmen is the worst, and devises many frauds contrary to the
benefit of travellers, we establish that the podestà is absolutely required,
twice each month, to conduct careful inquiry whether the boatmen
have any 'confederation', 'society' or band among themselves, covert
or explicit, in sailing boats by tacking or any other manner, and if he
finds any of them who have made any of the said conspiracies or
devices, or operate them de facto, the podestà is to fine them each L 100
for each occasion.

53 Non-guild-worthy occupations

Some crafts were allowed to form guilds, others – and not only low-skilled
occupations – were not: a response, according to Philip Jones, to growing
worker unrest and agitation.[31]

a. *Statuti di Bologna dell'anno 1288*, vol. 2, p. 220.

We order that bakers, innkeepers, sievers, wine-carriers, millers,
victuallers, gardeners, barbers, pork butchers, cheese-mongers, cloth-
weavers and cloth-beaters, dyers or wool-washers, sellers of
vegetables, fruit, poultry, straw, hay or wood may not enter or create
or organise any society or have officials, consuls, rectors or a captain
or other leader under any name whatsoever ...

b. *Statuti di Perugia* (1342), vol. 1, p. 122.

We establish and ordain that buyers and sellers of horses, sand-
diggers, limepit workers, makers of muslin, buyers of millstones,
sieve-makers and other crafts that are not accustomed to have rectors
may not have or create rectors, nor be regarded as a guild, nor be
reckoned among the community of guilds ...

54 Promotion of local industry

a. *Statuta communis Parmae* (Parma, 1855–6), p. 191.

This is an ordinance made regarding the craft of fustian cloth, in
agreement with ... the podestà and the whole Council of Parma ...
and the podestà of the society of merchants, namely: I, the podestà of
Parma, swear that ... I shall maintain the fustian craft in Parma ...

31 Jones, *City-State*, p. 255.

and I shall not allow any fustian to be sold in Parma or its diocese, except that made in the city or its suburbs. And no fustian made in any city of Lombardy may be brought to Parma or its diocese for sale, and if I know of anyone bringing such fustian, I shall seize it and have it burned ... [1211?]

b. *Le deliberazioni del consiglio dei rogati (Senato). Serie 'mixtorum'*, ed. R. Cessi and P. Sambin (2 vols, Venice, 1960), vol. 1, p. 94.

26 January 1303

As the craft of soap-making is the greatest and most profitable for shipowners and maritime merchants, and because of the practice followed up to now, this craft is almost lost in Venice, because our Venetians have gone to the Marche and Apulia to exercise this craft, it is proposed that no Venetian, for himself or another, may in any way or form exercise or cause to be exercised, this craft within the Gulf, except in Venice, on pain of L 1,000 ...

Also, lest anyone might have the alum with which to do this work in any part of the Gulf, no Venetian may, with any ship whether Venetian or foreign, carry alum within the Gulf, or unload it anywhere except at Venice, nor may any Venetian buy this alum from any foreigner, from outside or within the Gulf, except for carrying to Venice, on pain of 25 per cent of what the alum would be worth in Venice.

c. R. Cessi, 'Le corporazioni dei mercanti di panni e della lana in Padova fino a tutto il secolo XIV', *Memorie dell'Istituto veneto di scienze, lettere e arti*, 28 (1908), pp. 82–3.

18 October 1356

Measures are to be taken by all just and honest means to bring people to Venice. It is clear to all that the crafts of cloth and fustians, rather than others, are those which are good for the population of the cities of the world. It is also clear that before our war against Genoa a great quantity of woollen cloth and fustian was worked in Venice, but during the war it was given out that cloth from all places might be transported in ... ships within and beyond the Gulf, which redounds to the greatest damage of this city. Those who used to generate business for the said craft, with their workers, are so dispersed from this city and have moved to Padua to live, and similarly in the craft of fustians. Now in peacetime this should be corrected, so that cloth made in Venice may be transported in ... ships within and beyond the

Gulf, and any other cloth may not. Wishing to provide in this matter, that these crafts be done here rather than elsewhere, we propose that from now on all woollen cloth and fustians worked in any city not subject to us (or within 30 miles of such a city) which are brought to Venice by any person, must pay a due of 5s per lb, according to value.

55 The state promotes commerce

a. R. Cessi, 'Le corporazioni dei mercanti di panni e della lana in Padova fino a tutto il secolo XIV', *Memorie dell'Istituto veneto di scienze lettere e arti*, 28 (1908), 80–2.

May 1301

This order is issued for the honour of the commune of Padua and for the splendour and embellishment of the palace of the magnificent commune of Padua. Its purposes are that the palace, in its lower part towards the north, be inhabited by merchants, and resume its reputation, which was spreading through many parts of Italy a long time ago, for these workshops were a finer place for selling cloth than in any city of Italy;[32] furthermore, that between foreign and citizen cloth-merchants there be no discord. Therefore we establish and ordain that foreigners, whose trading in cloth and sendal in the stalls described below at present seems to be beneficial in the view of the stewards of the merchants' guild of Padua, may without penalty for five years sell at retail cloths and sendals, under the said palace and not elsewhere in Padua or its suburbs. This period may be extended if this satisfies a majority of the Paduan-born citizen merchants who have shops under the main palace of the commune towards the north … And if at the end of five years the majority of traders born in the city of Padua who then have stalls under the main palace on the north side wish that the foreigners … leave those stalls … then they must leave them within fifteen days of being notified by the stewards of the merchants' guild … and must fully empty and vacate the stalls … and no longer there or in any other place in the city or suburbs of Padua sell cloth or sendal, themselves or through another person …

And that henceforth no person or college or community may sell … at retail cloth or sendal in the city of Padua or the suburbs, except under the main palace in the stalls placed towards the north and south, and in the stalls under the communal chancery, and under the

32 See [2].

palace of the Greater Council, where it is customary for cloth to be sold. Saving only that citizens of Padua may in the said stalls ... sell all cloth except French and Florentine and sendal ...

b. *Codice diplomatico brindisino*, ed. G. M. Monti and A. De Leo (2 vols, Trani, 1940–64), vol. 2, pp. 162–3.

3 August 1359

Robert ... Prince of Taranto ... to the Captains and vicars of our district of Brindisi ... greeting. Turning our mind's eye with lordly compassion to the poor and depressed state of our city of Brindisi, and taking into due consideration that from the past hazards of war the state of this city is known to be so fallen into ruins that unless we graciously provide remedy, the city's desolation is to be foreseen, rather than (as is hoped) its continued existence ... We have been moved by the petitions addressed to us by the community (*universitas*), [reminding us that] this city, located in a most beautiful site, was of old called the metropolis of all Puglia, in which, because of its various skills and the inflow of goods, there was a port for individual shippers and a coming together of foreign traders of all sorts. Therefore, in order that it might be repopulated with citizens and foreigners, thus bringing an end to its desolation, we have granted by our special grace to all foreign merchants buying, selling or exporting any merchandise in and out of the city of Brindisi, from next September and thenceforth at our pleasure, those same immunities and freedoms regarding the payment of gabelles and other dues to our curia ... that Venetian merchants customarily enjoy who live and trade in our city of Trani.

[In 1360 Robert went on to grant further tax concessions, for trade on Mondays in the city market, and for two annual fairs, for six days around Corpus Christi, and for two days around St Antony's day].

c. *Problemi monetari veneziani*, ed. R. Cessi (Padua, 1937), pp. 127–8, 131–2.

22 January 1362

In the past, when gold was sold 'at the little bell'[33] on the Rialto, there were found eight or ten buyers, and at present there is only one, through whose hands all the gold passes that is brought to Venice for sale. This has caused the Germans, who used to bring good quantities

---

33 *ad campanellam.* On the importance of the bullion trade in Venice, see R. C. Mueller, *The Venetian Money Market: Banks, Panics and the Public Debt, 1200–1500* (Baltimore and London, 1997).

of gold here, to bring none at present, principally because when there were many buyers the gold was sold at a higher and more reasonable price than one buyer alone pays. On this matter it is necessary and beneficial to provide, as far as is possible, and to make every effort that gold be brought to Venice. It is proposed that all merchants and carriers of gold, who henceforth bring gold to Venice are wholly released from paying the impost of two *grossi*, imposed at the time of the recent war against Genoa, for every mark by those depositing gold in the mint, and ... from the *grosso* paid for not selling *ad campanellam*, and also from the 3½ *s* which they paid per 100 lb ... And the above are to last for two years and as long again, until revoked.

13 May 1367

From common report, all the buyers of silver at auctions *ad campanellam* at Rialto have an understanding among themselves and this is quite manifest. And it is said that they have a small chest from which they divide among themselves much money each year, and that they do much other dishonest dealing to the great cost of our state and in evident prejudice of merchants. These things are not in any way to be tolerated, rather to be wholly addressed to the honour of our state and the good and profit of merchants. It is proposed that henceforth whoever buys silver at auction *ad campanellam* may not dare or presume in any way or form to have or make a partnership or combination with others, but all are to conduct business for themselves, as in former times, on pain of 10*s* per lb ... and, in addition, of spending one year in one of the lower prisons ...

56 Demographic policy: controlling peasant immigration

The removal of peasants from the city was prompted by several concerns: at Parma, the concern to put back to work those peasants who had taken refuge in the city during warfare was followed by a more general fear 'lest all peasants become citizens'; at Perugia, the concern was to preserve the rural tax base from erosion through immigration.

a. *Statuta communis Parmae* (Parma, 1855–6), pp. 72–3.

That henceforth no one of the diocese of Parma is to come to live in the city of Parma and if he does, he is still to pay direct taxes as a peasant and a bad citizen.[34] And if anyone comes, the podestà, within

34 *pro malo cive.*

eight days of being notified, is to make him return to live in the countryside ...

All peasants who used to reside in the diocese of Parma before the last war [with Emperor Frederick II] must return to live with their families, wherever they might be, before the next octave of St Peter, and if any of them do not observe this ... all their property, movable and immovable, from that time on will be forfeit to the commune. And all the consuls and district officials of villages and castles [of the diocese] ... are to give in writing to the podestà within one month of this deadline the names of all peasants who have not obeyed, and are likewise to list all their possessions ... [Before 1254]

b. *Statuta communis Parmae digesta anno MCCLV*, ed. A. Ronchini (Parma, 1856–7), pp. 122–3.

Henceforth anyone originating from the diocese may not in any way become a citizen without the consent of the General Council, nor may it be proposed in councils that anyone become a new citizen from those who should be inscribed in the hearth registers with the men of the *contado*, lest in every respect all peasants become citizens. And this clause is absolute and is to be observed absolutely.

c. *Statuti di Perugia (1342)*, vol. 2, pp. 328–9.

We establish and ordain ... that no *contadino* or person of the *contado* of Perugia can be received as a citizen of Perugia on grounds of any statute of the *popolo* of Perugia ... nor enjoy the privilege of citizenship nor be regarded as a citizen on grounds of residence or habitation completed up to now or in the future with his family in the city or suburbs of Perugia, but he is to be regarded and treated as a true *contadino* ... We also will and ordain that each and every *contadino* who before 1319 came to Perugia and said that they had lived there for five years and who tried to prove their ... continuous residence ... with all their family, and who did not [in fact] live continuously with all their family according to the law, should be punished in L 100 each, and are to be regarded as true *contadini* and are to pay direct taxes in the *contado*.

57 Demographic policy: stimulating immigration of artisans

In the late thirteenth century, cities imposed high costs on residence (immigrants had to satisfy economic, fiscal, residential and political tests), but falls in population, experienced already in the first half of the fourteenth century, led to these being relaxed, even eventually for *contadini*, and replaced with inducements.[35]

a. *Statuta communis Parmae digesta anno MCCLV*, ed. A. Ronchini (Parma, 1856–7), pp. 122–3.

To the beauty and increase of the city, any foreigner who in the past ten years was made a citizen is to buy within one year in the city a house worth at least L 100 ... and the house is to be liable for direct tax and other public burdens, and may not be sold without the consent of the councils; and whoever does not fulfil this requirement, if he was made a citizen in the last ten years by authority of any General Council, is not to be understood to be a citizen and loses the privilege he has received. If anyone from outside the jurisdiction of the commune of Parma wishes to become a citizen ... he is to have a house built *de novo* in the city or suburbs worth at least L 100, which is to be liable to the commune's taxes ... And no one can become a citizen of Parma in any way who is not a true friend and member of the current regime of the Guelf party ... [1286]

b. *Corpus chronicorum bononiensium*, vol. 3, pp. 350–1.

1378: The government issued a proclamation that all foreign citizens who came to live in Bologna and exercise any craft in the production of woollen cloth, would not have to pay any imposition, save for the customary *dazi*, and would not be pursued for any debt for two years; save that this was not to apply to any rebel or bandit. And for this reason, it was prohibited to import any foreign cloth, except for Milanese cloth, worth 40*s* or more.

---

35 A. I. Pini, 'Un aspetto dei rapporti tra città e territorio nel Medioevo: la politica demografica "ad elastico" di Bologna fra il XII e il XIV secolo', in *Studi in memoria di Federigo Melis* (Naples, 1978). On Italian demography in general, see M. Gina-tempo and L. Sandri, *L'Italia delle città: il popolamento urbano tra Medioevo e Rinascimento (secoli XIII–XVI)* (Florence, 1990).

IV: SOCIAL ORGANIZATION AND TENSIONS

Urban society: nobles and *popolani*

One of the key elements of Philip Jones' interpretation of late medieval Italy is the importance attached to the feudal nobility and its chivalric values: For all the influence of merchandizing, he writes, 'it would be grossly wrong to visualize the nobility of communal Italy as somehow forming at any stage an alien species, a race apart, among the aristocracies of Europe ... Nobles and knights preserved all the pretensions and self-consciousness of a superior, separate caste'.[1] And it is the power of the nobility that contained and curtailed the growth of the 'bourgeoisie', and that resisted and challenged the achievements of republican Italy.[2] Franco Cardini has argued that there were three major elements of noble lifestyle in the communal period: knighthood, towers and vendetta. These three elements form the focus for the documents here.

In creating a sense of superiority, knighthood played an important, increasing part, and the ceremony of dubbing, by which new knights were created, because of its increasingly formal and sumptuous character, expressed the desire of the knightly class to close itself into a caste. The cost is attested by Folgore da San Gimignano, who wrote a series of loving poems on the ceremonies of knighthood; the formal character by an extraordinary document from the Sienese chronicles of the knighting of Francesco Bandinelli, that includes long lists of the guests, of what they had to eat, and of their gifts to the new knight.[3] This record, though exceptional in its detail, is but one of many records of formal chivalric ceremonies in fourteenth-century Italy: knightings were performed before battles and after victories, at the entries into cities of kings, emperors and princes, at specially convened chivalric 'courts' where they were part of dynastic festivities such as weddings, tournaments, banquets and dancing.

1 Jones, *City-State*, pp. 312, 315, and generally, pp. 298–321.

2 *Ibid.*, pp. 519–642.

3 F. Cardini, 'Vita comunale e dignità cavalleresca a Siena', in *L'acciar de' cavalieri: Studi sulla cavaleria nel mondo toscano e italico (secc. XII–XV)* (Florence, 1997).

Private towers distinguish the Italian city-state as no other artefact: they were raised in large numbers – one for each noble family at Ferrara, over three hundred at Rome, for example – and were ambitiously tall. Debate surrounds their origins and practical function: were they built by knights and nobles when they migrated into towns, in order to reproduce the type of fortified residence they already owned in the country? Or were they already a feature of towns – the headquarters of persons of prestige and power – before the great urban expansion of the twelfth and thirteenth centuries? Were their functions primarily military – for throwing and projecting missiles – or were they often built too close together for any useful military role?[4] On the symbolical role of towers there seems less debate: they 'came to represent the material symbol of common descent' (Venditelli) or 'symbolic capital' (Maire Vigueur), and this was evident in their scale and their location. In Rome, baronial residences were 'dominated by towers of a massiveness and height often disproportionate to any real need' and asserted the image of the rural castle;[5] at Verona the noble towers were concentrated in the old city centre (rather than in the newly expanding or incorporated suburbs) and around specific points of power (the main piazza, the market-place, the river bank). However, the role of towers changed with political circumstances: at Verona, the role of towers collapsed when political change caused rapid replacement of the traditional knightly élite first by the guilds and then by the emerging lordship of the della Scala family; at Milan the penchant for tower-building was 'bridled' by the early formation of *signorie*.[6] Noble families sold their towers to merchants, judges or notaries, or let them fall into ruin.[7] Something similar happens to noble pursuit of vendetta: we hear less of it in cities ruled by *signori* – indeed, Galvano Fiamma credits Lucchino and Giovanni Visconti with ending private war between families in Milan.[8]

4 A. A. Settia, 'Lo sviluppo di un modello: origine e funzioni delle torri private urbane nell'Italia centro-settentrionale', in *Paesaggi urbani dell'Italia padana nei secoli VIII–XIV* (Bologna, 1988); in the same volume, G. M. Varanini, 'Torri e casetorri a Verona in età comunale: assetto urbano e classe dirigente'.

5 S. Carocci, 'Baroni in città: Considerazioni sull'insediamento e i diritti urbani della grande nobiltà', in *Rome aux XIII et XIV siècles*, ed. E. Hubert (Rome, 1993), p. 154.

6 E. Saita, 'Una città "turrita"? Milano e le sue torri nel Medio Evo', *Nuova rivista storica*, 80 (1996), 331.

7 M. Venditelli, 'Note sulla famiglia e sulla torre degli Amateschi a Roma nel secolo XIII', *Archivio della Società romana di storia patria*, 105 (1982).

8 T. Dean, 'Marriage and mutilation: vendetta in late-medieval Italy', *Past and Present*, 139 (1997).

Knighthood is one thing that unites the nobility across Italy. Yet in other respects there would be more reason to differentiate. There are vast differences between, for example, the nobilities of Venice and Rome. In Venice a large and strongly mercantile aristocracy identified with the civic ethos of the state: Venetian noble families did not live in compact clan enclaves, but were scattered across the city in numerous households, and this meant that Venetian nobles did not look to create local clienteles in their neighbourhoods. The patron–client relation, where it existed, operated on a different level: the standing of nobles was based on state office and the procurement of state favours for clients, not on domination of a city district. 'Rather than cultivating neighbourhood clienteles and promoting family enclaves that could be mobilised and defended in times of civil strife, they jostled for power within the legal confines of government'.[9] The Roman baronage, by contrast, consisted of about a dozen families, of whom five or six were pre-eminent. They owned and inhabited closed fortresses within the city, huge blocks of land containing palaces, houses and squares, all held in condominium among various branches of the family. Their ownership also of properties and rights in the adjacent areas enabled barons to construct dense groups of local dependency, still formulated in the fourteenth century in feudo-vassalic terms, creating 'a network of fealties of unequivocal solidity and breadth'. At the same time, their rural possessions, of castles and estates, were equally important to them, and they did not identify wholly with the city.[10] Many cities probably resembled Rome rather than Venice: one thinks of the Peruzzi enclave in Florence, or the Perugian text that describes urban space as a series of feudal islands resembling 'castles'.[11]

From the late twelfth or early thirteenth centuries, political domination of cities by the noble-knightly class was challenged by popular societies – artisans and shopkeepers organised in 'paramilitary, neighbourhood societies' (Koenig), whose principal interest, it is argued, was not in using the city to protect and advance rural interests, but in pacifying the city and dominating the countryside.[12] The economic

9 D. Romano, *Patricians and Popolani: The Social Foundations of the Venetian Renaissance State* (Baltimore and London, 1987), p. 140.

10 Carocci, 'Baroni in città'.

11 A. Grohmann, 'Economia e società a Perugia nella seconda metà del Trecento', in *Società e istituzioni dell'Italia comunale: l'esempio di Perugia (secoli XII–XIV)* (2 vols, Perugia, 1988), p. 86.

12 J. C. Koenig, *The Popolo of Northern Italy (1196–1274): A Political Analysis*, UCLA Ph.D. dissertation, 1977 (published in Italian translation, Bologna, 1986).

and social interests of nobles and *popolo* were thus manifestly anta-gonistic. Popular societies expelled nobles, appropriated their juris-dictions, and demanded equal shares of political offices. The *popolo* has been seen behind communal efforts to wrest church offices from the hands of the nobility, to tax peasants, to force the countryside to supply the city's food needs, and to reduce church privileges and exemptions.[13] Unable to achieve peaceful coexistence, *popolo* and nobles disputed dominance of the commune: *popolani* were verbally abused in council meetings (as later was Cola di Rienzo in Rome: [68]), or removed and locked out. The outcome was division: expulsions and secessions, the rival appointments of chief officers, rival laws, rival councils, rival palaces, rival bells and banners. However, after 1250 the *popolo* in many cities won a permanent place in government through the institution of a committee of *anziani*, which came to share power with the podestà. In some cities, regimes of *anziani* achieved some successes, in reinforcing and maintaining public order through the creation of militias, through stronger means of reporting, prosecuting and punishing violent crimes, through efforts to keep government free of partisans, and through anti-magnate laws which sought to discipline and disarm lawless nobles while also dissolving their means of support (fiefs, vassals, etc.) and divorcing them from *popolani*. The purpose of such anti-magnate laws, it has been claimed, 'was simply to destroy the nobility as an organised force in public life. In other words, it was an attempt – careful, calculated, and completely serious – to make a revolution: radicalism at its best'.[14] These efforts were realised and reinforced through the institution of Captains of the *popolo* from the 1250s. In Perugia, the regime of the *popolo* achieved some sort of 'golden age' permanence, pursuing policies of 'equality, justice and public peace',[15] excluding the nobility, and even ending the greater merchants' dominance by the creation of Priors of the Guilds reserved to artisans and retailers (see [96]).

However, the class lines were not so clearly drawn, nor was the nobility so easily cowed as some historians claim. In some cities there were knights among the members of the *popolo*; in many cities the leaders of the *popolo* were local noblemen, who thus mobilised the people in their own interests. Even where leadership came from within

13 Jones, *City-State*, pp. 499–519.
14 Grundman, *The Popolo at Perugia*, p. 112.
15 *Ibid.*, p. 131.

the *popolo*, this could be instigated by noble families (as at Piacenza: [65]). In response to popular challenge, knights formed their own societies, and used their power bases in the countryside to disrupt the city's markets, food supplies and sources of water. In Asti they too adopted the slogan of equality and demanded equal treatment, not discrimination.[16] And nobles with greater ambitions, to lordship not equality, used the situation of *popolo*–noble conflict, to establish a new type of government altogether: the period of great popular successes is also the period of the institution of *signorie*, later known as despotisms (thus Uberto Pallavicino at Cremona, Uberto de Iniquitate in Piacenza, Azzo d'Este in Ferrara). And though city-lords sometimes came to power as leaders of the *popolo*, it was the *popolo* that often suffered from their advent to power: the *popolo*'s bell-tower (an important symbol) was destroyed in Mantua, the guilds were dissolved in Ferrara. The *signori* used some of the same methods to consolidate their rule: the creation of militias (Mantua, Ferrara), a harshening of police powers (torture, etc.), a reduction of magnates and feudal opposition, constitutional change (small councils to replace the large general councils of the commune), and building programmes in the political and spiritual heart of the city (see the example of Azzone Visconti: [13]).

In many communes though the *popolo* was weak to start with. The 'typical' Italian town was dominated by land, dependent on agriculture.[17] At Fermo in the Marche, for example, the guilds, even in the fourteenth century, were not well developed and lacked political weight. The economy was predominantly agrarian, and the most important artisan activities related to the processing of raw materials (wool, cheese). Expansion of the commune's control of territory meant a strengthening of agrarian interests in town. All the noble families were of feudal origin, having migrated to the town to ensure urban support in controlling their estates (for example, fugitive serfs). The fourteenth century accordingly saw a succession of attempts by these nobles to establish lordship over Fermo [102].[18]

---

16 *Gli atti della società del popolo di Asti dal 1312 al 1323 e gli atti della società dei militi del 1339*, ed. F. Gabotto and N. Gabiani (Pinerolo, 1906), p. 515.

17 Jones, *City-State*, pp. 271–3, 281–2.

18 G. Liberati, 'Dinamica della vita economica e politica a Fermo nel secolo XIV', *Studi urbinati*, 49 (1975).

Urban society: men and women

Women have sometimes been omitted from sourcebooks on later medieval Italy. My intention has been to include them as much as possible. But the sources for medieval women are, perhaps more than those for men, shaped by notions of what constituted behaviour appropriate to their gender. For understanding the moral literature setting down models for female behaviour, two figures have recently been proposed: 'the guarded woman' and 'the good wife'.[19] The guarding of women, Casagrande claims, had connotations of both enclosure and protection, and involved separation of women from externals (dress, body, public) and the stressing of internals (soul, home). Hence, efforts to control the ways that women moved (keeping eyes lowered, head and hands still), the ways that women dressed (avoiding 'vanities' that aroused male lust, disturbed social order and consumed family wealth), and the ways in which women talked (irrational, uncontrolled female talk being thought to imperil peace in the family and community). Hence too the value put on avoiding the sins of leisure by keeping women occupied, in either houseworks (spinning, sewing) or pious works. 'Women did not enter the law-courts, did not rule or teach or preach. The words of justice, power, culture and salvation had to remain male words'.[20] If the notion of 'guarding' women seems rather negative, the model of the good wife gave positive value to the wife's many roles: of taking on the task of creating good relations, of respect and assistance, with her in-laws; of loving her husband faithfully; of raising the children (with maternity seen as a 'natural' female inclination); and of running the household, as this was female space.

The reality, of course, could be rather different. Women could escape the 'iron fist'[21] of family marriage plans, through clandestine marriage, flight into the religious life, or resort to the ecclesisatical courts against forced marriage or violent husbands.[22] Among the lower classes, it is

---

19 C. Casagrande, 'La donna custodita', and S. Vecchio, 'La buona moglie', both in *Storia delle donne: Il Medioevo*, ed. C. Klapisch-Zuber (Rome and Bari, 1990), and translated in *A History of Women in the West*, vol. 2, ed. C. Klapisch-Zuber (Cambridge, MA, 1992).

20 Casagrande, 'La donna custodita', p. 121.

21 C. Opitz, 'La vita quotidiana delle donne nel tardo Medioevo', in *Storia delle donne*, p. 339, and generally for what follows.

22 *Marriage in Italy, 1300–1650*, ed. T. Dean and K. J. P. Lowe (Cambridge, 1997).

argued, both men and women had greater freedom to choose their marriage partners, because parental concern for the transmission of property was absent. Some women did have economic power, especially noblewomen during their husbands' long absences from home. Women did turn their backs on maternity, through abortion/ infanticide, abandonment of children, or through devoting themselves to God. The proportion of unmarried women in late medieval society was considerable, and, if widowed, there was some scope for freeing themselves from control by fathers or husbands. Though excluded from inheritance, women formed a 'regular part of the workforce'.[23] Female paid labour was normal: women worked in artisan production and retailing both inside and outside guilds, inside and outside the home, though mostly as wage-labourers or small-traders.

Both of these perspectives – the ideological and the actual – are reflected in these documents. On the one hand, Paolo da Certaldo voices extreme views on mistrusting and 'guarding' wives [81], while sumptuary laws enacted the moral concern of fathers and husbands at the seemingly uncontrolled female love of fine dress and ornament [88–9]. At the same time, women were excluded or marginalised: they were spectators at palio races and brought up the rear in processions [26], their dowries precluded them from inheriting the patrimony [83], their statements and accusations were not welcome in some lawcourts [84]. Authors blamed women and their 'bestial' love of finery for price inflation [77, 79], and made misogynistic attacks on slave girls and talkative wives [81, 94]. On the other hand, the servant class made their own marriages [82], and women disposed of unwanted children in hospitals [1]. Women performed heavy tasks such as carrying sand or water [5, 19]. Female innkeepers are mentioned at Bologna, female 'masters' in the Paduan wool guild, and female market traders in the Mercato Vecchio in Florence [19, 48, 51]. There were some female pupils and teachers, and Suor Manfreda in Milan for a number of years preached and acted as priestess of the cult of 'Saint' Guglielma [34]. Nevertheless, the repressive trend seems the more powerful, as the protective ideology sought to confine women within the bounds of 'decency': suppressing May day games that allowed young girls to meet their lovers [86], distancing women from contact with criminality in the lawcourts [84], and insisting on clearer gender definition through prohibition of cross-dressing [85].

---

23 Jones, *City-State*, p. 227.

Urban society: fourteenth-century tensions

Although worker unrest is evident in Italian towns from the late thirteenth century,[24] the second half of the fourteenth century saw a rash of working-class revolts, the most famous being that of the Ciompi in Florence, which, as one historian has said, has become the 'archetype' of worker insurrections.[25] In their influential book on the 'popular revolutions' of the later Middle Ages, Mollat and Wolff put the Ciompi firmly in the foreground of their discussion of the 'revolutionary years' of 1378–82. Debate over the origins and nature of the Ciompi 'revolution' has continued: from the Marxist position of Viktor Rutenburg (a workers' revolt against nascent capitalism) to Gene Brucker's reaction (minimising radical change, stressing the vertical solidarities of aristocratic clienteles), and from Sam Cohn's reassertion of the radical policies of the Ciompi government to Stella's reassertion of class solidarites.[26] Revolts in other cities have suffered in comparison, only partly due to a lack of comparable documentation. There was a tumult in Perugia in May 1371 in which dispute between workers and masters in the wool guild combined with protest at the government's policy towards the papacy and erupted in the ransacking of some patrician houses and the storming of the prisons.[27] Also in 1371, there was in Siena what Rutenburg called 'the first really important movement of the Italian pre-proletariat', when the wool workers of the Ovile quarter, under the name of the Compagnia del Bruco, rose up and, followed by the rest of the *popolo minuto*, brought down the government and constituted a new regime (the Fifteen); this, however, did not survive the first patrician plot against it, and a massacre in the Ovile quarter ensued.[28] Sam Cohn insists on differentiating the Ciompi from these tumults in Perugia and Siena: in neither city did the workers have a secret organisation, as they did in Florence, nor did they make independent demands. Both the timing

---

24 *Ibid.*, pp. 255–6.

25 F. Franceschi, 'La rivolta di "Barbicone"', in *Storia di Siena*, 2nd edn. 2 vols (Siena, 1996), vol. 1, p. 291.

26 V. Rutenburg, *Popolo e movimenti popolari nell'Italia del '300 e '400* (Bologna, 1971); G. A. Brucker, 'The Ciompi Revolution', in *Florentine Studies*, ed. N. Rubinstein (London, 1968); M. Mollat and P. Wolff, *Ongles bleus, Jacques et Ciompi: les révolutions populaires en Europe aux XIV et XV siècles* (Paris, 1970); P. Stella, *La révolte des Ciompi: les hommes, les lieux, le travail* (Paris, 1993).

27 R. Broglio d'Ajano, 'Lotte sociali a Perugia nel secolo XIV', *Vierteljahrschrift für Social- und Wirtschaftsgeschichte*, 8 (1910).

28 Rutenburg, 'La vie et la lutte des Ciompi de Sienne', *Annales*, 20 (1965).

and the form of the Ciompi revolt, he argues, were different. However, these revolts do share some similarities – in the role of labour conditions in the wool industry, in the role of flags – which distinguish them from revolt in non-republican cities. In the Ferrarese revolt in 1385, caused mainly by a proposed revision to the list of taxable property, there was no use of flags, no set of demands, no worker organisation: the angry crowd confronted and mutilated the ruler's evil counsellor, in a pattern of protest that was much more characteristic of monarchical regimes (and one that surfaced at Florence too in its more monarchical periods: for example, under the temporary dictatorship of the duke of Athens, 1343–5).

In Florence, Siena and Perugia the wool guild had substantial degrees of control over workers in each process of cloth production. In Florence and Siena these workers were subject (*sottoposti*) to the Wool Guild and lacked the right to combine. In Perugia, by contrast, the dyers, trimmers, wool beaters and washers formed separate guilds. Textile workers may be divided into three categories, following the three major phases in cloth production.[29] First, the wage labourers in the wool manufacturer's own workshop: these were largely unskilled workers performing the heavy tasks (beating, combing, carding) of preparing the raw wool for spinning. Second, the homeworkers: the spinners, often badly-paid women living in the countryside; the warpers, who set the initial threads on the looms; and the weavers, some of whom might possess their own looms. Third, the finishers: the dyers, stretchers, and so forth, who were skilled independent workers, sometimes guild masters, with their own workshops and equipment. Though the cloth passed through increasingly skilled hands as it advanced through these processes, it remained throughout the property of the wool manufacturer, and the wool guilds issued strict rules to prevent any loss of material or profit at each stage of production. Spinners were prohibited from working for more than one manufacturer. Finishers were prohibited from selling remnants. A 'pitiless system of fines was applied with the cruellest rigour' for breaking bobbins, not folding cloth correctly, dirtying the basins used for washing wool, failing to finish on time.[30] The bargaining power of the manufacturers was closely protected and the earning potential of *sottoposti* was undermined: they were not to tout for work, they were not to work for more than one

---

29 Franceschi, 'La rivolta di "Barbicone"', for what follows.
30 Rutenburg, pp. 99–100; and in general, see Jones, *City-State*, pp. 249–55.

manufacturer at a time and they were not to take on unfinished work begun by another wool-worker. Any dispute regarding wages was settled by the wool guild giving full credence to the manufacturer. Payment was at piece-rates, and employment was completely subject to demand. Work was monitored and inspected. What is surprising, in such conditions, is that open conflict was not more common.

58 The decadence of chivalry

Complaint about the alleged decline of the knightly class is common among learned and clerical circles in the later Middle Ages. Such complaint often centred on knights' avoidance of combat and pursuit of pleasure or comfort. In Italy, these themes were expanded to include the exercise of trade, as shown in extracts from the works of two academic lawyers, Odofredo from the thirteenth century, and Cino da Pistoia from the early fourteenth.

a. N. Tamassia, 'Odofredo. Studio storico-giuridico', *Atti e memorie della Deputazione di storia patria per la Romagna*, 3rd ser., 12 (1893–4), 368.

For anyone to be a knight many things are needed. He should be of noble blood (the northern Europeans observe this), which means that tradesmen cannot be knights unless they obtain dispensation from a monarch ... He must be belted with a sword. He must be a bathed knight, as the Tuscans say. He must not wear fur[31] at his neck as the Lombards do. He must swear on the divine gospels that he will not abandon his insignia [in battle]. This is said of knights who are chosen to go on military campaign, but those knights who are created today do not do such things ... Their instruments are dogs and hunting-birds.

b. G. M. Monti, *Cino da Pistoia giurista* (Città di Castello, 1924), p. 172.

What about the knights of our day? ... If they are knights who have time to devote themselves to arms, and who stand prepared to defend the public good of the city or king or their lord, as are the knights in Apulia, it seems it can be said that they are regarded as holding positions of chivalric honour. This can rarely be said of our knights who devote themselves to private trade and business: and many are found who do not know how to arm themselves and who have exercised the most base crafts, and yet they are belted with a sword, bathed in water, have precedence in drinking and in the honour of [wearing] squirrel-fur and beautiful spurs, and are greeted with some prerogative of reverence ...

31 *pelles.*

59 Complaint against moneyed parvenus

The Sienese poet Bindo Bonichi (c. 1260–1338) is an example of the so-called 'bourgeois realist' poets. He was a merchant who appears in official positions in Sienese institutions, and in his poetry he addresses moral problems regarding the values attached to money and nobility. His tone is that of common-sense wisdom, of the 'honest man scandalized'.[32]

Bindo Bonichi, in *Poeti minori del Trecento*, ed. N. Sapegno (Milan & Naples, 1952), p. 292.

Let no one think, when they hear the word 'rabble',
that it means only the despised poor.
For knights and counts and every ill-bred person
are numbered among the riff-raff now.

Whoever has more florins appears to have more worth:
the good man among the lower orders is thought base,
and squirrel-fur worn as a helmet-crest
takes the place of rotten straw.

Widows and orphans are very safe
on account of the oaths knights take,
but everyone makes sure they lock their doors.
For, though knights swear before friars
not to touch women and to live pure lives,
woe betide whoever trusts an old soldier.

60 The costs of knighthood

Knighthood also had its celebrants, as well as its detractors. The early fourteenth-century poet Folgore da San Gimignano is known for his poems celebrating chivalric themes. In a dream-like tone of impressionistic nostalgia, he depicts a world of material and sensual pleasures and of carefree enjoyment.[33]

Folgore da San Gimignano, in *Poeti giocosi del tempo di Dante*, ed. M. Marti (Milan, 1956), p. 382.

A squire is being made a knight just now,
and, wanting above all to be worthy,

32 E. Ragni, 'Bonichi, Bindo', in *Dizionario biografico degli italiani*, vol. 12 (Rome, 1970), pp. 87–8; N. Sapegno, *Il Trecento* (Milan, 1934), pp. 402–3.

33 *Ibid.*, pp. 98–104.

he mortgages his lands and castles,
in order to lay by what is required:
Bread, wine and victuals he gives to his guests,
Meat, partridge, and capon, as they wish,
with squires and servants in perfect order;
Rooms and beds, candles large and small.
He thinks of the many bridled horses,
the jousters and their fine companions,
the lances and banners, caparisons and bells,
the music-making grand and noble,
and jesters to lead them through the town,
ladies and maidens along every street.

61 Ceremonial knighthood: Siena, 1326

The formal ceremonies of knighthood also continued to be observed in Italy, as shown in this description from Siena. As Franco Cardini has recently argued,[34] there are many striking aspects of this extraordinary document: the importance of the spiritual formalities (the vigil and bath), the role of the father in financing for his son this rite of passage (resembling marriage), and the strongly civic character of the whole ceremony, through the participation of the civic authorities and of guests from all districts of the city.

Cronaca senese, pp. 443–51.

1326: This is the 'triumph' of magnificence of a Sienese nobleman of ancient family, the wise, rich and powerful Messer Sozo di Bandinello Bandinelli, of a family of knights and doctors, who had his son knighted on 25 December[35] 1326, and they began to hold a court eight days before hand …

Below is written [a list of] those invited to dine on 18th December … [63 names follow]. The food they had was pasta, boiled veal, roast capon, game, pears in syrup, all preceded and followed by sweets …

On St Thomas' day the jousting began and continued over the three days to Christmas, and everyone wore sendal tunics, and banners which were then torn up. Those who jousted on St Thomas' day, which was Sunday 21 December, came from the three *terzi*[36] of Città … [25 names], San Martino … [22] and Camollia … [41].

34 Cardini, *L'acciar dei cavalieri*, pp. 144–8.
35 The text reads 'November', but is clearly wrong.
36 City districts.

The food laid on the table for these was ravioli, boiled veal, game, exquisite[37] chicken cut diagonally, roast capon, pears in syrup, all preceded and followed by sweets ... The jousters on Christmas eve, were ... [42 names], and the food they had at table was: chickpeas with smoked tench, prepared tench, Sangalgano tart, roast eel, compote with syrup, pears ... preceded and followed by sweets ...

Below are those invited for the morning of Christmas: from Città ... [148 names], from San Martino ... [98 names], from Camollia ... [153 names] ... Invited to dine beside the knight were: the Captain of the *popolo* of Siena; count Simone da Battifolle, war-captain of the commune of Siena; Messer Pietro Andolfi da Roma, podestà, with all his officials; Messer Giovanni da Rodi, captain of justice with all his officials; and several ambassadors ... And we shall describe the food they had: first, ginger, *framangieri* in bowls, boiled veal, game, that is, boar, roebuck, venison, hare in large quantities and servings, roast capon ... partridge ... and pheasant, all preceded and followed by sweets ...

These presents were made to the said knight: Fazio and Forgia di Messer Naddo gave two peacocks, forty brace of partridge, twenty brace of pheasant, and two enormous marzipan cakes, with a large quantity of other game ...

And to the Franciscan friars was given veal and uncooked meats, for sixty people, for them to eat. Other friars were given bread, wine and meat. The preparations were so abundant that much food was left over and given away afterwards ...

Before Francesco was knighted, he and his father went to the Duomo to hear mass, on the morning of Christmas, and there Francesco was made a knight on the marble pulpit. Tommaso di Nello carried the sword, hat and spurs ahead of the horse. Messer Sozzo buckled the sword on his son. Messer Pietro Andolfi da Roma ... fitted the right-hand spur, and the captain of the *popolo* of Siena the left-hand spur. The count Simone da Battifolle then buckled his sword, handed it to Messer Giovanni da Rodi, who handed it to Messer Sozzo ... And you should know that the duke of Calabria, son of King Robert [of Naples], with the papal legate Giovanni Orsini, left Florence and reached Siena at the beginning of the banquetting, that is on Thursday before Christmas, and came to Siena to buckle the sword of the new knight, but Francesco did not want the duke to do this ... so they left on the following Saturday, returning to Florence in great indignation ...

37 *ad anbrosina.*

Below we shall list the presents and gifts Messer Francesco made to various people:

to Messer Antonio, minstrel, an overgown of silk and gold, a supertunic, a garment and hood, lined with vair, with a silken cord;

to Andreuccio di Meo del Mosca, an overgown, supertunic and doublet,[38] bright emerald green; the overgown was edged with paris braid of pure gold;

to the musician Saluccio, a grey overgown, supertunic, doublet and hood; the overgown was lined;

to the singer, Martino, 3 florins, a tunic and a sendal banner;

to Cardarello 3 florins ... and other money to other trumpeters and musicians;

to Salamone, a supertunic, hood, dark-red hose,[39] a lined buckram, wadded doublet, new underwear, a new coif, gloves, and a new belt. These were the clothes that Francesco took off when he bathed ...

Here below we shall list the stuff and equipment that the new knight had:

a pair of coverlets in imitation yellow sendal

a headboard of velvet, furbished

a mattress of red sendal, furbished

a bed-cover of red sendal embroidered with shields

a pair of sheets

two pillows of sendal, embroidered

a veil for the face, with gold braiding

an ivory comb

a pair of under-clothes

three pairs of dark serge hose

two pairs of flat shoes with buckles and prongs in gilded copper

silk underwear[40] ...

a pair of flat shoes

a pair of lightweight shoes with stamped decoration

an indigo samite doublet with gold braiding

a green-striped, samite doublet, for tournament[41]

a yellow sendal banner decorated with gold vine leaves

a pair of gold spurs furbished with silk

a pair of gold spurs, for tournament, furbished with leather

38 *corsetto d'uno dovagio.*

39 *calze di ligia sanguegna.*

40 *braghiere.*

41 *d'armare.*

a palfrey bridle, gold, furbished with silk
a war-horse bridle, gold, furbished with silk
a palfrey saddle, decorated with gold, and with fittings in red,
embroidered velvet
a tournament saddle, painted gold, and fittings in velvet ...
a shield decorated in gold
a hat of beaver-fur, lined in crimson velvet, embroidered with a
golden vine
a breast-strap and crupper-strap with bells, for tournament
a cuirass and arm-guards, covered in red velvet
a cuirass covered in deerskin and ornamented in gold
a pair of greaves, ornamented in gold
a pair of thigh-pieces, covered in velvet and ornamented in gold
a pair of gloves in steel platelets
a surcoat of crimson velvet, lined in sendal
a tournament hat covered in velvet and lined
a halberd lined with gilded velvet
an ivory-handled knife ...
a blue pennant with a gold lily
and many other things, armour and garments ...

And the court lasted for eight days before and eight days after ... such
that it was the most renowned court in Tuscany.

62 A miserly knight: late fourteenth-century Pistoia

Sacchetti inverts the theme of knightly largesse, in an unlikely tale from
Pistoia.

Franco Sacchetti, *Il trecentonovelle*, no. 23, in F. Sacchetti, *Opere*, ed. A. Borlenghi
(Milan, 1957), pp. 104–6.

Messer Niccolò Cancellieri was a knight from Pistoia, an experienced
and courtly man, who had spent most of his life with Queen Giovanna
of Naples, and with the barons and lords ... of that country. Having
returned to Pistoia, and making it his home, he was urged and pressed
by his kinsmen, who said to him: 'Well, Messer Niccolò, you're quite
a knight, except that greed spoils you. Why don't you throw a great
banquet and show the Pistoiesi that you're not as greedy as they
think?' At their urging, he sent out invitations, eight days in advance,
to all the notable men of Pistoia to dine with him one Sunday morning.
Five days before the day of the banquet, the time was approaching to

buy the food, but that night Messer Niccolò set to thinking and held fast once again to his avarice, because the following day he would have to start opening his purse. And so he said to himself: 'This banquet will cost me 100 florins or more, and if I did fifty like this, it would make no difference: it will not alter the fact that I am thought greedy. And so, since a reputation for avarice cannot be extinguished, I am not the right sort to spend money'. So he took a decision and, once he had got up in the morning, called the servant who had invited the citizens on his behalf, and said to him, 'You have the list of those citizens you invited to dine with me – take it with you and, as you invited them, go and disinvite them'. The servant said, 'Oh my lord, think about what you are doing, and think of the honour that will ensue [from holding the banquet]'. The knight replied, 'That's all right, honour can go to the devil; go and do what I have told you, and if anyone asks you why, say that I thought that the expense would be wasted'. And so the servant went and did this. After which, people talked about this for many days in Pistoia, with much mocking of Messer Niccolò. When this was reported to him, however, he said, 'I would rather they speak ill of me on an empty stomach, than on one stuffed with my food'.

63 Three social divisions

A teacher and preacher at the Dominican convent of Santa Maria Novella, Florence, fra Remigio de' Girolami was 'among the first writers to apply Aristotelian concepts to problems of the Italian city-states',[42] especially as regards the relation between individual and community, and the role of peace in achieving common welfare.

C. T. Davis, 'An early Florentine political theorist: fra Remigio de' Girolami', *Proceedings of the American Philosophical Society*, 104 (1960), 667.

The great city is broken into three pieces: one division is because the Guelfs speak ill of the Ghibellines, saying that they are unyielding, and the Ghibellines speak ill of the Guelfs, saying that they want to expel them. A second division is because the artisans speak ill of the great, saying that they are devoured by them, that they commit betrayals, that they protect the property of their enemies, and conversely the great speak ill of the artisans, saying that they want to dominate and are unaware that they bring the city to shame. A third division is between clerics and laymen, because the clerics say of

42 C. T. Davis, 'Remigio de' Girolami and Dante', *Studi Danteschi*, 36 (1959), 108.

laymen that they are traitors, usurers, perjurers, adulterers and thieves, which is true of many, and conversely laymen say that the clerics are fornicators, gluttons, idlers, thieves and vainglorious men, which is true of some. Only our lord Jesus Christ can, through his grace, unite and combine these divisions ...

64 Pisa brought low by its new citizens

Little is known of Guido da Pisa: apparently a Carmelite friar, born in the second half of the thirteenth century and still living in the 1330s, he was the author of a number of literary works, as well as of an early commentary on Dante's *Inferno*. Here, in his comment on *Inf.* XXXIII.89–91, he laments Pisa's downfall.

Guido da Pisa's Expositiones et Glose super Comediam Dantis *or Commentary on Dante's Inferno*, ed. V. Cioffari (Albany, NY, 1974), p. 698.

The city of Pisa has already fallen from a great, almost royal estate to the lowest, because of the discords among its citizens. For the kingdom of Sardinia, which it had seized from the powerful hands of the Saracens, and which it long ruled with mighty force, it has lost in a base and costly fashion because of the discords among its citizens.[43] And the dominion of the sea, which Pisa used to possess and rejoice in, has not only been lost, but Pisan ships can now barely cross it. It has lost ... that distinguished nobility that it possessed in abundance and which shone brightly in its noble citizens everywhere ... And, as we manifestly see, it has fallen into the hands of new citizens, who deprive it of all its old honour and high *status*, such that we can say of Pisa what Christ said of him who went from Jerusalem to Jericho, that he fell among thieves who robbed him, wounded him and left him for dead; in similar fashion, the city of Pisa has fallen among thieves, that is new citizens, who have robbed it of all its honour, *status*, riches and glory, and have either killed the old, noble citizens ... of hunger, allowing them to die in prison, or sent them into exile, or killed them by various methods. And so, wounded from head to foot, the city lies half dead.

43 Sardinia was occupied by Pisa in the course of the eleventh century, but ceded to Aragon in 1326.

66 The *popolo* of Piacenza, 1250

The history of the *popolo* of Piacenza is an example of swift domination and manipulation of a popular movement by members of the ruling class (especially the prominent families of Landi, Scotti, Anguissola and Fontana). The charismatic Guglielmo Landi was the first leader of the Piacentine *popolo* in the 1220s, but he was expelled in 1235. By 1250, the pressures of supplying grain to Parma triggered a new popular movement.

Annales placentini gibellini, in *MGH, Scriptores*, ed. G. H. Pertz, vol. 18 (Hannover 1863, Leipzig, 1925), pp. 499–501.

At the beginning of June, the Milanese army rode into the territory of Lodi with a great quantity of corn which they were sending to Parma, where there was a great shortage. They transported the corn as far as the Po and then handed it over to the Piacentines …

In 1250 the common people[44] of Piacenza saw that they were being badly treated regarding footstuffs: first, because all the corn that had been sent from Milan, as well as other corn in Piacenza, was being taken to Parma, with farm-labourers being forced to transport it without payment; second, because the Parmesans were touring Piacentine territory buying corn from the threshing floors and fields, which seemed very serious to the Piacentines. The Parmesans could do this in safety because Matteo da Correggio, a citizen of Parma, was podestà of Piacenza, and supported them as much as he could in having corn taken to Parma. Knowing about all this, on Friday 27 July early in the morning, Antolino Saviagata, at the instigation of the Scotti family, because he was their neighbour, and of others, gathered twenty or thirty leaders (consuls) of the popular societies of Piacenza in the church of San Pietro, with the purpose of going to the podestà and telling him to oppose this export of Piacentine corn to Parma. In the church they all swore to support each other if anything was said to them on account of this meeting. It was then maliciously reported to the podestà that Antolino Saviagata and others had gathered to cause damage and harm to the city of Piacenza. The podestà sent one of his judges … to the church; he arrested Antolino, but let the others leave. The podestà immediately held a general council and so maligned Antolino and his assembly that it was immediately decreed that no more than three people could assemble in the city, that the podestà had full power to inquire into Antolino's actions, and to put him to death if he deserved it. Some of those who had been at

44 *populares.*

Antolino's gathering, fearing death, convened their own societies and told them they had done nothing wrong in the assembly; and the societies decided to support their consuls within the law. Meanwhile, the podestà held Antolino in his home, not doing him any harm. The *populares*, inflamed by what had happened and by what was going on ... took up arms and banners, rang their bells, gathered together and came to the podestà. The podestà, in fact, wanted to release Antolino on surety, more out of fear than love, but Antolino refused ... His father was pressing him to let himself be bound over, and there were many magnates willing to stand surety for him, including Pietro Malvicini, Filippo Visdomini, Giacomo Visconti and Uberto 'de Iniquitate', but he refused them. The podestà, seeing the crowd coming towards him and hearing the bells ring, let Antolino go. Antolino was badly dressed, with shoes on his feet but nothing covering his legs. On his release, Antolino did not go home at once, but wishing to accomplish his desires, went well-supported to a certain well,[45] where he found a great crowd of men armed for battle, and he addressed them, provoking and inducing them to do what he desired, reminding them of the great harms that had been done to the *popolo* over the past fifteen years, how they had been killed, condemned and expelled from one city to another, and that they would rather die than suffer any more ... [The men of each of the six city districts] elected two consuls of the people ...

On the following Saturday, all the consuls, with a great number of the *popolo*, came to the communal council. Antolino excused their presence, arguing and explaining that what had been done by the *popolo* was not done as an affront to the podestà, but to his honour and that of the Roman church, of the commune of Milan and their friends ... The consuls of the *popolo* then assembled at Santa Maria del Tempio and resolved to issue statutes and to hold a council of the people. The statutes were passed, and on Sunday morning the council met in the church of San Pietro. There was such a press of people that they could not stay there, so they moved to the church of San Sisto. Among the first clauses [of the statutes] ... was one about electing a rector of the *popolo*. Many men believed themselves to be leaders of the *popolo*, namely Fredenzio da Fontana, Filippo Visdomini, Uberto Zanardi, Guelfo Stricto ... and when this clause was read out, great division arose among the *popolo*: some wanted one man, some another, and there was great clamour. Then [one man] said 'Why do you not

45 The *Puteum Fubertum*.

accept Uberto "de Iniquitate", for he has already suffered many injuries and losses on your behalf?' And so he was elected by acclamation. Those who had betrayed the *popolo* and Guglielmo Landi – and there were many of them among both the consuls and the others present – complained loudly and wanted to leave the church to raise uproar, but some of those who had been unable to enter the church closed the doors so that they could not leave. They regarded lord Uberto as an excessively 'imperial' man. Once things had calmed down, however, they resumed their seats and took part in the election of consuls of the people: one or two from each society, according to its standing, with other men from each district of the city. Unanimously these elected Uberto 'de Iniquitate' as podestà and rector of the *popolo* for one year. Envoys were sent to his home, and he came immediately and gladly took the oath of office, without consulting any of his relatives or friends. All of the *popolo* then accompanied him home with great rejoicing and honour. As he had been poorly dressed before, he later held a great meeting in the piazza San Pietro, dressed in scarlet with squirrel-fur. This was attended by a huge crowd of men of the *popolo*, at the news of which many knights and commoners were scared to death because of the harm they had done him and the *popolo* in the past. And from that day on, he began to lead the *popolo*. After a short interval, he held another council in San Sisto, saying what some of his friends had said to him, that 'a vassal of one year brings little profit and little loss', and so he was elected podestà of the *popolo* for five years, and after him his son Giannone. Men of the *popolo* who had relatives and friends among the Piacentine exiles began to tell them 'Come, come back, brothers, exiles from Piacenza'; others though … strongly opposed this. However, such was the number of the former that the latter could do nothing: people today delight in upsetting things. And at last, Uberto 'de Iniquitate' and his advisors were content to let the exiled *populares* return, but leaving the Landi … and other knights outside. Meanwhile, Antolino Saviagata … went to Milan as an envoy … on some business. There, either because he was offered money, or because he regretted what he had done, and fearing the return of the exiles whom he had persecuted and expelled, he sought to disobey and harm the *popolo*. Conspiring with others … he sought to return the city to its previous regime. When this was discovered by the podestà of the *popolo*, Antolino was captured and greatly tortured. But, because what he had done pleased Uberto 'de Iniquitate', who did not want the Landi and others to return, Uberto let him go unpunished, expelling him from the city. And thus faction arose among the *popolo*.

66 The *popolo* of Bologna, 1271 and 1287

In contrast, at Bologna, the *popolo* succeed in expelling the nobles and enacting harsh laws against them, prefiguring the more famous Florentine Ordinances of Justice (1293).[46]

a. Salimbene de Adam, *Cronica*, ed. Scalia, pp. 705, 937–9; ed. Holder-Egger, pp. 485, 643–4.

1271: In this year, there was formed in Bologna a society called the Society of Justice, and it was a very large society of the good and best of the *popolo* of that city; and they exiled eighty of the knights for the sake of the the good *status* of Bologna.

1287: The Bolognese *populares* enacted some harsh statutes against the knights and against all the nobles of their city: whoever of the knights or nobles harmed anyone of any society of *populares* was to be annihilated in the town and country, in houses, fields and trees, such that nothing should remain of all his property ... And into this curse they first thrust the sons of Niccolò Bazalieri, who were totally destroyed by the *popolo*. And from that point, the knights of Bologna, because of the vehemence of the raging *popolo*, fear to live in the city and reside in the countryside, on their estates, in the French manner; so that the *populares*, who live in the city, in the French manner can henceforth be called burgesses.[47] But it is to be feared for the *populares*, lest God's anger come upon them, because they are going against scripture: 'Judge your neighbour justly; do not seek revenge ... ' (Leviticus, 19). The world is destroyed by commoners and peasants; it is preserved by knights and nobles ... Keep in mind the example of the butchers of Cremona: one of them had a large dog, who patiently tolerated much pestering from the small dog of another butcher; but, because he would not cease the habitual injury, he eventually submerged and drowned it in the Po ... And thus are many in this world, who, if they would live in peace, are not harmed by anyone; but, because they go around industriously looking for trouble, they find it.

b. *Statuti di Bologna dell'anno 1288*, vol. 1, pp. 283–90, 299–300, 302–3, 308–9, 313, 317.

In the name of God, amen, to the honour and praise of his mother, the Blessed Virgin Mary, of the apostles Peter and Paul, of Saints Dominic

---

46 Translated in *Major Problems in the History of the Italian Renaissance*, ed. B. G. Kohl and A. Andrews Smith (Lexington, 1995).

47 *burgenses*.

and Francis, and of Saints Ambrogio and Petronio, the patrons and defenders of the city of Bologna, and to the honour and reverence of the pope and the holy Roman church, and to the good *status* and increase of the city of Bologna and of all its people and commune ... It is well known that the Holy and Most Holy Ordinances ... have ensured, since the day of their compilation [1282] until today, the strength, preservation and life of the *popolo* and commune of Bologna and its district ... The Bolognese people, in no doubt that without these ordinances the perils of many discords could easily have threatened the *popolo*, commune and district ... wishes to establish these ordinances with renewed firmness ... This is therefore the book of the Holy Ordinances, issued at the time of podestà Matteo da Correggio ... and of the Most Holy Ordinances, issued at the time of podestà Tebaldo Brusati ... all of which ordinances ... are to have the force of law ... up to 15 August next, and thenceforth for twenty years ...

1. First, they establish and ordain ... that the leaders of the societies of crafts and arms, banking and commerce of the *popolo* of Bologna, and the men of those societies, are required anew to swear to maintain and defend in good faith and without fraud, to the utmost of their abilities, the podestà, captain, Anziani and consuls, now or for the time being, in their offices and administrations, and to defend and maintain each other, and to observe all the following statutes and ordinances ... issued in favour and defence of the *popolo* and of the lands and men of the contado of Bologna. And that all the societies ... of the *popolo* are to be united and joined together ... and to ensure that all the following ordinances .. are observed in their totality ...

2. Item ... that if anyone of the *popolo* of Bologna, that is of the societies of crafts, arms, banking or commerce, or their sons, brothers or fathers, is henceforth wounded or killed or hit or captured by any of the magnates or knights or their sons or brothers, or by nobles or men of noble descent born in the city or district of Bologna – or if any of these magnates or knights ... causes the said crimes to be done – then the podestà is required without fail, immediately, as quickly as possible, on the same day as the crime is committed, to inquire into that crime on the basis of the statement of the victim (if he was not killed) and the victim is to be believed regarding the injury and the [identity of] the offending magnate or knight ... or noble, and to punish the criminal with a fine of L 1,000 if the *popolano* was debilitated, of L 500 if otherwise wounded or cut, of L 300 if hit without bloodshed. If any member of the *popolo* is captured or

detained – or his brother or sister, daughter, son or wife – the per-petrators are to be fined L 500 each ... And if the *popolano* has died, credence is to be given to his heirs, if the [direct] heir is male; if the heir is not male, then a brother or brothers are to be believed ... or the closest relative who is male; and if he has no close relative, then the ministers of his society are to be believed ... And these statements by the victim or his heir or relatives or by ministers of his society ... are to be taken as legitimate proof ... And if any of these criminals escapes into any house or courtyard of any magnate, knight ... or noble ... then he who owns that house or courtyard is required without fail to deliver the criminal or homicide to the podestà within three days, and if he does not, then the podestà will have that house and courtyard razed to the ground ... And meanwhile, until punishment is made for the homicide or wounding or abduction, no [other] trials are to be held by the podestà ... and all men of the *popolo* are to do no work nor open their shops ...

3. As many men of the *popolo* of the city and district of Bologna daily have their possession of farms and crops disturbed and impeded by magnates, they ordain and establish that if any *popolano* ... of the societies of crafts, arms, banking and commerce, or anyone who is the father, son or brother of anyone of those societies, or any peasant, widow, child or convent of nuns or friars is now disturbed or impeded or has been since the first troubles in Bologna in April 1274,[48] or is in the future for any reason ... or in any manner ... by any knight or magnate or noble ... or by any son of theirs or by any cleric, his or their statement under oath is to believed as regards the disturbance and the identity of the disturber ... and the podestà and captain ... are required, within eight days of being notified ... to ensure that the farm and crops are restored ... and to fine the disturber L 100 ...

9. If any man of the city or district of Bologna wishes to keep one or more men as bodyguards, taking them armed or unarmed with him, he is required to give to the podestà and commune good, suitable guarantees that they will not injure any other men in their persons or property ... and he is to show and present to the podestà the man or men whom he wants to keep, and surety of L 500 is to be taken from and on behalf of each. This ordinance applies only to those born to great families or who have special hatred or [private] war. And that

48 The long struggle between the two factions of the Lambertazzi (Ghibelline) and the Geremei (Guelf), which ended in the mass expulsion or flight of the Lambertazzi (12,000 according to one chronicle).

no one of the societies of crafts, arms, banking and commerce is to go armed with any such men ...

11. As it is manifest and notorious what nobles and magnates of the *contado* of Bologna do to peasants and inhabitants of the villages ... to the point that they are virtually forced to go begging, we provide and ordain that all legal deeds of fief or vassalage ... or perpetual or conditional dependence ... or generally of whatever obligation, on account of which anyone in the *contado* is required to provide any material or personal service or to make any annual render to any knights, or the sons, brothers or nephews of a knight, or to any nobles or magnates or man of noble descent ... or to anyone on their behalf ... from the time that the Lambertini party first left Bologna in April 1274, are, as from now, cancelled, void and of no effect or value ... and are to be so regarded in perpetuity ...

12. In order to protect villages of the contado and their men, they ordain that no knight or son of a knight, no noble, no commoner or *popolano*, cleric or lay, citizen or foreign, male or female, is henceforth to dare or presume to impose, demand, collect or receive, themselves or through another, anything in money, grain, wine, hay, wood or carriage, or any other thing whatsoever, in the name of tribute, fee, payment, gift, gratuity, rent, goodwill payment or exaction ... from any commune of any place, village or castle of the *contado* ... or under the title of a sale, gift, fief, recognition of a fief, or vassalage ... or any other contract ... however named, to acquire or receive from the said village commune anything which is public or belonging to the public [property] of that commune ...

16. Wishing and intending that the rapacious wolves and the mild lambs should walk at an equal pace, they ordain ... that all those named below, whether of the city or district, are required within one month of the publication of this ordinance to give good, suitable guarantee to the podestà of the commune of Bologna of L 1,000 or more ... that they will obey all the orders and commands of the podestà, captain and commune ... and to present themselves in person before the podestà and captain whenever required ... and not to keep or permit to stay in their houses ... courtyards or churches ... any criminal bandit of the commune of Bologna, or any rebel of the Lambertazzi faction ... and not to attack or cause to be attacked anyone in their property or person ... And each of the below-named is required [to give surety] both for himself and for those of his house, whether clerical or lay, namely fathers, sons, brothers, nephews,

legitimate or illegitimate ... [There follows a list of 83 names, including six members of the Galluzzi family, four of the Lambertini, Malavolti and Bazalieri, and two of each of the Caccianemici, Ariosti and Ghisilieri]

18. That no man who has entered any craft society, since the first troubles in Bologna in April 1274, who has not exercised that craft with his own hands, in retail or wholesale, may not hold for that society any office in the *popolo* or commune, nor be *anziano* or consul of the *popolo* ... nor attend any assembly of the *popolo* or commune for that society.

24. As the *anziani* and consuls ... and the two *savi* for each society of crafts, arms, banking and commerce of the *popolo*, who [issued] many statutes and ordinances ... against the magnates, knights and nobles ... are on this account held in hatred and enmity by many, they and their fathers, sons, brothers and nephews who are of the ecclesiastical, Geremei faction of Bologna ... may, each and every one, carry offensive and defensive weapons in the city, suburbs and district of Bologna, day and night ...

67 Social tensions in the kingdom of Naples, 1338–9

In Naples, as the city grew under the Angevin dynasty, tension developed over participation in local government between the older districts (*piazze*), predominantly inhabited by noble families, and the new districts of artisans and *populares*. In 1339 these tensions erupted, requiring the intervention of King Robert.

a. Giovanni Villani, *Cronica*, vol. 3, pp. 169–70.

In 1338 there began in the kingdom of Naples, ruled by King Robert, a great disturbance and nuisance in the city of Sulmona, and also in the cities of Aquila, Gaeta, Salerno and Barletta. In each of these places factions were created, and they fought against each other, with one faction driving out the other. These towns and their environs were devastated, and consequently the countryside filled up with robbers and brigands, who robbed everywhere. Many barons of the kingdom had a hand in these disturbances, supporting one side or the other. The greatest disturbance was in Barletta, where it lasted longer and involved heavier fighting. One faction was led by the Marra family, and with them was the count of San Severino and all his followers; in the other faction was the Gatti family and the count of Minerbino, called 'the Paladin', and his followers, who did much damage, devastating the town and its environs. The king was much criticised on account of these disturbances ... because of his tolerance of the devastation of his kingdom, out of his personal greed for the fines and compositions that would be paid as a result of these misdeeds ... Then, only when these towns were well ruined, did the king send his troops to besiege Minerbino and the count; and the count's brothers came to Naples and threw themselves on the king's mercy. All their property was confiscated to the crown and then sold, and they were held prisoner in Naples ... These counts of Minerbino were originally of low birth, being the sons of a son of Messer Gianni Pepino, who was the son of a lowly, small-time notary in Barletta. He had prospered through hard work in Charles II's reign, and came to run the whole kingdom, profiteering and enriching himself to such an extent that he left his sons as counts, but they, as has been said, quickly came to a bad end through their pride and arrogance.

b. M. Schipa, 'Contese sociali napoletane nel Medio Evo', *Archivio storico per le province napoletane*, 32 (1907), 361–7.

Robert, etc. ... At the instigation of the devil, serious discord and 'scandal' has been incited between the men of the piazze of Capuana and Nido, on the one hand, and those of the other piazze of our city of Naples, on the other, regarding the discussion, handling and government of the city's business and other matters. Such discord was often produced by the congregation of citizens as they tumultuously rushed together for the business of the community. Subsequently, various blows were exchanged, then wounds, homicides, injuries and assaults. These have been reported to us and our court by the disruptive complaints of both sides. From these, rancour and hatred grew, and from the multiplication of crimes greater quarrels and turbulent divisions flourished. Abhorring the proliferation of discords and hatreds among our subjects, and wishing by our lordly benevolence to spread the benefits of peace, we have sought to settle these quarrels and to bring each side to peace, by removing the obstacles of discord ... We have effectively intervened, through acceptable mediators, such that, by God's grace, both the men of the piazze of Capuana and Nido, and those of the other piazze, freely and fully put the matter in our hands to be terminated as it seemed best to us ... We have decided, determined and declared ... that all those things contained in the following terms of peace and concord are to have force and efficacy in perpetuity and to be observed inviolably by the men of each side and their heirs and successors now and in the future, such that, with the quarrels put to rest on both sides, their embroilment in conflict and scandal may cease and the delight of joyful peace take the place of hatreds ...

First, that, having for themselves forgiven each other all past blows, wounds, homicides, injuries and assaults, they are to keep and observe a true and firm peace, inviolably and in perpetuity, reserving to royal decision the satisfactions to be made by each side.

Item, because justice consists in restoring to each man what is his, from which peace ensues, we declare that the men of the piazze of Capuana and Nido are to have one third of all burdens and honours of the city, and the rest, of the other piazze and their *populares*, are to have two thirds ...

Item, in electing officials and deliberating the business of the city, as far as legally pertains to them, the men of the piazze of Capuana and Nido may not assemble with the men of the other piazze, but are to elect and deliberate separately ... so as to avoid the 'scandals' which recently arose from such assemblies ...

Item, because equality usually generates concord, it is granted that in royal offices and services men be appointed and advanced equally and in equal number from the other piazze as from Capuana and Nido.

Item, it is requested and granted that the Captains for the time being in the city will not be men suspect to the other piazze (that is, Portanuova, Porto Sant'Arcangelo, etc.), nor to Capuana and Nido.

Item, it is requested and granted that men of the city may not disturb its tranquillity, nor carry prohibited weapons by day or night, nor congregate in crowds, nor march through piazze with weapons, nor commit violence on peers or inferiors, openly or stealthily, in public or private places. For such actions the statutory penalties are to apply, and other penalties reserved to our royal pleasure, any privilege to the contrary notwithstanding.

Item, this peace is to be sworn by the citizens of Naples ... and supported by the addition of great penalties to be decided by the king.

Item, twelve of the elder, more powerful and more wealthy men of Capuana and Nido, and twenty-four from the other piazze are to swear on the gospels that they will work to ensure that royal justice can operate and penalties against transgressors can be exacted ...
Dated Naples, 29 June

Because whoever has the right to legislate has the right to interpret the law, we declare: lest in future any doubt arise from the mention, in the text of peace, of *populares* ... that we intend by the *popolo* that which is commonly called the *popolo grasso*, and not the *popolo minuto* and the artisans, who are not accustomed to be associated in such things, nor is it useful to them to be so, but we wish and intend that they may enjoy the tranquillity of peace and be ready for all things required of them by us and our officials ...

Dated Naples, 5 July

68 Social tensions in Rome: Cola di Rienzo

At Rome the *popolo* was much weaker than in northern Italy. There are nevertheless obvious similarities between the public action of Cola di Rienzo and that of Antolino Saviagata of Piacenza [65]. Here an anonymous Roman chronicler recounts the early stages of Cola's action and the initial baronial reaction.

Anonimo romano, *Cronica*, ed. G. Porta (Milan, 1979), pp. 143–57; *Vita di Cola di Rienzo*, ed. A. Frugoni (Florence, 1957), pp. 31–70. There is a full English translation: *The Life of Cola di Rienzo*, trans. J. Wright (Toronto, 1975).

Cola di Rienzo was of humble origins: his father, Rienzo, was an innkeeper; his mother, Matalena, made her living washing clothes and carrying water. Cola was born in the district of Regola. His house was by the river, amid the mills ... In his youth he was fed on the milk of eloquence, good grammar, better rhetoric, good familiarity with ancient texts ... He often read Livy, Seneca and Cicero ... and took delight in telling of the magnificent deeds of Julius Caesar. All day long he pondered over the marble carvings that lie around in Rome. No one but he knew how to read the ancient inscriptions. He tried to translate all these ancient writings, and to identify correctly the marble figures. As he often used to say: 'Where are these great Romans now? Where is their great justice? That I might have lived in their time!' He was a handsome man, and on his lips always appeared a somewhat excited smile. He was a notary. It happened that his brother was killed and no one was punished for his death ... Cola long thought of avenging his brother's blood; and he long thought of setting the badly-led city of Rome on the right path ... Cola went to Avignon as ambassador to Pope Clement on behalf of the [popular magistracy of the] Thirteen Goodmen of Rome. His speech was so excellent and beautiful that Pope Clement liked him immediately. Pope Clement much admired the fine style of Cola's language, and wanted to see him every day. So Cola spoke to him at great length and told him that the

barons of Rome were highway-robbers and allowed homicides, robberies, adulteries and all kinds of evil, and that they wanted that city
to lie desolate. The pope greatly took against the nobles.

Then [1343], at the instigation of cardinal Giovanni Colonna,
Cola fell into such disgrace, poverty and sickness that he was little
different from the inmate of a hospital. With his jacket on his back he
would stand in the sun like a snake. But the man who had pushed him
down then raised him up: Messer Giovanni Colonna brought him
back before the pope, he returned to favour, and was made notary of
the *camera* of Rome [1344] ... He very quickly returned to Rome,
making threats under his breath.

After his return from the papal curia, he began to exercise his office
courteously, and he saw clearly the robberies of the dogs of the
Campidoglio and the cruelty and injustice of the nobles. He saw the
commune in danger, with no good citizen willing to help it. Therefore
he himself rose on one occasion in the Roman assembly, where all the
councillors were, and said: 'You are not good citizens, you who devour
the blood of the poor and refuse to help them'. Then he warned the
officials and governors that they should attend to the good state of
the city of Rome. When Cola's splendid speech was over, one of the
Colonna rose up ... and gave him a resounding slap; and another man
... who was the recorder, made the tail at him [an obscene gesture].
This was the outcome of his speech.

Afterwards, Cola wanted the governors and *popolo* to behave well
by having a picture painted on the Palace of the Campidoglio in front
of the market. On the outside, above the Camera, he had painted a
picture of a huge sea, rough with horrible waves. In the middle of this
sea was a ship, almost sunk, without a rudder or a sail. On this ship in
peril was a woman, a widow dressed in black, with a belt of mourning,
her dress split open at the chest, her hair torn, as if she wanted to
wail. She was kneeling, her hands piously crossed on her chest, as one
praying for the danger to relent. Above this a caption read: 'This is
Rome' ... To the left were two islands: on one was a woman, sitting
in shame; the caption read 'This is Italy' ... On the other were four
women, with hands to their cheeks, kneeling in act of great sadness ...
These were the four cardinal virtues, Temperance, Justice, Prudence
and Fortitude. On the right-hand side was a little island, on which
was a kneeling woman, holding out her hands to the sky as if in
prayer. She was dressed in white, and her name was Christian Faith
... On the right-hand side, at the top, were four rows of different
animals with wings, holding horns to their mouths, and they blew as

if they were winds making the sea rage ... The first row consisted of lions, wolves and bears, and the caption said 'These are the powerful barons, evil governors'. The second row had dogs, pigs and roebucks, and the caption said 'These are the evil councillors, followers of the nobles'. The third row had rams, dragons and foxes, and the caption said 'These are the *popolari*, thieves, killers, adulterers and plunderers'. The fourth row had horses, cats, goats and monkeys, and the caption said 'These are false officials, judges and notaries' ...

The city of Rome was in great distress. It had no governors; men fought every day; there were robbers everywhere; virgins were insulted; there was no shelter. Little girls were abducted and led away to dishonour. Wives were taken from their husbands in their own beds. [Field]workers, leaving the city to go to work, were robbed at the very gates of Rome. Pilgrims, coming to the holy churches of Rome for the sake of their souls, were not protected but killed and robbed. Priests were engaged in wrongdoing. All lust and evil, no justice or retribution. There was no remedy anymore; everyone was perishing. Whoever had the strongest sword had the most right. There was no other salvation except through everyone defending himself with his relatives and friends. Everyday there were armed assemblies. The nobles and barons did not stay in Rome. Messer Stefano Colonna had gone with the knights to Corneto for grain. That was at the end of April. Then Cola on the first day [17 May 1347] issued a decree, at the sound of trumpets, that every man should, when the bell rang, assemble without arms for 'the good state'. On the following day, from midnight on, Cola heard thirty masses of the Holy Spirit in the church of Sant'Angelo in Pescheria. Then, at the hour of half terce [7.30 a.m.?], he came forth from that church, fully armed, but with his head uncovered. He issued forth in a fine, public manner, with a crowd of youths behind him, all shouting. Before him banners were borne by three good men of his confederation. The first banner was very large, red with gold lettering, on which was depicted Rome, sitting between two lions, with the world in one hand and a palm in the other. This was the banner of liberty ... The second was white, on which was St Paul with a sword in his hand and the crown of justice ... On the third was St Peter with the keys of peace and concord. Another man carried the banner of St George the knight: because it was old, it was carried in a box on a pole.

Now Cola became bold, though not without fear, and went up to the Palace of the Campidoglio, together with the pope's lieutenant ... In his support he had a force of one hundred armed men. When a huge crowd gathered, he stepped up to the rostrum and spoke, making a beautiful speech about the misery and servitude of the Roman *popolo*. Then he said that, out of love of the pope and for the sake of the *popolo* of Rome, he was putting himself at risk. Then he had a document read out in which were the ordinances of the 'good state' ... These were some of the clauses:

1. That whoever killed should be killed, without any exception.

2. That lawsuits should not be drawn out, but should be expedited within fifteen days.

3. That no house in Rome should be razed for any reason, but should be forfeit to the commune.

4. That in each district of Rome there should be one hundred footsoldiers and twenty-five knights at the commune's expense, that they should be given a shield worth 5 *carlini* and a suitable stipend.

5. That orphans and widows should be assisted by the camera of the commune.

6. That a boat should be kept constantly in the Roman marshes and lakes, and off the shore, to guard merchants.

7. That the revenue from the hearth-tax, salt-tax, ports, tolls and fines should, if necessary, be spent on the 'good state'.

8. That the Roman forts, bridges, gates and castles should not be guarded by any baron, but only by the leader of the *popolo*.

9. That no noble may have any fortress.

10. That the barons must keep the roads secure and not give shelter to thieves and criminals, and that they must provide foodstuffs for Rome on pain of 1,000 silver marks.

11. That assistance should be given to monasteries from the revenues of the commune.

12. That in each district of Rome there should be a granary, and that grain should be stored for the future.

13. That if any Roman were killed in battle serving the commune, he should have L 100, or, if a knight, 100 florins.

14. That the cities and towns within the territory of the city of Rome should receive governors from the *popolo* of Rome.

15. That when anyone accuses another and fails to prove the accusa-

tion, he should receive the punishment that the accused would have had to suffer, whether in person or in money.

Many other things were written in the paper, at which, as they greatly pleased the *popolo*, everyone raised their voices, shouting joyfully that Cola should be lord along with the pope's lieutenant. Also, they gave him authority to punish, kill, pardon, appoint to offices, make laws and treaties with other states, and determine borders; and they gave him full and free authority, as far as the boundary of the Roman people stretched.

When these things came to the ears of Messer Stefano Colonna, who was in Corneto ... with a small company he rode to Rome without delay. Arriving in the piazza of San Marcello, he said that he did not like what had been done. On the following day, early in the morning, Cola sent to Messer Stefano a command that he leave Rome. Messer Stefano took the note, tore it into a thousand pieces, and said 'If this madman provokes me any further, I shall have him thrown out of the windows of the Campidoglio'.

69 Food shortage and food riot: Siena, 1328

The food shortages of 1328–9 were among the greatest of the fourteenth century, and caused political and social problems in many cities.

Cronaca senese di Agnolo di Tura del Grasso, in *Cronache senesi*, pp. 483–5.

1328: There was the greatest food shortage throughout Italy. In Florence and its *contado* a *staio*[49] cost 1 florin, and it was not prized by those with money to buy, which was a great hardship and pain for the poor. And Siena, Perugia, Pistoia and other towns in Tuscany, afraid that they could not sustain poor beggars, removed and expelled them from their cities, with the result that many beggars went to Florence, where the commune received them and allocated provisions to sustain them. And the Florentines set up many stores of food, and sent to Sicily for grain, importing it by sea via Talamone ... and they offered it on the piazza at half a florin per *staio*, mixed with barley. And because of popular uproar, the staff of Florentine officials had to stand armed guard of the stores, with the executioner's block and axe at the ready, to punish any who ran up in tumult. And a good number were mutilated in punishment. In two years Florence sank 60,000 florins into the sustenance of the people and the poor ...

49 24 litres, dry measure.

At Siena too the populace was restless and ran in uproar to the Campo, and in this way the shortage spread, for in January a *staio* cost 40*s*, and then rose to a florin (67*s*). As a result, by April 1329 there was hardly any grain to be seen in Siena. It had not rained ... and because of the bad look of the crop, grain could not be found at any price, and everyone was dismayed. Anyone who had any grain kept hold of it, so as to sell at the highest price; and many kept their grain so that their families did not go short. So the government of the Nine instructed the Captain of the People to order all those who had grain to sell to place it in the Campo, and so day by day it was arranged who was to sell, and they sold it by a ticket-system to those in the tax registers, and whoever was not registered could not have any, and they sold it at 60*s* per *staio*. The commune also made a bread of mixed grain, barley and millet, weighing 4 oz each and selling at 2 *quattrini*. The commune also had bread made of pure grain, weighing 6 oz and selling at 2*s* each, though throughout the *contado* ... they cost more than in Siena as the shortage was greater. And many foreign beggars left Siena, and many people came from Florentine territory and secretly bought grain and bread. Though the commune and the Captain of the People had ordered that neither grain nor bread should be traded and that no-one should take them out of the Sienese *contado*, many craftily did so, saying that they were residents of the *contado*. Because of this, guards were placed at the city-gates, and foreigners leaving were searched. Many hid bread and grain, as much as they could, in sacks under their cloaks; others emptied their pack-saddles, and filled them with grain and bread. One day the guards, informed of this fraud, searched and found two men who had emptied their animals' pack-saddles: they were arrested and taken to the podestà, who at once had a platform raised over his door, and put them on it, with chains round their necks, and the pack-saddles full of grain and bread for all to see, and they stayed there most of the day, but were then released without further action. This was done as an example to others ... but many good men thought it was cruel, as the grain and bread had been bought out of hunger and necessity.

The hospital of Santa Maria della Scala distributed bread on its usual days, and such a large crowd of poor came from the city and countryside, as well as from Florentine territory, that there was a tumult ... And on 12 May 1329 the uproar and sheer number of poor people was so great that it seemed the crowd would overwhelm those who were handing out alms at the hospital gate. So, afraid that the poor might force their way in and ransack the hospital, they locked the doors. Seeing this, the poor shouted out 'Mercy!' and other words. And some of them said 'Let's go to the Campo and take whatever grain and bread we can find'. And so, with such an uproar that it seemed the earth was opening up, the poor ran to the Campo and ransacked the tubs holding grain and bread, shouting 'Mercy! We're dying of hunger'. The podestà and his staff came out to restore order, but could not. The poor took up stones and threw them at the podestà's staff, and then hit them with poles they had seized from stalls, so that they retreated to the podestà's palace. So the poor looted all the grain and bread in the Campo; and the shopkeepers around the Campo, afraid of having their shops looted, locked them up ... and there was a great clamour of shouts, ... such that the Nine feared that houses and shops might be wrecked. So they sent for their captain of war, but he with his men ... could not restore order, and three of the podestà's constables and a squire were killed. And the crowd of poor went on growing: now they were throwing stones at the windows of the podestà's palace and of the government. The government and the citizens were very much afraid that Siena would be sacked by the poor. Seeing that they could not restore order or calm the crowd, whose numbers were incredible and who terrified everyone, the captains withdrew from the Campo, posting armed guards to prevent other disturbances. So it was decided that the rector and friars of the hospitals of Santa Maria della Scala and of the Misericordia should go to the Campo and persuade the poor to go to the hospital, where they would be satisfied. And so they did, saying 'Come everyone: we shall give you all the bread you want. Don't create a disturbance and everyone will get some'. And so, at this invitation, they all went to the hospital ... and everyone received all the bread they needed for that day.

Then the Nine announced that citizens should put more grain for sale in the Campo; the bishop sent a great quantity, as too did the hospitals of Santa Maria della Scala and the Misericordia ... and everyone was able to have grain and bread because of the [lower] price-level (everyone, that is, who was tax-registered).

Then the captain of war seized six poor men, who had been the first to incite others, to lead them from the hospital to the Campo, or to loot the grain-tubs and baskets ... and he hanged them at Pecorile as an example to others ...

It followed that many citizens sent so much grain to the Campo that the price came down. And this was because Siena had sent to Sicily for a large quantity of grain, which arrived on 20 June, so that the price fell to 40s per *staio*.

70 Revolt in a lordly city: Ferrara, 1385

The Estensi lords of Ferrara were one of the long-surviving of Italian princely dynasties, but their sense of security was shaken by a revolt in 1385, prompting them to construct a new fortress near the centre of the city to 'reinforce their lordship in stone'.[50] The local chronicler, in describing this event, uses a 'monarchical' model for his narrative, in which full responsibility is laid on an 'evil counsellor', the crowd is anonymous, and the lords themselves appear as either attempting pacification or benevolently granting the crowd's wishes.

Chronicon estense, ed. L.A. Muratori, *RIS*, vol. 15 (Milan, 1724), coll. 509–10.

1385: On 3 May Tommasino da Tortona, the lieutenant of Niccolò d'Este, lord of Ferrara, eyeing maliciously the tranquillity and concord existing between the lord and his people and subjects, acted as follows, in order to sow weeds among them. He pleased the lord by saying that large revenues could be produced if the tax assessments of the community of Ferrara were revised, taking into account not only immovable wealth, but also movable property, that is, money, rents and suchlike, property with which merchants traded in their crafts and businesses. The lord leant his ears to this, not heeding future dangers. So it was that the tax assessments [*estimi*] were drawn up in writing by a select group of citizens led by Tommasino himself. And because they did not compile them equally, another twelve citizens were elected to correct them. And as the assessments were neither well-compiled by the first group, nor well-corrected by the second, the people felt that great burdens would fall on them, so an assembly of about a thousand, unarmed but angry, came to the piazza, shouting 'Viva Niccolò! Death to the traitor Tommasino!' Tommasino, seeking to escape their anger, fled to the lord's chancery. But the people, already incensed with anger and looking to bring about the death of Tommasino, violently broke down the door to the chancery and, not finding the traitor, because he had retreated to the top floor, they disgracefully sacked the chancery and its many books and documents, amid continuing shouts against the traitor. Then Niccolò's brother, Alberto, came down to them, unarmed, and addressed them with many smooth words, in order to mitigate their anger and violence, and he surrendered to them all the records of the gabelles and *estimi*, both new and old. Immediately a fire was lit in the piazza, next to the

---

50 J. E. Law, 'Popular unrest in Ferrara in 1385', in *The Renaissance in Ferrara and its European Horizons*, ed. J. Salmons and W. Moretti (Cardiff and Ravenna, 1984).

church of San Romano, and they burned all these books and documents. Then they went to Tommasino's house, looted all the goods and totally wrecked the interior. Not content with this, they ran to the houses of the gabelle collectors and other officials and looted them like plunderers. As evening came, and the tumult was in no way calming down, they returned in uproar to the piazza, their voices growing stronger, roaring now and screaming 'We want the traitor!' Niccolò, fearing that the worst could befall him, and considering that with smooth words and promises he could not calm such a fury, having taken counsel for the safety of his state, ordered Tommasino, the author of the disaster, to be freely given to them. As he was cast out of the palace gate, he was received by them with rejoicing. And on the spot, some mortally wounded him with their swords, others put him to death; some hit him with cudgels and staves, and rained stones on him, others shamefully dragged him with hooks and ropes to the fire on which the books had already burned, and burned his corpse; but some cut out his heart and liver, and inhumanly fed on them, throwing his intestines down for the dogs and birds to eat, and others carried bits of the body around the city on poles, and some parts were taken as far as Francolino and placed there for all to see. Around midnight ... with the tumult altogether quietened and the popular fury spent, all left the piazza and returned to their homes in silence.

4 May: Niccolò d'Este with his brother, Alberto, early in the morning mounted their horses and rode to the piazza with twelve others. The people came to him there in great reverence, and asked that Tommasino's death should not be blamed on them, as they had acted for the preservation of Niccolò's state and for the sake of peace, and for no other cause, as they were always his loyal and obedient servants. The lord accepted this and, having made his usual circuit of the city, returned to his palace with his usual retinue.

71 Revolt in a republic: Siena, 1371

By contrast, the Sienese chronicler reports the multiple miseries of the Sienese people in the months before the uprising, and condemns the cruelties inflicted on the rebels. The contending political groups in Siena were known by the names of the regimes in which they or their families had taken part: thus the Nine (*Nove*), in power 1287–1355, the Twelve (*Dodici*), and the Reformers (*Riformatori*), in power during the revolt of 1371. In addition, there were the magnates or nobles (*Gentiluomini*) excluded from government, and including the families of Salimbeni, Malavolti, etc.

Cronache senesi, pp. 633–43.

1370: There was a great shortage of all foodstuffs in Siena and its territory: grain cost 28*s* a *staio* ... and the grain officials in Siena issued a proclamation that whoever wanted to bring grain to Siena could sell it at whatever price they wanted, and the price rose to 52*s* ...

The government of Siena created a *bargello*[51] with great arbitrary powers and with forty footsoldiers, four horses and two notaries. And he resided in the house of the sons of Salamone Piccolomini and there held his lawcourt ...

Wine at this time cost 3 florins per load in Siena. The Sienese decided in Council that the wine tax should be halved ... Then, on 10 December, they decided in Council that it should be one third: for every 3*d* that had been paid in the past, only 1*d* would now be paid ...

The [so-called] *Compagnia del Bruco* was uncovered in Siena on the 26 August. It was in the district of Ovile, and 300 or more swore an oath together, and their leader was Domenico di Lano, a second-hand clothes dealer. They said that they wanted peace and plenty, and that they would go for grain to whoever had it, and who had it would give it ...

The grain officials were dismissed on 7 October ... and members of the *Nove* and *Dodici* who had been grain officials were fined 500 florins each. A *staio* of grain then cost 52*s*. The grain office was reformed, with members only of the *Riformatori*, and the grain price came down to 34*s* ...

The *balìa* of Siena removed from the Salimbeni all their armed men and ordered that they could not keep more than twenty-five men, who were all to be their kinsmen ...

1371: 26 January: A plot was discovered in Siena. Those who discovered it were rewarded ... and on 8 February two men were tortured on a cart by the podestà ...

There was great fear in Siena of a *chevauchée*, as the Florentines and Perugians had dismissed many of their troops. And a proclamation was issued in Siena that everyone should take care of their livestock and place it in safe-keeping ...

March: All foodstuffs were dear at this time: grain cost 40*s* a *staio*, meat 2*s* a pound ...

---

51 A police-chief, often a bandit-catcher.

The Florentine and Perugian troops came into Sienese territory on 7 March ... The Germans, Count Luzio and Messer Anasi, were captains of the Perugians' troops, and the whole company was called 'the company of Count Luzio' ... They took plunder and prisoners ... and burned as far as Fonte Becci near the city ... The Sienese sent to many places to recruit soldiers against this company, and ordered that all the straw in the *contado* be burned in order that the company should not be able to find quarters ... On 14 March, the podestà and the Captain of Justice left Siena with a large force drawn from the *popolo* ... The company moved to the Berardenga out of fear of the Sienese *popolo*, who were over 4,000 in number and well-equipped ... On 22 March Siena made an agreement with the company: it received 8,000 florins and 20 *moggia* of bread from the commune ... And I want you to know that many people left Siena and surrounded these troops, and they killed all those they captured. More than 200 were killed. All were questioned, and they said that they were being paid by the Florentines for twenty days, that they had made this raid at Florence's instigation, and that, for every house they burned, they received 1 *grosso* from Florence ... The company departed 31 March and went into the territory of Volterra ...

16 April: Siena decided to mint coins, as it was more than twenty years since they had minted any, and there was a shortage of them ...

The Sienese, seeing that the officials of the commune were consuming all its revenues, decided to sell them off ... and so they were auctioned for 106,000 florins per annum, beginning on 1 August ... Many citizens bought them: members of the *Nove, Gentiluomini, Popolari* and *Dodici* banded together and bought them ...

The workers and carders of the Wool Guild of Siena had a dispute with their masters, demanding to be paid according to the commune's ordinance, and not that of the Wool Guild. They went to the government palace, and were not admitted, and they made a great uproar, threatening to kill their masters and others. For this [three named men], carders of the *Compagnia del Bruco*, were detained: the Captain of Justice tortured and questioned them, and they said things that would cost them their lives. For this reason, all the *Compagnia del Bruco* and others gathered together. On Monday 14 July they ran armed to the palace of the Captain of Justice and demanded [the release of] these three detainees; not being able to have them, they wanted to burn the palace. Hearing this, the Captain of the *popolo*, Francesco di maestro Naddo, came out of his palace, preceded by his banner and trumpets, and went to the palace of the Captain. There was then a great fight, with many of the latter's men being killed or wounded. And the Captain obtained the release of the three men ... The Compagnia del Bruco then went, in great uproar, to the government palace ... and around the city, shouting 'Death to the *Dodici*! Long live the people!' ... They met Nannuccio di Francesco, who had been Captain of the *popolo* for the months of November and December 1370, and they killed him, because he had done many disgraceful things at the request of the *Dodici* and the Salimbeni when he was Captain; and it was Feraccio, Captain of the *Compagnia del Bruco*, who killed him. They then went to the house of the Salimbeni and took away the banner of the *popolo*, which the Salimbeni kept as partners of the *popolo*, and they wounded one of the Salimbeni. And the banners were taken from the standard-bearers and placed at the windows of the Palazzo of the Signori ... ; later they were returned to them ...

Six citizens of the *popolo* from each *terzo* were called up to calm the city, but the *Riformatori* sent them away ... and it was remitted to the *Riformatori* to settle the city and reform the offices as they saw fit. And 24 July they had the banner of Camollia taken from Lorenzo Casini, a member of the *Dodici*, and given, to the sound of trumpets, to Giacomo armourer, and the banner of San Martino from Bertaccio shoemaker to Nanno d'Alesso, because he had been in the action at the Salimbeni house; and they sent to take the banner of Città from the house of Nanni di Pietro, [but] Agnolino di Giacomo, a second-hand clothes dealer and member of the *Riformatori*, said 'I've got that banner', and it stayed with him ... Then on 28 July they had the banners taken from the other standardbearers, that is, Magio, Paschuino and Migliorino, and appointed two captains in each *terzo* to guard the city, and these captains issued tickets to those who left Siena day or night. And certain citizens of the nobles, *Nove*, *Dodici* and Salimbeni, who had been detained, were released ...

29 July: Some of the *Compagnia del Bruco* went to the *Signori*[52] and, putting their hands to their swords, they said that they wanted certain gentlemen whom the *Signori* had detained, and if they did not have them, they would cut the Captain to pieces. They also wanted Niccolò d'Ambrogio, one of the *Dodici*, and Antonio di Bindotto, of the *Nove*, to be beheaded ...

It followed that the *Dodici* plotted with the Salimbeni and their supporters, and they were able to arrange, both through their scorn

52 The government.

for recent happenings and through money, that Francesco di Nado, who was Captain of the *popolo*, and all three of the *maestri* standard-bearers, and many others of the *popolo*, were with them. Their plan was this: the Captain was to place, on the night of 31 July, on the tower and in the palace ... thirty weapons,[53] and on the morning of 1 August the standard-bearers were to arm themselves and the *Dodici* would do likewise, each in his own *terzo*, and then they would come to the Campo, each group also occupying his own *terzo* so that no one else could come to the Campo. And the Salimbeni would come in from outside with all their forces on horse and foot ... and would occupy the streets so that no one could enter or leave the city, and they would then cut to pieces the *Compagnia del Bruco*, the Tolomei, the *Nove*, the bishop and others, and reform the city creating a regime of the *Dodici* and good men, as they wished.

The Signori, noticing their happy faces and hearing the words they were using and their bad behaviour, detained some gentlemen, some members of the *Nove* and *Dodici*, and some *popolari*. The plotters, fearing discovery, at once brought things forward, and on the night of 29 July the Captain put some of the men in his chamber, and then stood on his own at the palace door waiting to let the others in, as arranged. By chance, one of the Signori got up that night and heard the noise and clanging of weapons in the Captain's chamber, and immediately called to his companions and told them. At once they looked for the Captain and found him alone at the door with the keys in his hand. They said to him: 'What are you doing here, Captain?'. Lost for words, he did not know what to say. They took the keys from him, and when his band of men arrived, they sent them away and locked the Captain in a room.

On the following morning, Wednesday 30 July, the standard-bearers, Magio di Giacomo, shoemaker [from the district] of Città, Paschuino, potter of San Martino, and Migliorino ... of Camollia, armed themselves, got the *Dodici* and their followers armed, and came each with more than 600 armed men ... and began to assault the Palace. The Signori defended themselves. A stone was thrown from the tower and bounced off Paschuino's helmet: he fell, such that the crowd thought him dead and almost took flight. Many had gone to Ovile, as planned, to fight with the *Compagnia del Bruco*. They broke them up and chased them through that part of town with lances, bows and swords ... Some fled here, some there, some hid, others threw

53 *zapardi, spinelli e cotali.*

themselves from the walls. Their women, dishevelled and screaming, fled in fear, with cradles on their heads and children in their arms ... There never was such a piteous sight, and it had to be seen to be believed. The *Dodici* in person, that is Giovanni Fei, Ambrogio Binducci, Francia and others, robbed and cut cloth from the looms, and set fire to about eight houses and ... were turning to go back to the Palazzo, when some of the *Compagnia del Bruco* began to cry out to the noblemen and *Nove* 'Help your people!' At which the gentlemen and *Nove* at once took up arms and put themselves at the head of the crowd. The Ugurgieri, with the Tolomei and the Malavolti ... opposed and fought the *Dodici*, and quickly routed them ... The men of Città set upon Paschuino [and his followers] and routed them: they could not sustain any blows and melted like the mist – all the standard-bearers, the *Dodici* and their followers fled. And Domenico and Giovanni Fei, and the merchant Francia di Lenzo were captured ...

The government, having duly learned the truth of this whole matter, had ... four men, including Antonio di Bindotto and Niccolò d'Ambrogio, who had been detained for several days on suspicion, beheaded on the Campo ... And while the execution was taking place, the crowd shouted 'Take the Captain'. So Francesco, the Captain of the *popolo*, was taken, dressed in scarlet, and was beheaded in the middle of the Campo on a scarlet cloth on 1 August ... In his place, Landino, a smith from the suburb of San Marco, was made Captain of the *popolo* ... Magio di Giacomo, the standardbearer of Città, was taken on that very day at Camporegio, having fled and hidden there ... He was beheaded on the 11th, along with Giovanni di Meo and three others ...

The *Riformatori* ordered the electoral bags to be destroyed, and resolved, at a meeting on 12 August, that the government should consist of Fifteen, that is twelve *Riformatori* of the *popolo*, and three of the *Nove*, and that it should be called a popular government. And so a new electoral bag was made for five years ... And they resolved that all the *Dodici* and their descendants could not become members of the government for five years. They also appointed three citizens with full power to convict all the guilty and whoever they wanted ... These three made the two standard-bearers, Paschuino and Migliore, rebels; they were also painted in the Council chamber and their houses were razed to the ground ... In addition, 131 of the *Dodici* and 85 of the *popolo*, who were their friends or friends of the Salimbeni family, and twelve of the *Nove*, were fined, and all these beastly supporters of the *Dodici* paid, together, about 20,000 florins ... Almost all of them were exiled, and those who did not pay within a certain time were declared rebels. And the three citizens who were appointed to pass these sentences received 200 florins each ...

22 August: The *Riformatori* inaugurated the new electoral bags ... The newly elected *Riformatori*, with many trumpets, olive branches and garlands, and with all the Gentlemen and the staunch *popolo*, carried the box in great joy to the Hospital of Santa Maria della Scala. And on the following day, the Riformatori instructed all the Gentlemen and staunch *popolo* to accompany them in making an offering to the Hospital in praise and reverence of the Virgin Mary. And there was no one in Siena who did not go, carrying a candle.

72 Social tensions in a southern town: Chieti

As the account of unrest in Barletta shows [67], disturbances in southern towns were mainly the result of aristocrats, their landed interests and political rivalries.[54]

G. Ravizza, *Collezione di diplomi e di altri documenti de' tempi di mezzo e recenti da servire alla storia della città di Chieti* (4 vols, Naples, 1832–6), I, pp. 23–4.

Giovanna, by the grace of God, queen of Jerusalem and Sicily ... to the Captain general and justiciar of the province of Abruzzi ... On behalf of the whole community [*universitas*] of the men of Chieti ... it has recently been shown by their petition to our Majesty that a dispute arose between the count of San Valentino and the men of Chieti on account of some men from the count's lands who had gone to live in Chieti. The count demanded them back, and two envoys were sent to the count to negotiate a settlement. The count detained them and refused to release them until the community obliged itself on pain of 400 *onze*[55] to remit and expel his vassals from the city. This the community, keen to liberate its citizens, undertook to do, under duress ... In the same petition, it is added that the count busied himself ... to proceed against the community and notified you, as royal justiciar, of the penalty and pressed you to exact it ... Mindful that if the undertaking was made under duress, as claimed, the community is not legally held to observe it, we ... therefore order that if you find the matter corresponds to this petition ... you are ... not to trouble the community at the request of the count in any way ...

Naples, 6 August 1362

54 Jones, *City-State*, p. 290.

55 The *onza* (or *uncia*) was worth 30 *tari*: P. Spufford, *Handbook of Medieval Exchange* (London, 1986), pp. 59–64; and see above, [44].

73 Fist-fights: Florence and Siena

Much of the violence in Italian cities came from young males, some of it in organized fighting games, as here, some in feuds and vendettas, as in the next document.[56]

a. *Alle bocche della piazza: diario di anonimo fiorentino (1382–1401)*, ed. A. Molho and F. Sznura (Florence, 1986), pp. 64–5, 148.

1387: On 18 April there was a fight of young Florentines at the Santa Trinità bridge, one side coming from the quarter of Santa Maria Novella and led by the Strozzi, Altoviti and other families, the other side coming from the quarter of Santo Spirito and led by the Capponi. The bell rang for the end of day. All the families of Florence were there, as well as the Otto di Guardia, the XII and the Gonfalonieri, and they could not manage to halt the fighting, which carried on, by torchlight, for several hours into the night. At the end they began to fight with stones and staves, and to shout 'To arms' and 'Fire' at the Capponi house. Several on each side were wounded, others were arrested and convicted.

1393: On 12 April there was created a band of youths from Santa Maria Maggiore who called themselves 'della Berta', and another band from Santa Maria Novella calling themselves the Magroni, and each evening they invited youths from all over Florence and held fist-fights at Santa Maria Maggiore. The numbers multiplied so much that there were over 500 brawlers on each side and the fights lasted several hours at night. Suspicious, the government issued a proclamation that no one should make assembly ... and a large number of people were detained in the podestà's palace.

b. *Statuti della repubblica fiorentina*, vol. 2: *Statuto del podestà dell'anno 1325*, ed. R. Caggese (Florence, 1921), p. 200.

As, because of fist fights which often happen in the city of Florence and its suburbs, sedition, tumults and many wounds are committed, it is established that no one in the city or suburbs of Florence is to fight with fists or at fist-fighting games, and if anyone contravenes, he is to be detained and not released until he pays ... 100*s* if aged fifteen or below, or L 10 if aged over fifteen ... And the podestà and Captain of Florence must send their staff and footsoldiers to any places in the

56 For this theme, see *Gioco e giustizia nell'Italia di comune*, ed. G. Ortalli (Treviso and Rome, 1993); R. C. Davis, *The War of the Fists: Popular Culture and Public Violence in late Renaissance Venice* (New York and Oxford, 1994).

city or suburbs where they hear or know such fights are taking place, and they are to arrest ... whomever they find fighting, and also anyone else they find there or around the fight or fleeing from it ... And all [other] deliberations regarding this matter are altogether rescinded.

c. *Cronaca senese*, p. 416.

1324: On the Sunday before the end of Carnival, 3 February, there was a fist-fight in Siena between those of the districts of San Martino and Camollia, 600 on each side, and those of the district of Città. And so there were many people on the Campo, stripped to their doublets, with cloths wound round their heads and side-pieces covering their cheeks, to protect the face and head, and cloths wound round their hands, as is customary. As the fist-fight progressed, those of San Martino and Camollia chased those from Città from the Campo, and then began to fight with stones and staves, and then with shields, large and small, with sallets and lances, swords and arrows, and there was so much uproar and so many people on the Campo that it seemed that the world was turning upside down. All the commune's soldiers came armed to the Campo, as did the podestà and his staff, and the Nine issued a proclamation that the fighters be separated, but there was so much uproar that they could not be ... Rather, some soldiers and some of their horses were killed. And all the time more people swarmed into the Campo with crossbows, axes and swords, and the fighting spread, with neither the Nine nor anyone else able to restore order. Seeing this, the bishop of Siena summoned the priests and friars of the city and, with a cross borne before them, they entered the Campo and began to pass through the middle of the fighting ... At the bishop's entreaties, and those of the priests and friars, the fighters began to let themselves be separated, so that the fighting ceased. While the fighting was still going on, before the bishop arrived, the Saraceni and Scotti had thrown many stones from their windows facing onto the Campo, so that there was a move to set fire to their houses, and a son of Ser Nello da Gallena killed an axe-master of San Martino, at which the men of San Martino set fire in two places to the shops on the Campo ... And when the fighting stopped, four men were found dead. Once the tumult was calmed, the Nine held a Council meeting to consider what to do regarding the fight, the killings and the arson, and it was decided that the podestà should banish those who had killed and those who had set fire to shops. And they decided that in the future there should be no such fist-fights ...

74 The origins and conduct of vendetta

These stories from Pistoia illustrate several common elements in vendetta: for example, the role of youths in instigating attacks, and the equivalence of injuries exchanged. However, the second story also shows that vendetta was not tolerated by the lawcourts.[57]

Storie pistoresi, ed. S. A. Barbi, *RIS*, vol. 11, pt. 5, pp. 3–7.

[1286–8] In this city [of Pistoia] there were many noble and power-ful citizens, among whom was a clan of powerful citizens and gentle-men, called the Cancellieri, and this clan had at that time among its members eighteen knights and was so mighty and of such power that it overcame and defeated all the other *grandi*, and, on account of their power and wealth, the Cancellieri became so proud that there was no one in the city or *contado* whom they did not hold down. They insulted everyone, committed many cruelties, and had many people killed or wounded. Out of fear of them no one dared complain.

It happened that some youths, all from this one family, but from two different two branches, one called the Amadori and the other the Rinieri, were gathered at a shop where wine was sold, and, having drunk to excess, a dispute arose among them as they gambled. They exchanged words, then blows, and the Rinieri lad had the better of the Amadori lad. The latter was called Dore di Messer Guglielmo, one of the leading members of his branch; he who injured him was Carlino di Messer Gualfredi Rinieri, also a leading member of *his* branch. Dore, seeing that he was beaten, disgraced and vituperated by his kinsman, and unable to avenge himself there and then, because Carlino's brothers were there, left, resolving to take vengeance. And the same day, late in the evening, Dore was on the look-out and there passed by on horseback one of Carlino's brothers, called Messer Vanni, who was a judge. Dore called to him. Vanni, not knowing about what his brother had done, went over to him. Dore went to strike him on the head with his sword, but Vanni raised his hand to parry the blow, such that Dore cut his face and hand, removing all of it except the thumb. Vanni left and went home. And when his father and brothers and other kinsmen saw him wounded in this way, they and all their friends and relatives were greatly aggrieved ...

The father of Messer Vanni Rinieri and his brothers resolved to make vendetta and to kill Dore, his father, brothers and kinsmen. For

57 For Pistoia, see D. Herlihy, *Medieval and Renaissance Pistoia: The Social History of an Italian Town, 1200–1430* (New Haven and London, 1967), pp. 201–3.

the Rinieri were powerful and well-connected by marriage, and the Amadori feared them greatly, indeed so afraid were they that they did not leave their house. Dore's kinsmen, thinking that they could get out of this quarrel, decided to give Dore up to Vanni's father and brothers, for them to do as they pleased, believing that they would treat him like a brother. So they arranged for Dore to be seized and sent to the house of Messer Gualfredi and his sons and put into their hands. But they, as pitiless and cruel men who disregarded the good intentions of those who had sent Dore, put him in a stable, and there one of Vanni's brothers cut off his hand, the one with which he had attacked Vanni, and cut his face on the same side as Vanni had been injured. And thus wounded and mutilated, they sent him home to his father. When his father and brothers and kinsmen saw him in this state, they were plunged into grief, and this was considered by everyone to be too cruel and severe a thing, to shed their own family's blood, especially as they had put him in their mercy. And this was the beginning of the division of the city and *contado* of Pistoia, from which followed killings, the burning of houses, castles and villages, and the emergence of the faction names Black and White … and war multiplied such that neither in Pistoia nor in its *contado* did there remain anyone who did not belong to one party or the other, and often neighbour fought neighbour …

The parties within the city often fought together, and on one occasion a hard fight began in the Porta Guidi district, to which Messer Detto di Messer Sinibaldo of the Black Cancellieri hurried. He was one of the most wealthy and wise members of his side, and he rode a large horse, well-armed. But during the fight, one of the White party threw a block of stone out of a window and this hit Detto on the head, such a great blow that he was completely stunned and fell forward onto his horse's neck, staying there for a long time such that he was thought to be dead. But when he came to, he left and at once each of the parties went home. Back at home, Messer Detto decided to avenge himself on one of those from whose house the stone had been thrown and, with the advice of his brothers and kinsmen, he resolved to avenge himself on the leader of that house. Messer Detto had a nephew called Messer Simone, who was a knight, young, courageous and pitiless beyond measure, and with him Detto arranged to make vendetta. Simone promised to do it, as one who attended to these things more than to anything else. Having given the order, Messer Simone provided himself with many bold and experienced troops, and one day a judge called Piero of the Pecoroni family, from whose house

the stone had been thrown, went from his house to the palace of the
podestà of the city, and there, at the bar, before one of the podestà's
magistrates, Messer Simone, with his band of men, killed him. The
podestà's officers were powerless to defend him because of the goodly
band with Messer Simone. And with his company, Messer Simone
then returned home, meeting no one on the way who challenged him.
The death of Messer Piero was considered a great injury, for no one
thought he had deserved to die. The podestà prosecuted Messer
Simone and fined him. He paid the fine and went into exile, and it was
five years before he could return to Pistoia.

75 The pacification of vendetta

Despite the image given above, of families united in their resolve to take
revenge, and revenge as an indelible family duty, these were not the
dominant features of vendetta, as shown by this account from San Miniato.

Diario di Ser Giovanni di Lemmo da Camugnori, in *Cronache dei secoli XIII e
XIV*, ed. C. Minutoli (Florence, 1876), pp. 173, 201–2.

Monday evening, 30 December 1309: Nelluccio di Nuccio dei
Tobertelli of San Miniato, who was working for the Priors of Lucca,
killed Manarduccio di Andrea Manardi of San Miniato, who also
worked for the same Priors. Afterwards, on 3 January, all the Tobertelli
gathered on the piazza of Santa Maria, and, in the presence of the
Manardi, repudiated Nelluccio as their friend and kinsman, declaring
that they wished to be friends and servants of all the Manardi. And
the Manardi said and promised that, on account of the death of their
kinsman Manarduccio, they would take no revenge against any of the
Tobertelli family except Nelluccio, and that they would regard
Nelluccio (but no other of the Tobertelli) and all who helped and
supported him as enemies ...

1318 January or February: Because Filippo di Nuccio Pallaleoni of
San Miniato had quarrelled with Piricciuolo di Stefano Tobertelli and
had wounded him with a sword-point to the forehead, several days
later Piricciuolo wounded Filippo in the shoulders with a knife. Later,
in revenge, Bindino Pallaleoni wounded Stefano [Tobertelli] with a
lance in the hand and chest while he was at Nuova, and in revenge
Stefano di Andreuccio wounded Andrea di Mazzo Pallaleoni with a
sword, many blows but without bloodshed. Andrea, returning home,
came across Astanuova son of Buccio Tobertelli, who, along with his

brother, was trusted by the Pallaleoni, and worked with them in collecting the gabelles, which they had jointly farmed from the commune. Astanuova had not joined his Tobertelli kinsmen in this war, but Andrea, moved to anger and breaking a promise not to offend, wounded him with a knife in the shoulders, which his other Pallaleoni kinsmen much deplored. Eventually, the two parties came to an agreement: all the Tobertelli, except Astanuova and his brother, made peace with the Pallaleoni, except for Andrea, whom the Pallaleoni repudiated in public. Subsequently, Andrea, who had been abandoned by his kinsmen, came to a public assembly of the commune, dressed in black like a dead man. He kneeled before Astanuova and, holding his unsheathed sword by its point, said 'Astanuova, here I am to confess that I attacked you in a false and treacherous manner. Take my sword and do with me what you will'. Astanuova's brother stepped up to the podium and spoke at length against Andrea, but concluded that, out of love of God and Saint Francis, he wished to spare him if he undertook to wear forever the habit of a lay brother. This Andrea promised to do: he put on the habit and peace was made.

76 Legal penalties against vendetta: Florence, 1325

Florence was unusual in the complexity of its laws against vendetta, though laws similar in intent were also passed by many communes in central Italy.
Statuti della repubblica fiorentina, ed. R. Caggese (2 vols, Florence, 1910–21), vol. 2, p. 278.

It is established and ordained that, if any assault is made against anyone's person, and such assault is public and manifest, or is the subject of a judicial sentence, and he on whom such assault is made, or someone else of his family, while the original attacker is alive, takes revenge for the assault against someone else, not the one who made the manifest and public assault, then the podestà is to convict such an avenger in the following way: if, from the vendetta, death follows, the avenger is to be beheaded and all his property to be given or adjudicated to the sons or heirs of the dead man; ... but if, from the vendetta, not death but debility of limb or disfigurement of face results, then the avenger is to be sentenced to twice what he would be fined if he had attacked someone else, and in addition he is to be fined L 1,000 ... In other cases, such an avenger is to be fined twice what he would be fined if he attacked some other person.

77 The customs of the citizens of Piacenza, 1388

The praise of times past (the *buon tempo antico*) was a literary–historical commonplace of the thirteenth and fourteenth centuries, used, from its first formulation by Riccobaldo of Ferrara, to condemn luxurious comforts and to extol the rugged virtues of past heroes.[58] In the late fourteenth century, Giovanni de' Mussi, while broadly following Riccobaldo's outline, provides a variation on this well-worn theme, by both celebrating and condemning present luxuries, and by centring the condemnation of extravagance more on women and their ruinous dowries.

Johannis de Mussis, Chronicon placentinum, in *RIS*, ed. L. A. Muratori, vol. 16 (Milan, 1730), coll. 579–84.

Now, at the present time, that is in 1388, the men and ladies of Piacenza make the most lavish expenditure on food and clothing, and in all things more than is customary. For the women wear long, wide garments of crimson silk velvet and of gilded silkcloth and of cloth of gold and of plain silk cloth alone and of scarlet and reddish-brown[59] woollen cloth … and of other most noble woollen cloths. These fabrics of red cloth or velvet or silk cost from 25 to 60 florins for a sleeved cape or loose overgarment. These garments are made with wide sleeves all round, from top to bottom, so long that the sleeves cover half the hand and some hang down to the ground, open only at the back, pointed at the ends in the manner of a long Catalan shield, which is wide at the top and narrow and pointed at the bottom. And on some of these garments are set from 3 to 5 oz of pearls worth up to 10 florins an ounce. On others are set great, wide fringes of gold around the throat in the manner of neck collars worn by dogs. And [likewise] around the sleeves and the cuffs. And they wear small hoods with wide fringes of gold or pearls around them and beautiful belts of silver-gilt and pearls, worth 25 florins more or less; and sometimes they go without belts. And some ladies commonly have so many rings and bands of gold with precious stones, that are worth 30 to 50 florins. At least such garments are decent, for with them they do not show their breasts; but they have other, indecent garments, called 'Cyprians', which are very wide towards the feet and from half-way up the body are tight, with long, wide sleeves like the other garments and of a similar value … and they are dappled in front from neck to

58 Jones, *City-State*, p. 214; C. T. Davis, 'Il buon tempo antico', *Florentine Studies*, ed. N. Rubinstein (London, 1968), esp. pp. 65–7 (for a translation of Riccobaldo's text).

59 *pavonazzo*, 'brownish red': J. Herald, *Renaissance Dress in Italy, 1400–1500* (London, 1981), p. 224.

hem with silver-gilt spangles or pearls. These 'Cyprians' have a neckline so low that they show the breasts, and it seems that the breasts are about to fall out of these dresses. These dresses would be beautiful if they did not show the breasts and if the neckline was decently narrow so that at least the breasts could not be seen by others. These ladies also wear on their heads jewels of great value: namely, some wear chaplets of silver-gilt or of pure gold with pearls and precious stones, worth from 70 to 100 florins, others wear plaited strings [*terzollas*] of large pearls worth 100–125 florins, while others wear bundles of pearls worth 50–100 florins. *Terzollae* are so called because they are made from 300 large pearls arranged in three strings. And in place of inserts of gold and silk which they used to wear intertwined with their hair, these ladies now mostly wear what are called *bugolos* [turban-shaped headgear] which they cover with their hair, tied to the *bugolos* with ribbons of silk or gilt cord or with silk cords covered with pearls. Some women wear short cloaks or capes coming down only to their hands, lined with sendal or vair; and beautiful strings of red coral or amber prayer-beads. Matrons or old ladies wear a fine mantle or a wide, ground-length cloak, round towards the bottom, pleated throughout and open at the front, sprinkled for a handsbreadth around the throat with silver-gilt spangles or pearls, and usually with a collar. And some ladies have up to three mantles: one blue, one reddish-brown and one of wave-patterned camlet, lined with sendal and edged with gold braid or lined with vair. And some wear hoods and some do not; and some, whether they are wearing a hood or not, wear beautiful, fine, white veils of silk or cotton. Widows wear similar garments, but all dark and without gold or pearls, and only with spangles of dark cloth, and they wear dark hoods and fine, white veils of cotton or linen.

Similarly, the young men wear long, wide, ground-length over-garments, with fur linings from wild and domesticated animals, many made of woollen cloth alone, others of silk or velvet. These garments cost from 20 to 30 florins. They also wear large and long mantles down to the ground and short capes covering only their hands. The old men wear similar garments and double hoods, over which they wear beautiful red hats, neither woven nor sewn, but knitted. The young men wear other garments, some short and wide, some short and tight, so short that they show half their buttocks and their genitals, except that they wear hose so long, and tied in five places to their short, tight-fitting doublets (worn beneath other garments) that they cover their buttocks and genitals. And underneath, they have very tight linen underpants and nevertheless, they show the shape of their buttocks and genitals. These tight garments are, some of them, of linen ... and on them they have embroidery of silver thread or pearls, some more and some less. And some of these garments are of velvet or silk, crimson or other colours, or of camlet. And these short garments are somewhat longer at the front and back than at the sides. Sometimes the men wear belts over all these garments, sometimes not. For the most part they do not wear hoods, though they do in the winter – hoods which are very small with long liripipes almost to the ground. These are seen to be stylish ... Soled hose are worn, with plain leather shoes under them, both in summer and winter, and sometimes they wear shoes and soled hose with long pointed toes [pikes], three inches beyond the foot. All other Piacentine citizens, both men and women, used to wear shoes without pikes, but now wear them with short pikes; and these pikes, both long and short, are filled with oxhair.

Item, there are many ladies and young men who wear at their necks torques or circlets of silver, silver-gilt or pearls or red coral. And the young men are clean-shaven, and also shave the hair round their necks to half-way up the ears; from there up they have a great, round head of hair.

And some of them keep one roncey or horse, others keep up to five horses, according to their means; some keep no horse. Those who keep more than one also have one or more servants, who earn up to 12 florins every year in wages. Female servants earn up to 7 florins each per year, and also receive food, but no clothing.

In food all citizens of Piacenza do marvels, especially at weddings and feasts, because most of them give these ... and first they serve good red and white wine, and before everything they serve sugar confections. For the first course they serve one or two capons and a large piece of meat for each table-setting in a sauce[60] made of almonds, sugar and other good spices. Then they serve large quantities of roast meat, capons, chicken, pheasant, partridge, hare, boar, wild-goat and other meats according to season. After this they serve tarts and junket with sweets of sugar on top ... Then, having washed their hands, and before the tables are removed, they serve drinks and sugar confections and more drinks ...

The men of Piacenza currently live in a splendid, well-appointed and elegant fashion. In their homes they use finer and better tableware and utensils than they did seventy or more years ago ... and have more beautiful houses than they did then, because there are in their

60 *ad lumeriam.*

houses beautiful rooms, rooms with fireplaces, storerooms, courtyards, wells, gardens and solars, for the most part. And there are several chimneys in each house, whereas in earlier times there would have been none, as there would be only one fire in the middle of the house, under the tiles of the roof, and everyone stayed around this fire and the cooking was done there. This I have seen in many houses. Nor did they have wells in their houses (or almost none) and few solars and courtyards. And all the citizens of Piacenza drink better wines than their predecessors. The mode of eating for the majority of Piacentine men is as follows: at the first table eats the lord of the house, with his wife and children in a room with a chimney-piece or fire, and their servants eat after them in another part with another fire, or mostly in the kitchen. Two eat off one table-setting, and everyone has a plate[61] and a glass goblet or two for himself, one for wine and one for water. And there are many who have their servants serve them with large table-knives, with which they cut the meat …

Furnishings, which used to be few seventy and more years ago, are now multiplied twelvefold in the houses of Piacentine citizens. And this has come about through Piacentine merchants who trade, or used to trade, in France, Flanders and even Spain. Commonly used are large tables, 18 inches wide, which used to be no larger than 12 inches; also napkins which used to be used by few, and cups, spoons, silver forks, bowls and plates of stoneware and large table knives, bronze vessels, basins, large and small bedspreads and cloth curtains around the bed, and arasses and bronze or iron candelabra, and torches or candles of wax and tallow and other fine furnishings and vessels. And many have two fires, one in the room with a chimney-piece and the other in the kitchen or in the bedchamber. And many keep good confections of sugar and honey in their houses. All of which makes for great expenditure.

For which reason, it is now necessary to give large dowries and commonly 400, 500 or 600 florins or more are given. All of this, and sometimes more, is spent by the groom on adorning the bride and on the wedding. And he who gives the bride away spends, over and above the dowry, about 100 florins in making some new clothes for the bride, on gifts and on the wedding. For this reason, if such expenses are to be met, illicit gains have to be made. And thus there are many who are impoverished, who spend more than they can afford out of desire or necessity. Indeed, at present, if one has in one's family nine mouths and two ronceys, one spends every year over 300 florins

---

61 *menestram.*

... namely in food and clothing, wages of servants, direct and indirect taxes and other extraordinary expenses that arise every day and cannot be avoided. Certainly there are few who can meet such expenses; and there are many who, for this reason, have to abandon their homeland and go into service, whether as servants, merchants or moneylenders, etc.

No one should think that manual workers are included in what I have said, but only nobles and merchants and other good, old citizens, who exercise no craft. Yet even manual workers spend more lavishly than they are used to, especially in clothing for themselves and their wives. Craftwork always sustains those who want to live honourably. At present, people cannot live without wine, so much has everyone become used to drinking it.

78 Fine clothing only conceals the dirt

The poet Antonio da Ferrara (1315–c. 1373) wandered around the courts and cities of northern Italy, and created a genre of desperate, bitter poetry, taking inspiration from moments in his personal life. Here, as he left Venice having failed to find work, he attacks Venetian personal hygiene.

E. Levi, 'Antonio e Nicolò da Ferrara, poeti e uomini di corte del '300', *Atti e memorie della Deputazione ferrarese di storia patria,* 19 (1909), 245; *Rimatori del Trecento,* ed. G. Corsi (Turin, 1969), p. 349.

There are people who wear outfits
of ermine lined with sendal,
but they don't have money to pay the rent
and there's no bread or wine in their homes.
They haven't got a change of underwear,
their cloaks are worn-out and shortened,
their socks and stockings are coarse.
They even pawn their purses and knives.

Now I'll turn the page and address their wives.
They walk around with four rings on their hands,
which would be enough if they were knights.
If you could get a sight of their lingerie,
you'd find their blouses much blacker
than really dark blackberries.
They stuff themselves with apples and pears,
but don't do their laundry in a twelvemonth.

79 'Greed was greater' after the plague

The condemnation of greater materialism was a feature of social comment after the Black Death, as in this extract from the verse chronicle of Buccio di Ranallo (*c.* 1300–1363), an obscure townsman from the central Italian city of L'Aquila.

Cronaca aquilana rimata di Buccio di Ranallo, ed. V. De Bartholomaeis (Rome, 1907), pp. 185–6.

When the plague was over, men revived:
Those who did not have wives, took them now,
And women who were widowed got remarried;
Young, old and spinsters all went this way.

Not only these women, but many nuns and sisters
threw away their habits and became wives,
Many friars ruined themselves to do such things;
And men of ninety took spinsters.

So great was the rush to remarry,
That the numbers by the day could not be counted;
Nor did many wait for Sunday to hold weddings,
They did not care for things, however dear they were.

Who sees the meat prepared in the butchery
Never in any city saw it so fine;
So many loads came out that it seemed a bordello!
Who did not have money killed young pigs.

As there was a great market of things,
prices rose so, I say, because of these brides:
Clothes and silver and whatever was needed
Were so dear that they became outrageous.

I saw 7 *carlini* given for slippers
four or five for earrings;
rings I saw for 4 and 5 *soldi*.
I shan't tell you how dear cloth was.

People were fewer, but greed was greater:
From now on women who had dowries,
were sought after and requested by men …
Worse than this: some were abducted.

When men had come through that great fear

of short illness and hard glandules,[62]
few there were who cared for their souls;
they put their care and energy into getting rich.

80 Civil law on clandestine marriage

During the fourteenth century many Italian cities issued laws insisting on parental consent to marriages. Such laws ran expressly counter to the established canon law on marriage, by which, although the contract was to be made in public, the consent of the couple alone was required and should not be in any way impeded.

Statuti di Verona del 1327, ed. S. A. Bianchi and R. Granuzzo (Rome, 1992), p. 468.

On clandestine marriages, and how transgressors are to be punished.

We decide as law that, if anyone marries or takes as a wife any woman who has a father, mother, brother or elder relative, secretly and without their knowledge or consent, he shall be fined L 100, and more or less at the discretion of the lord or of the podestà and his court ... having regard to the nature of the fact and of the persons. With the same penalty will be punished anyone who gives his or her daughter, sister, niece or cousin, or arranges for her to be betrothed, whether secretly or openly, to any man who has a father or grandfather [without consent], except if he is emancipated. And the witnesses who are present, and the notary who draws up the contract, shall also be punished, the witnesses L 25 each, the notary L 50.

81 Advice on the management of wives and daughters

Advice books proliferated in late medieval Italy. One of the most famous of these is by the Florentine Paolo da Certaldo, of whom little is known (son of a notary, perhaps a grain merchant), but whose views are crystal clear.

Paolo da Certaldo, 'Libro di buoni costumi', in *Mercanti scrittori: ricordi nella Firenze tra medioevo e rinascimento*, ed. V. Branca (Milan, 1986), pp. 36, 43, 59, 71, 90–1 (nos 155, 209, 300, 331, 374).

Sons ... at six or seven years should be put to learn to read. Then they should be put to school or to whichever craft most pleases them, and they will become good craft-masters. Young girls should be taught to

---

62 *blandullia*.

sew, and not to read, for it is not good in a woman, knowing how to read, unless you want to make her a nun. If you do want to make her a nun, put her in the nunnery before she has the guile to discover the vanities of the world, and there she will learn to read. Feed boys well, and dress them as you can, in a decent fashion, and they will be strong and vigorous ... Girls should be dressed well, but it does not matter how you feed them, as long as they get enough to live: don't let them get too fat. Teach them all aspects of housework: bread[-making], washing capons, sieving and cooking, doing the laundry, making beds, spinning, weaving purses, embroidering silk, cutting linen or woollen cloth, darning stocking-soles, and all similar things, so that when you marry them off, they don't seem fools and it won't be said that they were brought up in the forest.

Good horses and bad horses need spurs; good women and bad women need masters and the stick.

The young and virgin woman should live following the example of the Blessed Virgin Mary ... She did not stay out of the house, wandering up and down, here and there, listening to and watching vain men and other vanities, but stayed enclosed and locked up in a secluded and decent place.

I remind you again, if you have girls or young women in the house, that you should discipline them and keep them on a tight rein. And if, as often happens, any of them is looked at by young men, don't get angry with such youths, but punish and warn the girls ...

If it were to happen that you fell ill and, in fear of death, came to the point of making a will, leaving behind you your wife and children, avoid like the fire leaving your affairs and those of your children solely in your wife's hands, even though she is their mother, for women are almost all vain and light-headed, easy to distract. And for many reasons it can happen that she will leave your children and take with her their inheritance, or will treat them badly or will watch and keep quiet while someone else treats them badly, for the financial profit either of herself or of her children by a previous husband or of her natural kin or of a friend with whom she is enamoured or out of fear of some man intent on usurping their property. In one way or another almost no woman ever stays loyal and true ...

82 Sorrowful marriages

The 'bourgeois realist' Bonichi (see above, [59]) here depicts a lower-class marriage, while Tedaldi (above, [46]) adds his variation to the well-worn theme of wife-hating.

a. Bindo Bonichi, in *Poeti minori del Trecento*, p. 294; *Rimatori del Trecento*, ed. G. Corsi (Turin, 1969), pp. 650, 664.

The hired hand is in the house as a servant,
she is a wet-nurse or a young housemaid;
the manservant eyes her and says nice things;
she makes to rebuff him, but then consents.

The 'wifing' is done, but both soon repent:
The dowry is a pallet and a chest;
The new bride has no escort of trumpets;
he feels he is wretched, she feels mournful.

If she doesn't soon become pregnant,
he can't rest till he takes her to a spa.[63]
One carries the water, the other chops wood.

They breed poor little ones and are short of money,
and don't have enough bread to feed themselves.
She hates him and they are always complaining.

[An alternative ending concludes:]
For this reason there's no greater sorrow
for the poor man than to have taken a wife.

b. Misogynistic complaint against marriage and wives was common in poetry, and can, of course, be seen as the outcome of frequent arranged marriage. Here, Pieraccio Tedaldi offers rewards for news of his wife's death. Pieraccio Tedaldi, in *Poeti giocosi del tempo di Dante*, ed. M. Marti (Milan, 1956), p. 725.

If someone were to bring me the news,
true, either by sight or hearsay,
that my wife had departed
this life, having first lost her tongue,
I'd give him a robe and a tunic,
a belt and a purse full of money,

63 Spas were thought to aid fertility.

and always thenceforth while I lived,
I'd serve him with prompt pleasure.

I was never as desirous
of joining with her in matrimony
as I am craving to leave her.
If God or the devil will separate me from her,
I shall never marry another
with witnesses and contract.

83 Women and the patrimony: dowry law

Exclusion of women from the patrimony was the counterpart to the
extension of dowry practices (to the extent that it could be proverbially said
that there was no marriage without a dowry).[64]

Statuti di Perugia (1342), vol. 1, p. 334.

If any woman is given a dowry by her father, mother, brother,
maternal or paternal uncle or any other person, such a woman and her
descendants cannot and may not have any reversionary claim on the
inheritance of any of those who endowed her, or of their descendents
in the male line, while any male descendant survives. Moreover, if a
woman is given a dowry by her brother or brothers, and one of those
brothers dies without sons, then the other brothers or nephews
succeed and the woman and her descendants are excluded from the
inheritance. Except in all cases the last will and testament of any of
the above: if they leave anything to an endowed woman, this is to be
observed. And except that, in time of need, women can have food and
clothing from the inheritance, as its resources allow.

84 Women in the lawcourts

King Robert of Naples excluded women from the lawcourts in 1332, and
Perugia followed suit, but there is little evidence of such a restriction
applying in northern Italy, except as regards testimony from nuns.[65]

---

64 D. O. Hughes, 'From bride-price to dowry in Mediterranean Europe', *Journal of Family History*, 3 (1978), esp. pp. 278–81.

65 B. Schnapper, '*Testes inhabiles*: les témoins reprochables dans l'ancien droit pénal', *Tijdschrift voor rechtsgeschiedenis*, 33 (1965), 579, 583.

Nevertheless, Sam Cohn has argued that from the late fourteenth century on, women suffered a 'decline in power and status' on the urban streets.[66]

Statuti di Perugia (1342), vol. 2, p. 48.

And because it does not seem either legitimate or decent for women to go to the palace of the podestà or captain for the purpose of giving evidence in trials, we are led to ordain that no woman, of whatever condition, should be compelled to go to the palace of the commune or the residence of the podestà or captain in order to give evidence as a witness in any criminal or civil trial. Instead, when a woman is called as a witness, she should go to the church of San Lorenzo, or to her own parish church, and the podestà or captain or their judge should send a notary there to take the woman's oath and testimony.

85 Cross-dressing

The view that gender, occupation and social rank should be visible from people's dress, and that the dress of one gender, occupation or rank should not be used by another, was commonly asserted by churchmen, and is here illustrated in legislation and chronicle.

a. *Statuti della repubblica fiorentina*, ed. R. Caggese (2 vols, Florence, 1910–21), vol. 2, p. 416.

It is established that no woman is to go about the city or suburbs dressed in 'virile' clothing, nor any man in female clothing. And the podestà is required, in the first month of his term of office, to have it proclaimed through the city that no woman or man is to dare or presume to do this, and that she who contravenes is to be whipped through the city, from the communal palace to the place where she was found.

b. Salimbene de Adam, *Cronica*, (ed. Scalia), pp. 911–13; (ed. Holder-Egger), pp. 626–7.

In Carnival 1287 the people of Reggio did not play games according to the custom of other Christian cities, who all at such time behave stupidly and foolishly, but kept silent, as if mourning their dead. However, in Lent, when time is dedicated to God, they began to play games ... when it is the time to give alms and do pious works ... to confess, to listen to sermons, to visit church portals, to pray, fast and weep, as the scriptures say, which at this time are read out in church,

66 S. K. Cohn, *Women in the Streets: Essays on Sex and Power in Renaissance Italy* (Baltimore and London, 1996), p. 37.

as in Joel II.12: 'Turn ye even to me, with all your heart, and with fasting, and with weeping and with mourning' ... and our lord in Luke, VI.25: 'Woe unto you that laugh now, for ye shall mourn and weep' ... The people of Reggio did not apply themselves to pious works or do the good works mentioned above, but 'walked after vanity and are become vain' (Jeremiah, II.5). And though the lord prohibited that 'The woman shall not wear that which pertaineth unto a man, neither shall a man put on a woman's garment: for all that do so are abominable unto the lord thy God' (Deuteronomy XXII.5), they did the complete opposite and walked around 'after their own inventions' (Psalms, LXXX.13). For many of them borrowed some female clothing, and dressed in it they began to play and to charge around the city jousting. And the better to look like women, they whitened some masks with lead-white, and put them on their faces, not expecting punishment for such acts. For scripture says of sinners: 'All faces shall gather blackness' (Joel, II.6), 'And the faces of them all gather blackness' (Nahum, II.10), and 'Their visage is blacker than a coal; they are not known in the streets' (Lamentations, IV.8). Woe to such wretched Christians who strive to turn ecclesiastical worship into frivolity and empty talk.

86 Women in the streets

The mistreatment (or misbehaviour?) of women in the streets led to efforts to control or protect them, either by circumscribing their activities or penalizing their harassers.

a. *Statuti di Perugia* (1342), vol. 2, pp. 120–1.

As it is said that, at the time of the indulgence granted by Pope Benedict to all who attended the church of the Dominicans of Perugia, on the [feast of] the translation of the blessed Santo Stefano, many insults and verbal injuries, disparagements, violence and assaults were done to women, both those of the city and *contado*, and foreigners, wishing to go to [receive] the pardon, and both in the church and outside it, and both going and coming back, such as indecent touching, kissing, hugging, embracing, pinching, lifting of head dresses, pushing over, colliding, and not permitting to proceed or to leave freely, we enact that whoever does any of these things in future is to be punished by the podestà or captain in L 500 in *denari piccoli*, if before 29 July, and L 1,000 if between 1 and 5 August.

b. N. Tamassia, 'Odofredo. Studio storico-giuridico', *Atti e memorie della Deputazione di storia patria per la Romagna*, 3rd ser., 12 (1893–4), 374.

It used to be customary in Rome and Bologna in the month of May to play a game in the following way: a girl, adorned, decked-out and well-dressed is placed on a cart full of flowers and foliage, and below her she has other girls standing in the piazza, and they seize men passing by and ask for money for the queen, because the queen who is there commands it. And wherever they are, their lovers go and give them large gifts, and enjoy this game, both because they speak with the girls, and because they touch them. This game used to be done in Rome, and later it was ordained that it should be not done.

c. *Statuti di Bologna dell'anno 1288*, I, p. 249.

We establish that May queens,[67] countesses or counts, are not to be created in the city or suburbs of Bologna, nor is the game involving these to be played, or tents or curtains to be put up for this purpose. And whoever allows them to be done in his house, under his portico or in front of his house, is to pay as penalty 100*s*, and the countess or count 20*s* ... And the podestà is required to have this proclaimed throughout the city in the months of April and May. And fathers are to be held responsible for the fines of their daughters.

87 Confinement of prostitutes and pimps

Statuti di Verona del 1327, ed. S. A. Bianchi and R. Granuzzo (Rome, 1992), p. 495.

We issue as law that all public prostitutes and pimps are to stay in the Arena, and if they are found anywhere else, they are to be fined L 10 each on each occasion. And that each prostitute and pimp must wear on the head a hood half a foot long and particoloured white. And if any prostitute is found without the hood, she is to be fined 60*s*. If anyone held by common report to be a prostitute or pimp is found to be staying in anyone's house, the householder is to be fined 100*s*. In all these matters, anyone can make an accusation and receive half of the penalty.

67 *maiume*.

88 Sumptuary law: Parma, 1258

Sumptuary laws are found throughout late-medieval and early-modern Europe, but the Italian cities legislated more often and in greater detail than states elsewhere. Though the early laws, from the mid-thirteenth century, were fairly simple and addressed many types of spending considered excessive (on wedding parties, funerals and wakes, etc.), the later laws were much longer and came to focus more on women's dress.

Statuta communis Parmae (Parma, 1855–6), p. 406.

That from this time forward women's garments are to be made as long only as to reach the ground, plus a quarter of a *braccio*, and no more; and tailors are to be held under oath to observe this and not to cut longer robes; and if they transgress, they are to pay L 3 on each occasion.

89 Sumptuary law: Bologna, 1288, 1398

Sumptuary law at Bologna underwent significant evolution between the thirteenth and fourteenth centuries: the 1288 law issued a blanket ban, but allowed the rich to keep their illicit clothes while paying fines; the fourteenth-century laws made exceptions for certain social groups, so that money could no longer buy them license to dress in the manner of their superiors.[68]

L. Frati, *La vita privata di Bologna* (Bologna, 1900), pp. 271–2, 275–9.

1288

We decree that no woman in the city, suburbs or district of Bologna may dare or presume to wear furs or any garment that has a train that trails more than ¾ of a *braccio* along the ground, or a stole[69] longer than one *braccio*, without tassels, and if any such garments are found already made, they are to be reduced to the said measurements ... on pain, for each person in contravention and for each occasion, of L 25 (and the garment is still to be altered as above). And no citizen or foreigner in the city or district may dare or presume to tailor any garment contrary to the above ... on pain of L 100.

Item, that no woman of the city or district, great or small, may dare or presume to wear any chaplet or diadem composed of pearls, or

---

68 M. G. Muzzarelli, *Gli inganni delle apparenze: disciplina di vesti e ornamenti alla fine del Medioevo* (Turin, 1996), pp. 139–43.

69 'Regoglum': 'A sign of pomp and inane glory, that Bolognese women used to wear over their shoulders on their cloaks, which they called in common speech a *regolium*': Salimbene de Adam, *Cronica*, (ed. Holder-Egger), p. 436.

a circlet of beaten gold or silver, or wear or have any ornament of pearls on any part of her person, except on a ring, nor have any hairbands or nets in which there is gold inserted or interwoven ... on pain of L 25 for each occasion, and forfeiture of the chaplet, circlet, or ornament of pearls.

Item, no person, whether a male older than 12 years or a married female ... may dare or presume to have or wear any decorated braids or any sort of edging on any garment on pain of L 10 for each occasion. We do, however, out of urbanity, permit and allow unmarried girls to have and wear four embroidered braids ... up to the value of 2s, but from that value upwards we prohibit them, under the said penalty.

Moreover, we order that no woman, of high or low status, of the city and district of Bologna, may dare or presume to have or wear on any garment fastenings of gold or silver at the collar or at any other point, if they are worth more than 20s (on a garment without a surcoat) or 11s (on the surcoat) ...

1398

Wishing to remove the immoderate expenditure on women's clothes and ornaments, which not even husbands can afford, and desiring that the community be strong and behave well and honestly, and especially in those things pleasing to God, [the government] has ordered that no woman, of whatever condition and estate, may for the sake of ornament wear or have on her any gems or precious stones, pearls, gold or silver-gilt, whether enamelled or not, nor any coronet, chaplet, garland or net[70] of gold or silver or pearls ... However, they may wear on the head 1½ oz of silver or gold wire, in any manner they please, combined or not with any other (non-prohibited) object; and it is allowed to women of over forty years to wear braids, both gilded and not, in the customary way.

Item, they may not wear or have on them gold or silver for the sake of ornament, save that they may wear silver, whether gilt or not, or enamelled, in or on ornaments, up to the weight of 12 oz ... not counting any gilded cords ... which they may wear, for ornament, up to the weight of 6 oz ...

Item, they may wear, beyond the said 12 oz and 6 oz, one belt of silver gilt or enamel, provided that the weight of the enamelled silver or gold ... does not exceed 10 oz ... and provided that ... fixed to it is no pearl or precious stone.

70 *frascatam.*

Item, that they may not wear any wide edging wider or higher than the stomach of a loose overgown ...

Item, that they may not wear on their fingers more than three rings which they may wear with gems, pearls and other precious stones, or not.

Item, they may not wear any garments of figured velvet, or velvet with a high pile in any fashion, whether brocaded with gold or silver, or in any cloth of wool or silk, or in any mixed fabric, interwoven with gold or silver ... nor any garments decorated with circles, waves, almond-shapes, twills, steps, chevrons or similar ... nor wear a loose overgown with edging at the neck or hem wider than one inch, and the sleeves of any garment may not be wider than 1⅓ *braccia* in circumference, nor extend beyond the hand (except for old garments, already made, which have been sealed).

Item, they may not wear or have any garment embroidered in any part or with embroidered buttons or pins unless they are old and sealed garments, ... nor show at the neck, chest or arm any jewel, device or collar of any value.

Item, they may not wear any garment lined in any fur, namely ermine, vair ... or marten, entirely or partly sewn on to the garment ... nor lining of any kind, of the same or greater value, save that they are allowed to wear furs (except ermine) for the edges of sleeves ... However, this clause does not apply to women, of whatever condition, aged 40 or over (of whose age their own statement should suffice), nor to the wives and unmarried daughters of knights and of doctors of law or medicine.

Item, they may not wear tippets on any of their garments in any way wider than three inches ...

Item, they may wear garments already made at the time of this proclamation, notwithstanding that they are prohibited by the terms of the present decree, provided the sleeves that are wider or longer than above stated are reduced and sealed in the permitted form, and provided there are not on them pearls or any silver above the permitted weight, not counting embroiderings or braids. Such garments may be worn only up to eight years from the date of this proclamation ... in such a way, however, that such old garments ... should be given and produced in writing to the podestà and Captain, or other deputed official, within the deadline announced, and sealed ... Of which garments a register should be kept ... in which should be recorded the type of cloth and the name of the woman and her husband, if she is married, otherwise her father, and the district where she lives ...

Adding and declaring that the present statute does not extend to wives or unwed daughters and nieces living together in the family of any foreign officials or hired troops resident in the city for less than five years (provided that such wives and daughters are also foreigners) ...

Item, that no citizen, inhabitant or foreigner may have at any time, even on the occasion of a marriage agreed or made, more than thirty women in his house, including the women of his own household, except on the day when the women go to escort the bride from her father's or mother's house ...

And the podestà and Captain should each depute one of their notaries to inquire diligently and effectively into all the above, and should also send out their officials, especially on feast days, to churches, and especially to the church where a solemn festival is being held, or where a new priest is celebrating his first Mass, to enforce all the above.

Item, the said notaries and officials are to go to the houses of each and every bride and groom at the time of a wedding, and diligently inquire into contraventions ...

Item, wishing to provide for the immoderate expenses of widows, which are made at the time of their widowhood, they decree that no widow ... of any citizen, resident or inhabitant, who enjoys the benefits of citizenship, may, even at the time of the funeral, or after, have or wear sombre widow's garments valued at more than L 50, nor any garments lined in squirrel-fur, ermine, or marten, or have veils on their heads for ornament ... of value greater than L 10 ...

90 Women cleverly evade the law

Research on the registers of civic officials who had the task of inspecting women's dress has shown that sumptuary laws were resisted, both by husbands and lawyers, and by the women themselves, who gave false names, prevented inspections, and argued that officials had made mistakes.[71] Sacchetti – who was indeed, as he says, one of the Florentine Priors in 1384 – spins and elaborates such material into a story.

Franco Sacchetti, *Il trecentonovelle*, no. 137, in F. Sacchetti, *Opere*, ed. A. Borlenghi (Milan, 1957), pp. 421–4.

71 R. Rainey, 'Dressing down the dressed-up: reproving feminine attire in Renaissance Florence', in *Renaissance Society and Culture: Essays in Honor of Eugene F. Rice*, ed. J. Monfasani and R. G. Musto (New York, 1991), pp. 224–6.

In this story I wish to show how the law of ladies has defeated great legal minds, and how they are great thinkers, when they want to be.

Not long ago, while I was (though unworthy) one of the Priors of our city [Florence], a judge arrived whose name was Messer Amerigo degli Amerighi, from Pesaro, a very handsome man, who was even more outstanding in his learning. Having presented himself at our office on his arrival, with the requisite formalities and speeches, he began his term of office. A new law had just been passed on women's ornaments, and he was sent for within a few days and reminded to enforce those regulations as expeditiously as possible. This he agreed to do. Having gone home, he looked over the ordinances and for several days his patrolmen went out searching [for transgressors]. When his notary returned from such expeditions, he would tell the judge, when he had found any woman, how he had tried to take her name and the objections she had made, and the notary appeared almost beside himself [at their responses]. Messer Amerigo noted and considered all his notary's reports.

By chance it happened that certain citizens, seeing women wearing what they wanted without any restriction, and knowing of the new law, and hearing that a new judge had arrived, went to the Priors and said that the new judge should do his job well so that women did not in future overstep the mark, as they were now doing in their attire. So the Priors sent for the judge and expressed their surprise at his negligence in the matter of the ordinance on women. To which Messer Amerigo replied as follows:

'My lords, throughout my life I have studied to learn the law, and now, when I thought I knew something, I find that I know nothing. For, searching for ornaments forbidden to your women by the ordinances you gave me, I have never come across defence arguments like those given by these women. I would like to give you some examples. A woman was found with the liripipe of her hood dagged and twisted around her head. "Tell me your name", my notary said to her, "because you have a hood with a dagged liripipe". The good lady took this liripipe, which was attached to the hood by a pin and, holding it in her hand, claimed that it was a garland! Later on, he found a woman wearing many buttons. She was told, "You cannot wear these buttons", and she replied, "Yes I can, Sir, for these are not buttons, they are cupels; and if you don't believe me, look, they don't have shanks, and there are no button-holes". The notary went to another woman wearing ermine, and thought as he did so "What objection will this one make?". "You are wearing ermine", he said, and wanted to take her name, but the woman said "No, don't write down my name, for this is not ermine, but suckling fur".[72] And the notary said "What is this suckling fur?", to which the woman replied "It comes from an animal." ... '

And so, amid many arguments, Messer Amerigo was told that for the rest of his term of office he should look to do what was right and to let anything else go. And this was said in such a way that from that time on almost no judge has given himself trouble in this matter, letting pass the garlands and cupels and suckling fur ...

91 Assistance to converted Jews: Perugia, 1298

Having grappled in the 1270s with the problems of implementing a statutory order expelling the Jews,[73] the commune of Perugia is to be found in the 1290s granting money to a Jewish convert.

A. Toaff, *Gli Ebrei a Perugia* (Perugia, 1975), pp. 224–5.

25 January 1298 [proceedings of the General Council]

The Captain of the *popolo*, in the presence of the guild consuls and with their consent, made proposals and asked for advice ... [in various matters]. There is a petition from fra Giovanni, who was a Jew and is now voluntarily imprisoned, to serve God, in the prison at the San Pietro gate, that he be assisted from communal funds, out of piety, in obtaining a tunic so as to avoid the cold and to serve God.

In the Council's deliberation, ... it was decided that the Captain and consuls should give to fra Giovanni the Jew, who returned to the faith and is now in service[74] at the prison by the church of San Pietro, at his own choice to serve God, L 3 from communal funds for a tunic.

---

72 *lattizo.*

73 A. Toaff, *Gli Ebrei a Perugia* (Perugia, 1975), pp. 211–13.

74 *nuncupatur.*

92 Exemptions and privileges to Jews

Toaff argues that the Black Death, far from unleashing greater anti-Semitism against presumed Jewish poisoners of Christian society, led to a greater appreciation of the useful services performed by Jews for the city.

a. A. Toaff, *The Jews of Umbria* (3 vols, Leiden, 1993), vol. 1, pp. 117, 170–1.

19 June 1351

In order that the city of Perugia always be full of sufficient and useful people, and in order that the Jews and physicians master Gaudino, son of master Bonaventura, and master Musetto, son of Salomone, have cause to reside in Perugia and to aid Perugian citizens freely and faithfully with the benefits of their profession, the Lords Priors of the city of Perugia ordain that henceforth the said Gaudino and Musetto are to be, by the authority of this law, exempt and immune from all burdens, imposts, forced loans or contributions that will be imposed in future by the commune of Perugia specifically on Jews living in the city ... except that this will not apply when such burdens are imposed on other citizens, in which case they are required to pay as other citizens are.

14 July 1383

As the Perugian Jew Matassia was a true partisan of the government of the city of Perugia, and showed this in word and deed, coming to the commune's aid with his money, investigating keenly those things that would harm the government in any way, reporting them to the Lords Priors so that they could take appropriate remedies and prevent rebels and traitors from bringing their evil intentions into effect, because of which he has earned the favour of all citizens, and recently, as God pleased, he has gone the way of all flesh, his son Salomone and his kinsmen have humbly asked us to grant, out of special favour, that they might wear black mourning dress as a sign of sadness and mourning of the said Matassia. We therefore, gratefully acceding to this request ... grant to Salomone and three of his kinsmen full licence freely to wear the said dress, with impunity, notwithstanding the relevant statute ...

b. C. Santoro, *La politica finanziaria dei Visconti*, (3 vols, Varese & Gessate, 1976–83), vol. 2, p. 47, doc. 69.

We Gian Galeazzo Visconti, count of Vertù, imperial vicar of Milan etc., make known to all ... that, having received the following requests on behalf of the brothers Menelm, Isaac and Vinelm and of another

Isaac, Jews, who wish with some other Jews to come and live in the
cities and territories of our dominion, we have confirmed and
approved their requests and are content that they come to live in our
cities and lands, at their pleasure, under the following terms and conditions as expressed in their request ... The tenor of their request
follows: first, they request exemption from all impositions on their
persons and property, excepting only indirect taxes; item that they
may lend at interest and give money on loan at whatever price they
wish ...; item that they may sell just as the lord's other citizens and
subjects buy and sell, and enjoy the same rights, in those places where
they will be ...; item that in civil litigation the law will be administered
to them, whether as plaintiffs or defendants, as it is administered to
the lord's other citizens and subjects, and that if any injury is done to
them, the lord will defend them ... except if they be found *in flagrante*,
in which case justice will be done to them by the podestà of the city
where they live as to the lord's other subjects; item that they cannot
be prosecuted in a criminal case without the lord's prior notification,
and after prosecution the lord will order their punishment according
to the seriousness of the crime, as he pleases; item that they be given
a cemetery outside the city and a synagogue inside the city and a
house where they can live for rent; item that meat and other
foodstuffs will be sold to them at the same price as they are sold to
others ... ; item that they be not forced to baptize any of their sons
unless he is thirteen years old; item that, if it happens that they wish
to leave and to go elsewhere, they be issued with safe-conducts, to
secure their persons and property thoughout the lord's territories ...
Issued in Pavia, on 5 November 1387.

93 Jews as the enemies of the cross: Florence

By the early fifteenth century, however, official anti-Semitism was once again
leading to restrictions, reconsidered only when convenient.[75]

U. Cassuto, *Gli Ebrei a Firenze nell'età del Rinascimento* (Florence, 1918), pp.
362, 364–5.

24 January 1406

Considering that Jews are enemies of the cross, of our Lord Jesus
Christ and of all Christians, and that they practise usury contrary to

75 For these and other documents on Jews in Florence, see *The Society of Renaissance
  Florence*, ed. G. Brucker (New York, 1971), pp. 240–50.

the commandment of the holy Church, [the Signoria of Florence] has deliberated and ordered that no Jew, wherever he comes from, may himself or through another, directly or indirectly, secretly or openly ... lend at usury ... or make any usurious contracts in the city, *contado* and territory of Florence, or in any city, land or place in which the commune of Florence has jurisdiction ... on pain of L 1,000 each on every occasion.

12 June 1430

Lest the poor of the city of Florence be ruined by such high interest rates – as they have been by usurers – especially at this time of plague, and in order that they can meet their necessary expenditures at a lower cost, the magnificent lords Priors of the Guilds and the Standardbearer of Justice wish to introduce Jews into the city and, having made serious deliberation on this ... they ordain and provide ... that they, together with the Gonfalonieri of the societies of the *popolo* and the Twelve Buon'Uomini (and a two-thirds majority of them), may from now up to 15 September next ... permit any Jew or Jews to lend and to stay in Florence for the purpose of lending, for those periods of time ... with or without payment of 4*d* per pound to the Company of the Magi, and with those concessions, exemptions, freedoms and agreements ... as will seem fitting to the said lords ... and to order suspension of the deliberation against Jews made in January 1406 ...

94 'The domestic enemy': female slaves

Though slavery began to reappear earlier in southern Italy, the mid-fourteenth century saw the legitimation and growth of slave-ownership in the towns of the north and centre. With the import of non-Christian, 'infidel' slaves famously approved by Florence in 1364,[76] the numbers of Eastern European, Tartar and African slaves – mostly young females – multiplied. Here Antonio Pucci is witness to the sexual tensions that resulted within slave–owning households.

Antonio Pucci, in *Poeti minori del Trecento*, ed. N. Sapegno (Milan and Naples, 1952), p. 357.

Female slaves have advantages in every way,
and better conditions than free women,

---

76 Text in Brucker, *Society of Renaissance Florence*, p. 222.

for, if a free woman wants a husband,
he has to be bought according to an agreement.

Whereas the slave is bought first of all,
and has no marriage ring on her finger,
but she satisfies her desire better
than her mistress, whom she humiliates.

It's true she does much hard work about the house,
as is her job, in the morning and the evening,
but she also feeds her mouth to the full.

And, if she breaks something in the kitchen,
it is almost as if she is not to be blamed,
as a Florentine woman would be.

Let fever kill whose who first brought them to Florence,
for one could say that they have destroyed the city.

95 Contract of sale of a slave, 1388

Slave-owning, even by churchmen and women, became common, but
Christian charity did at least encourage emancipation, though this often took
delayed and conditional forms, as here.[77]

Amalfi: Sergio de Amoruczo, 1361–1398, ed. R. Pilone (Naples, 1994), pp. 159–60.

19 October 1388

We Giacomo Boccaforno of Amalfi, judge ... and Sergio de Amoruczo
of Amalfi, notary ... make known and attest [that] in our presence
appeared the reverend religious woman, lady Maria, by the grace of
God, abbess of the Monastery of Santa Maria of Amalfi ... for the one
part, and Lorenzo di Guttafrede ... for the other part, and that the
said abbess freely sold and granted on behalf of herself and her
monastery to the said Lorenzo ... the labour and services of a female
slave belonging to the abbess, now a Christian, which slave the abbess
asserted belonged to her in full property, and has assigned to serve
Lorenzo for the next eight years, for the agreed price of 3 *onze* and 10
tarì ... which the abbess acknowledges she has just now received by

---

77 I. Origo, 'The domestic enemy: the eastern slaves in Tuscany in the fourteenth and
fifteenth centuries', *Speculum*, 30 (1955), 353. For more recent work on slaves: J.
Heers, *Esclaves et domestiques au Moyen Âge dans le monde méditerranéen* (Paris, 1981).

hand from Lorenzo ... With this condition agreed between the parties: that if the said slave within the next two years commits any fault or misuses her own body, then Lorenzo may sell her labour and services for the remainder of the eight years, and no more, and that after this period is finished, the said slave is to be free ...

V: POLITICAL STRUCTURES

From *commune* to *signoria*, from independence to subjection

The Italian communes of the thirteenth century have been celebrated for their recreation of the institutions and methods of ancient democracy. Political participation was widened beyond the families of a narrow élite. Appointment to executive boards and committees was based not on wealth or rank or seniority but on election or the drawing of lots. Above all, the influence of powerful individuals and families was restricted through secret ballotting, short terms of office, compulsory 'vacations' from office and limits on kinsmen serving together on the same committees (see [96–7, 99]). At the same time, rules of procedure for councils and assemblies aimed to create conditions in which polite, balanced and expeditious discussion of proposals could take place [100]. All this produced a 'broader democratic base ... than in any known regime before the French Revolution'.[1]

These achievements were soon, however, under threat. 'Democracy' did not bring peace, and the baleful power of division and faction grew stronger.[2] From the middle decades of the thirteenth century, political life in northern Italy began to be dominated by a new breed of political and military leaders, generally known as tyrants or *signori*. At a time of intense military activity and pressure during and after the reign of Emperor Frederick II, such men provided internally-divided cities and their incomplete communal 'states' with the beginnings of a more stable political order. In an accelerating development, as Frederick II's efforts to reimpose imperial authority failed, monarchical authority was recreated at the local level, in the persons first of Frederick's former political and military lieutenants, then of local faction chiefs (Azzo d'Este in Ferrara, Martino della Torre in Milan, Mastino della Scala in Verona). Though their power often remained informal, they passed that power to their heirs, who formalised their position through popular 'elections' and technical transfers of

1 Jones, *City-State*, p. 403, and generally pp. 403–12.
2 *Ibid.*, pp. 600–16.

arbitrary power (Ferrara 1264, Mantua, 1299 and so on). In the course of time, some of these lordships developed into principalities and regional states. By 1300, most cities of northern Italy were under signorial rule; those that were not soon followed (Padua, Parma), while attempts to create city-lordships were also made in Tuscany.

At the same time as political instability was producing new constitutional solutions in many cities of the north, in others the same process was leading to a strengthening of communal government. In Florence, most famously, a new government by 'Priors of the Guilds' was instituted in 1282 [99], which was to become the 'pivotal magistracy for 200 years'[3] and was a victory for what Najemy has called 'corporatism', that is control of membership of executive committees by the professional and commercial corporations. This was strengthened in 1293 with the Ordinances of Justice which, in the declared interest of 'equality', excluded magnates and restricted eligibility for the priorate to non-knights and guildsmen who 'continuously exercise a craft'.[4] However, the method by which the Priors were elected continued to vary, from simple co-option to combinations of nomination and election by voting, until the settlement of a four-stage electoral process in 1328 [99]. This reform, however, came to operate more in the direction of oligarchy: by periodically creating lists of those eligible for office, it designated in advance a 'whole political class', giving it the certainty of future office, thus creating a one-class 'monopoly' on government.[5] In this respect, constitutional development in Florence coincided with developments in Venice, were the much-debated 'closure' (*Serrata*) of the Great Council defined and fixed membership of the ruling class. 'Democracy' was defended through exclusion.

If the major political developments of the thirteenth century were the appearance of city-lordships and the consolidation of communes, the major political development of the fourteenth was the construction of regional states, in which one dominant city came to control several formerly independent city-states. This process, it is true, had already begun in the thirteenth century, and already by 1350 Milan dominated much of Lombardy, including the cities of Pavia, Cremona,

3 J. M. Najemy, *Corporatism and Consensus in Florentine Electoral Politics, 1280–1400* (Chapel Hill, 1982), p. 17.

4 A translation of the Ordinances is available in Kohl and Smith, *Major Problems* (see above, ch. 4, note 46).

5 Najemy, *Corporatism*, pp. 115–16.

Brescia, Bergamo, Piacenza, and parts of Piedmont (Asti) and Emilia (Parma); while Venice had taken control of Treviso in 1339. In the second half of the century the process continued, with Florence taking Prato in 1351 and Arezzo in 1384, and Milan briefly extending its dominion to include Genoa (1353–6), Bologna (1350–5) and Verona (1387–1404). Meanwhile many submissions had proved temporary: thus Lucca's to Pisa (1347–68), Reggio's to the Gonzaga, lords of Mantua (1335–71), or Ancona's to the Malatesta, lords of Rimini (1348–55). Then in the early fifteenth century both Venice and Florence made lasting, key gains, respectively of Verona, Padua and Vicenza, and of Pisa. The submissions of Pisa to Florence and Padua to Venice illustrate the two principal means by which dominant cities reduced others to subjection: by purchase and by conquest. The harshness of Venice's treatment of Padua and its lords in 1405, with the *carroccio* smashed and Francesco da Carrara killed, further contrasts with the gentle treatment by Florence of the lords of Pisa in 1406, the Gambacorta, who were granted border castles, houses in Florence, tax exemptions and so on [107–8]. The contrast is, however, deceptive on two levels. First, because both Florence and Venice, for all that they proclaimed liberty as their justification or rested their conquests on the spontaneous submission of the people, occupied subject towns through military power: one of the first acts of Florence in newly-subject Prato was to build a new citadel.[6] Second, the dominant city's attitude when occupying subject towns differed from its subsequent interventions. Florence 'amputated' subject towns' *contadi* and imposed on them its own fiscal system and its own weights and measures; Venice made few exiles and stressed continuity; the Visconti of Milan, a third variant, recognised and created fiefs and gave separate status to small towns. Pisa under Florentine rule 'sickened and shrivelled' (Schevill), the Pisans being treated 'worse than Jews' (Sercambi): existing downward economic trends were reinforced by Florence, which exiled over a hundred families, suppressed competition from the Pisan wool guild and increased taxation. The Pisan *contado* was annexed to Florence, the Pisan fiscal system was appropriated, offices in the Pisan church and state were engrossed by Florentines. Florentine artisans were not obliged to enrol in Pisan guilds; Florentine élite families bought up land; the archbishops of Pisa were all Florentine. Florentine stimulus to the

6 G. Pampaloni, 'Prato nella repubblica fiorentina', in *Storia di Prato* (3 vols, 1980), vol. 2, p. 8.

Pisan economy, through shipbuilding (galley fleet, 1421) and the transfer of university faculties (1473), came rather late.[7] At Padua, by contrast Venice immediately transformed the long-established university into an institution of state.[8] At the same time, its recognition of Paduan statute law ensured the preservation of Paduan urban councils and government procedures (in matters such as taxation), while the political class was largely unchanged, the subjection of the countryside to the city was maintained, and Padua's economy preserved.[9] This contrast should not perhaps be pushed too far. Venice too did come increasingly to intervene in Paduan life: statute law was gradually supplanted by rulings from Venice, new fiscal burdens were imposed, and the political class was denied real power. It is also true that Venice's treatment of its subject cities could vary, as James Grubb's study of Vicenza has shown.[10]

96 A guild-based regime: Perugia

Perugia achieved one of the most successful of guild regimes, and Grundman has argued that the creation of government by the Priors of the Guilds in 1303 wrested power out of the hands of the *popolo grasso*, the greater businessmen, and transferred it to the *popolo minuto*, or small traders and artisans.[11] This is not, however, borne out by the record of lesser guildsmen among the Priors: whereas the Mercanzia (and later the bankers too) had regular places as of right, most of the other guilds – some of them numerous, for example the fish-mongers and the cobblers – very rarely succeeded in getting a member elected.[12]

Statuti di Perugia (1342), vol. 1, pp. 93–7, 127–8, 129–30, 132–3.

7 M. E. Mallett, 'Pisa and Florence in the fifteenth century: aspects of the period of the first Florentine domination', in *Florentine Studies*, ed. N. Rubinstein (London, 1968); G. Petralia, '"Crisi" ed emigrazione dei ceti eminenti a Pisa durante il primo dominio fiorentino', in *I ceti dirigenti nella Toscana del Quattrocento* (Impruneta, 1987).

8 P. Denley, '*Signore* and *Studio*: Lorenzo in a comparative context', in *Lorenzo the Magnificent: Culture and Politics*, ed. M. Mallett and N. Mann (London, 1996), p. 205.

9 M. Knapton, 'Capital city and subject province: Financial and military relationships between Venice and Padua in the later fifteenth century', University of Oxford, D.Phil. thesis, 1978, pp. 11–16.

10 J. S. Grubb, *Firstborn of Venice: Vicenza in the early Renaissance State* (Baltimore and London, 1988).

11 Grundman, *The Popolo at Perugia*, pp. 213–38.

12 G. Mira, 'Aspetti dell'organizzazione corporativa in Perugia nel XIV secolo', *Economia e storia*, 6 (1959), 382–6.

Starting on 1 November next are to be elected ... ten good, loyal and sufficient men of the *popolo* and guilds of the city and suburbs of Perugia, two from each gate[-district], who are to be called Priors of the *popolo* and guilds, of whom two are always to be from the guild and college of the Mercanzia, but the other eight Priors are to be from the other guilds ... such that the guild which has a prior for two months, cannot have a prior in the following two months ... and that none of the guilds can have more than one prior (but this does not apply to the Mercanzia). The two Priors of the Mercanzia are to rotate among the gates every two months, so that from the gates where Priors of the Mercanzia come for two months, Priors cannot come in the following two months ... Anyone under 25 years cannot be a prior ... And no one can be a prior ... who is not native of the city or suburbs or *contado* of Perugia ... And no one can be a prior ... who has not had for a year previously a good and sufficient house in the city or suburbs ... worth at least L 200 ... and a tax assessment of at least L 100. And no notary or official of the commune is to dare or presume, after the election of the Priors, to inflate anyone's tax assessment ... And whoever is prior may not be a prior again for three years ... And we ordain that at the time of the election of the Priors, the Priors for the time being may not be present ... but there should be present two literate Franciscan friars and the Priors' notary ... and one of the Captain's knights, who will administer to the rectors of the guilds the oath to elect as Priors the wisest, best and most loyal artisans of the city and suburbs ... who are registered in the books and member-lists of the guilds ... and not to support anyone from whom they have received entreaties ... The voting papers are to be given out by the two Franciscan friars, first to the gate which happens to have a merchant, then to the gates without a merchant, and so on among the gates ... And no one of the city or suburbs or *contado* may be a prior ... who is not registered in the member-lists of the guild whose craft he works and has worked for five years ... continuously ...

In order that the city of Perugia be governed by the *popolo*, and in order that its state advance from good to better, we say and ordain that all the guilds and artisans of the guilds of the city and suburbs included in the above statute [50] ... are obliged, at the request of the Priors ... to convene together as one body and to swear an oath to stay together as one, and not to abandon the other guilds, but to maintain, defend, aid, support and favour each and all of the guilds and their artisans, as much as they can; and to give to the Priors ... aid, council and support against any person, and to follow them wherever they wish, with or without arms, at their pleasure and command, for the good and peaceful *stato* of the commune and *popolo* of Perugia ... And we will and command that when the Priors ... proclaim an assembly of the guilds and artisans ... and ring the bell, each *camorlengo*, rector and artisan of each guild must go to the meeting in the specified place; and while the meeting lasts, no shop is to open, but they are to remain closed and locked.

In order that the officials (*camorlenghi*) and rectors of guilds can attend meetings at their due time, without the need for taking men in from the squares and streets to hold meetings, we ordain that when a meeting of officials and rectors of guilds is to be held, they must come to the meeting before the bell ceases to ring, on pain of *5s* ... And that a judge ... of the captain of the *popolo*, immediately the bell stops ringing for the meeting ... (which is to be held at least once during every priorate) ... is to read out [the names of] the officials and rectors, and all those who are not found in the meeting or those who are there, are to be written down, so that those present and those absent may be known; and from those who are not present ... unless they make a valid excuse (that is, of illness or absence ...), he is to take *de facto* the said penalty of *5s*.

The consuls of the Mercanzia, and the auditors of the *Cambio* ... and the officials of the other guilds may meet wherever they wish, and the podestà and captain may not forbid them ... when they meet for the good *stato* of the city and commune of Perugia ... And the rectors of the guilds ... with their guilds, or alone without the guilds, may meet when they wish, though with the licence of the Priors, and not for any other purpose than to treat and provide for the peace, tranquillity and good *stato* of the city and *contado* of Perugia. And the podestà and captain cannot forbid this ... Nevertheless, each official may assemble his guild when he wishes for the business of his guild and for the peaceful *stato* of the city ... provided that no more than one guild may assemble in the same place without the licence of the Priors ...

97 Elections of the doges of Venice

The Venetian nobleman Andrea Dandolo (1306–54) was elected doge at an unusually young age in 1343, having impressed with his political skill and legal learning. He was an example of a rare type, the ruler who also wrote history. In his major (unfinished) historical work, which covers Venetian history up to 1280, he aimed to provide an authoritative version of the city's history, for the practical needs of government.[13] In this passage he describes modifications made in 1268 to the method of electing the doge. These have been variously interpreted: according to the famed 'myth of Venice' that stressed the stability of Venetian politics, they had the aims of removing the dogal election from the popular assembly, of blocking the formation of aristocratic clienteles, and of ensuring equal participation in government. According to Cracco, however, they were a (failed) attempt by aristocrats to *prevent* the election of the popular Lorenzo Tiepolo: an explanation that focuses more on the divisions among the Venetian political class.[14]

Andreae Danduli ducis venetiarum Chronica, ed. E. Pastorello in *RIS*, vol. 12, pt. 1 (Bologna, 1938), pp. 315–16.

Lorenzo Tiepolo was proclaimed doge in 1268. For ... refining the process of electing a doge, the dogal councillors, and the heads of the [Council of] Forty, along with the Greater Council and with the praise of the people, established the following rules: that anyone younger than thirty would not be able to attend these councils, and that when the Greater Council was convened and everyone was counted, as many waxen ballots should be placed in a hat as there were members present, and in thirty of these ballots should be enclosed a ticket on which would be written the word 'Elector'. And as the name of each person coming to the hat was signalled, a child would extract a ballot which he would give to one of the officiating councillors, and all those, at whose name an electoral ballot was drawn, should enter a [separate] room, until the number of thirty was reached. Then thirty ballots should be placed back in the hat, and enclosed in nine of them should be a ticket, with an inscription, and those nine, in whose name these engraved ballots are drawn, should stay in the room, and the rest should depart. The nine are to elect forty wise men, by at least seven votes in favour. By the same procedure of ballots, twelve of the forty are to remain, the rest departing, and they are to elect twenty-five prudent men, by at least eight votes in favour. The twenty-five are to be reduced to nine by drawing lots, and they are to elect forty-five prudent men (with agreement of at least seven out of the nine). The forty-five are to be reduced to eleven, and these are to elect forty-one (with agreement of at least nine of the eleven). These forty-one are to elect the future doge, with at least twenty-five votes being in favour of the successful

13 G. Ravegnani, 'Dandolo, Andrea', in *Dizionario biografico degli italiani*, vol. 32 (1986), pp. 432–9.

14 G. Cracco, *Un 'altro mondo': Venezia nel Medioevo* (Turin, 1986), pp. 92–5.

nominee. In any election, however, there may not be more than one member per family [on any of the above electoral panels] ... The forty-one electors, having held the election, on 23 July announced the result at the public rostrum. The doge, having received the banner and sworn to observe the terms of his office [the *promissio*], was enthroned in the palace, and then, speaking to the people, he gave thanks to God and St Mark for the honour bestowed on him, and offered himself ready to pursue the honour and profit of Venice. All the people showed great joy at his election, and one by one the artisans' *scuole*, in customary fashion, paid reverence to him, and, once the dogess had come to the Palace, an honourable banquet was given to them.

98 Bell-ringers

Bells had many different functions in Italian towns: calling people to religious services and political assemblies, marking the beginning and end of the working day, and sounding the alarm in event of fire or disturbance are just some of these. Ownership and control of the bells was therefore a matter of public interest (see [**2**]). In the following extract the commune of Perugia seeks to ensure the prompt service of its bell-ringers.

Statuti di Perugia (1342), vol. 1, pp. 201–3.

We establish and ordain ... that Martinello de Cilglarello ... [and six others] are to be the bell-ringers of the commune of Perugia, and are obliged ... to be continuously near the palaces of the podestà and captain, such that they can always be got hold of when they are needed ... and they must ring the bells in the service of the commune for all things as will be needful, and as and when the podestà and captain, or either of them, and the Priors command, day or night. They must ring the large San Lorenzo bell for sermons, when they are due to be given in the piazza of the commune and daily in the church of San Lorenzo ... and they must ... ring the bells, especially the large bell of the *popolo*, for all things that will be needful, such that they are well and sufficiently rung. And they must ring the large evening bell three times ... and on the last of these three times they must ring the bell so that a man can easily go from the church of San Pietro to the church of Sant'Agnolo outside the gates ... so that immediately before the last ring they do three chimes, with a space between each chime, long enough to say three paternosters. And they must ring the morning bell at dawn ... And the above bell-ringers are

to have from the commune, in fees and wages, each per year ... L 30
and a hood of scarlet cloth worth 100s. bearing an image of the bells
... And so that the ringers can better be got hold of ... we order that
one of the above ringers should continuously be and reside in the
palace of the *popolo*, on pain of 20s.

99 Constitutional reforms at Florence

The institution of the Priors of the Guilds in Florence was 'a revolutionary
innovation imposed on the city's patriciate'.[15] However, the method by which
the Priors were elected remained unfixed, and varied in the following
decades, until the further reform of 1328, which, in introducing a settled
electoral process, constituted 'the most far-reaching innovation in the history
of Florentine political institutions'.[16]

a. Giovanni Villani, *Nuova cronica*, ed. G. Porta (3 vols, Parma, 1990–1), vol.
1, pp. 532–4 (VIII.79).

In 1282 the city of Florence was governed by the regime of the
Fourteen Goodmen, that is eight Guelfs and six Ghibellines, as
Cardinal Latino had left it.[17] This office of the Fourteen seemed to the
citizens of Florence too great a mass and confusion to bring such
discordant minds together as one, especially because the Guelfs did
not like having to share office with the Ghibellines, given recent
events such as Charles d'Anjou's loss of Sicily, the arrival in Tuscany
of an imperial vicar, and the wars begun in Romagna by the ...
Ghibellines. So, for the salvation and well-being of the city, they
annulled the office of the Fourteen and created a new office to govern
the city, and this was called the Priors of the Guilds. The name meant
the first elected above others, and derived from the gospels, where
Christ said to his disciples 'Vos estis prior'. The pressure for this
change and innovation began with the consuls and the council of the
Calimala guild, of which the wisest and most powerful citizens were
members, with the greatest following of *grandi* and *popolani*. They
attended especially to the pursuit of trade, and most adhered to the

15 Najemy, *Corporatism*, p. 42.

16 *Ibid.*, p. 99.

17 Cardinal Latino, 'a man of great authority and learning' (Villani) had been
despatched to Florence by the pope in order to pacify noble feuding there. Between
late 1279 and early 1280 he pacified many families, restored the Ghibelline exiles
and instituted a governing committee of fourteen (who held office for two months
at a time).

Guelf Party and the Holy Church. And the first Priors of the Guilds were three in number, their names being Bartolo de' Bardi, from the *sesto*[18] of Oltrarno and for the Calimala guild, Rosso Bacherelli, from the *sesto* of San Piero Schieraggio and the Bankers' Guild, and Salvi Girolami for the *sesto* of San Brancazio and the Wool Guild. And their term of office began in mid-June and lasted two months ... and so, every two months, there were to follow three Priors for the three major guilds. They ate, slept and gave audience in secure lodgings in the Badia, at the commune's expense, where the *anziani* of the old *popolo* used to meet, and after them the Fourteen ... And these Priors, with the Captain of the *popolo*, had the task of governing the great and weighty affairs of the commune, of convening councils and issuing ordinances. During the first two months, the citizens liked this office, so for the next two months six Priors were appointed, one per *sesto*, and to the three major guilds were added those of physicians and spicers, of Por Santa Maria and of furriers. Then successively other guilds were added, up to the number of the twelve major guilds, and they included *grandi* as well as *popolani*, men of good reputation and deeds, who were artisans or merchants. And so it continued, until the second government of the *popolo* was instituted in Florence ... from which time no more *grandi* were included and a Standard-bearer of Justice was added ... Election to the office of Prior was made by the outgoing Priors with the leaders of the twelve major guilds and with certain additional members elected by the Priors from each *sesto*; they elected by secret ballot, such that whoever got most votes was made prior; and this election was held in the church of San Piero Scheraggio.

b. Giovanni Villani, *Nuova cronica*, ed. Porta, (X.108).

After Florence had heard the news of the death of the duke,[19] they held various councils and discussions on how they should reform the city's government along communal lines, so as to eliminate factions among citizens. And, as it pleased God, those who were then Priors, with the advice of one good man from each *sesto*, agreed on the following method of electing the Priors and Standard-bearers: that the Priors, with two additonal *popolani* from each *sesto*, should make a choice and list of all the citizens — Guelfs, *popolani*, and men aged over thirty — who were worthy of the office of the priorate; and likewise, the *gonfalonieri*, with two additional *popolani* from each

18 Quarter of city (literally 'sixth').
19 Charles, duke of Calabria, son of King Robert of Naples, died 9 November 1328.

gonfalone,[20] should do the same, as should the Captains of the Guelf Party and their council, the Five officials of the Mercatanzia with the advice of the seven leaders of the major guilds and two consuls per guild. Once these lists were done, the Priors and Standard-bearers should convene in the Priors' council-chamber at the beginning of December, along with the Twelve Goodmen (the Priors' advisors in serious business), the nineteen *gonfalonieri*, two consuls from each of the twelve major guilds, and six additional members from each *sesto* appointed by the Priors and the Twelve Goodmen: the total of all these was ninety-eight. Each man listed should be put to a secret ballot of black and white beans, gathered by wise, discrete foreign friars (two Franciscans, two Dominicans, and two hermit-friars), some of whom should be in the chamber by turns to collect the beans and count them. And whoever had sixty-eight votes [or more], that is sixty-eight black beans, was approved for the office of Prior, and his name was written both into a secret register that remained with the Dominican friars, and on to a small ticket placed into a bag according to his *sesto*. These bags were then placed in a strongbox locked with three keys and kept in the Franciscans' sacristy. The *conversi* friars of Settimo kept one key ... the Captain of the *popolo* another, and the Minister of the friars the third. And when, every two months, the office of Priors finished – or rather three days before they left office – the outgoing Priors, with the Captain, convened the council, had the strongbox brought in and opened, and, *sesto* by *sesto*, the bags were opened, the name-tickets mixed up, and tickets then drawn at random. Those who were drawn became Priors, though observing the following prohibitions: of two years, during which the same person could not again be prior; of one year, during which his son, father or brother could not be prior; of six months, during which anyone of his wider family could not be prior. And this arrangement was decided first by the requisite councils, then in a full public assembly[21] on the piazza, on 11 December 1328, when many people gathered, and when many speeches were made praising and confirming it ... And [it was decided] that every two years in January the whole process should be started again, but that whoever's name was still in the register as not having been drawn [from the bags] should stay there, and those names approved in the new process should have their tickets mixed with those that had not yet been drawn ... In this way, the city's

20 banner district (of city).
21 *parlamento*.

government and officials were reformed ... and from this ensued for a while a very tranquil and peaceful state ... but, as wanting to make frequent changes is a Florentine habit, these good arrangements were very soon corrupted and vitiated by the factions of wicked citizens, who wanted to rule over everyone else.

100 Regulations for councils in Pisa, 1286 and 1317

a. 'Breve pisani communis an. MCCLXXXVI', in *Statuti inediti della città di Pisa dal XII al XIV secolo*, ed. F. Bonaini (3 vols, Florence, 1854–57), I, pp. 65–6, 67–9, 71.

We [the podestà and captain of Pisa] agree and permit that the *Anziani* of the *popolo* and of the companies of the Pisan *popolo* may hold one or more councils, as they decide and please; and that they can assemble as often as they please, in whatever manner they wish. And all the ordinances and statutes of the ... Pisan *popolo*, and of the provisions of the Anziani of the *popolo* ... already made and ordered, or made and ordered in the future ... we shall have and hold as settled and fixed ... And that no one can be a councillor of any council of the Pisan commune or *popolo* who does not pay taxes and do other services in the city like other Pisan citizens, unless he has a privilege or exemption from the Pisan commune. And that no one may or should be elected [to office] by any council unless he or his father was born in the city or *contado* of Pisa, or is assessed for tax in the city and has lived there for twenty-five years with his family and belongings, paying taxes and imposts and doing services ...

Whenever any business of private persons or communities ... has to be put before the council and that business runs contrary to the ordinances or deliberations of the Pisan commune or contrary to public utility or does not seem to be of benefit to the commune, and when no councillor speaks ... in defence of the communal ordinances and deliberations, or for the utility of the commune and in defence of the law, or to impugn and reprove whatever is contained in the petition or motion, we shall order and compel, under oath and penalty, one or more councillors to speak against what is contained in the petition or motion, and in defence of the ... public utility and the law of the commune, adducing necessary and beneficial reasons on behalf of the commune ... And if this is not done, the deliberation is not valid and should not be implemented. If, conversely, there is any business pertaining to the commune, and the only speeches made are in favour, we shall, if it seems beneficial and profitable to the commune, order and compel ... one or more of the council to speak against and to the contrary, and to give suitable reasons ... And we shall not allow those [private persons] petitioning for a deliberation to be present in the council, or those whom the matter in hand touches, or any of their kinsmen up to the fourth degree ... nor any of their partners or supporters ... And when general councils are held in the cathedral, we shall have the doors guarded ...

We shall not put or allow to be put any motion on one and the same business more than once without first referring it to the councils of the senate and Credenza, or to the minor council of the *anziani* of the *popolo* (and it cannot be referred to them more than twice). We shall not prevent or impede anyone from speaking on the motion all that seems to him beneficial to the Pisan commune or *popolo*. We may fine any councillor between 2*s* and 100*s* ... if he impedes any speaker, or does not have patience or understanding, or if he speaks outside the motion, of he does not say something new, or stands outside the columns in the cathedral ... And we may fine a councillor 5*s* for not coming to council; and 5*s* for leaving the council without our permission (unless with a reason that seems just to us) ...

b. B. Casini, 'Magistrature deliberativi del comune di Pisa e leggi di appendice agli statuti', *Bollettino storico pisano*, 24–5 (1955–56), 189–90.

5 August 1317

At any greater or general council of the Pisan commune there must be present at least four hundred councillors, and with that number or more this council may be held as often as is necessary, and any greater or general council, and any council of the senate and Credenza ... can be held with a majority of the councillors, except in the months of July to October when it suffices if in the council of the senate there are present seventy councillors ... And for the council of the *popolo* convened to draw the name tickets for the months of August and September, it suffices that a majority of the councillors are present, and similarly for July and October, such that henceforth the council of the *popolo* in the months July to October may be held with a majority of the councillors, as this is summer time and citizens, on account of harvests and vintages, go into the *contado* and reside there more than in the other months of the year.

And in councils of both the commune and the *popolo* ... it is not useful henceforth for the names and speeches of councillors to be written down, so that everyone can fully advise as he believes to be to the best advantage of the Pisan commune, without record or memory being kept of his name or speech.

101 A short-lasting lordship: Pisa, 1365–8

Like many cities, Pisa experienced a succession of short-lived native lordships, under various names, before falling under the permanent control of a larger neighbouring city (below, [107]). In 1365, an economic and military crisis caused by Pisa's war with Florence led to an attempt to reconfigure Pisan politics around a dynastic dogeship, held at first by Giovanni dell'Agnello. Here, this experiment is described by the contemporary Florentine chronicler, Filippo Villani. Villani's narrative – complete with its novellistic, bedroom scene and its quotation from Dante – is a much more consciously literary version than other accounts, for example that of the Pisan merchant–diarist Ranieri Sardi who was more concerned with cataloguing in a precise and non-partisan way the sequence of actions that laid the legal basis for the new doge's rule.[22] Such sources suggest that Giovanni dell'Agnello's dogeship was more an uncontested, factional seizure of power, rather than the piece of individual opportunism, backed with foreign money, that Villani describes.[23]

Matteo Villani, *Cronica*, ed. G. Porta, vol. 2, pp. 740–5.

Giovanni dell'Agnello was a citizen of Pisa of popular stock and obscure descent, who by rank was a merchant. He was more cunning and shrewd than wise, astoundingly pretentious and eager for new things, and above all quick to act. He had just returned from an embassy, on behalf of the commune of Pisa, to Bernabò Visconti, lord of Milan. With this tyrant he had secretly negotiated for the Pisans to become his allies and for Bernabò to help them by ensuring the return of some of their territory [following Florentine victory over Pisa in July 1364]. And for this reason Giovanni received a grant from Bernabò of 30,000 florins. From this negotiation arose Giovanni's bold plan to make himself lord of Pisa, imagining that, if Pisa were going to submit to a tyrant, Florence would be happier with him as tyrant than with Bernabò Visconti.

22 Ranieri Sardo, *Cronaca di Pisa*, ed. O. Banti (Rome 1963), pp. 158–61, 163, 171–3, 175, 181.

23 M. Tangheroni, 'Dell'Agnello, Giovanni', *Dizionario biografico degli italiani*, vol. 37 (Rome, 1989), pp. 49–55.

With Pisa in a state of undecidedness, fear and trembling, its hope of peace repeatedly frustrated, the Pisans held a great council of the most important and notable citizens, to decide on measures to strengthen the government. Present at this meeting was Messer Piero di Messer Albizzo da Vico ... and among the others was Giovanni dell'Agnello, who was regarded as a good merchant and loyal citizen. Giovanni stood up and boldly said that it seemed to him necessary to submit to a lord for a year, giving his opinion that this lord should be Messer Piero da Vico ... Messer Piero, with all the pleading he knew, refused the burden ... Giovanni, seeing his suggestion rebutted, as he had reckoned, by Messer Piero, reiterated the advice that it was necessary for one of the others to take on this responsibility ... Then ser Vanni Botticella, from an old family of butchers, offered to take this role; Giovanni said that though he was good and worthy, he needed to have 30,000 florins now to pay the troops. Vanni replied that he did not feel capable of doing this. So it was concluded that day, that everyone should think of someone who might be capable and that the council should reconvene at another time.

From this strange reasoning and frightful advice, in the following days suspicions arose of Giovanni's speaking so insincerely and insistently in the council, and rumours were current among the people that Giovanni was assembling armed men. So, one evening, many good citizens armed themselves and went to the Palace of the *Anziani*. This at once came to Giovanni's notice, as he constantly kept his ear to the ground. Giovanni, guessing what they would do next, astutely and quickly took measures to cover himself: he distributed his armed men among the houses of his trusted, special friends; and he instructed his wife and household servants in all that they were to do. With a weapon concealed in his clothing, and a thick cap on his head, he went to bed, and made his wife come to bed beside him. When night came, the citizens, with the consent of the *Anziani* ... came to Giovanni's house. As Giovanni had ordered, the door was at once opened to them. The citizens made straight for Giovanni's bedchamber and heard him snoring, apparently fast asleep, like a man who really needed his sleep. His wife, as instructed, got up and sat, bare-breasted, on the bed, and said to the citizens that Giovanni needed to rest, but that if they wanted her to wake him, she would. The citizens, ashamed at the sight of this lady, and trusting in the free entry they had been given to the house and the chamber, took her words at face value and left, returning to the *Anziani*, to whom they reported all that they had found. With suspicions allayed, everyone went home, put down their weapons, and turned their thoughts to sleep.

Giovanni dell'Agnello, who was acting in concert with John Hawkwood,[24] feared that delay might be damaging to him and give time for his intentions to become clear, so that very night, with John Hawkwood and his friends and assembled soldiers, he went to the piazza and, noiselessly took the entrance to the Palace of the *Anziani* with one part of his company, leaving the rest to guard the piazza. He then entered the room where the *Anziani* meet, and sat in the Provost's seat. One by one he had the *Anziani* woken up and brought before him, and he told them − this would have been a foolish thing had it not been backed up by the force of John Hawkwood − that the Virgin Mary had revealed to him that, for the good and peace of the city, he had to take the Signoria and government of Pisa, with the title of doge, for one year. And so he had taken it ⌈he told them⌉, and had, with his 30,000 florins, satisfied the troops, who were with him in the Palace and the piazza. And so he was confirmed by the *Anziani*, and without further ado, he had them swear oaths in his hands, under the gleam of swords. And, through the *Anziani*, he sent for those citizens he thought might oppose him and when each arrived he told them how and why he had taken the Signoria. Courteously received, in such a way that they could not leave, he made them promises: to one the vicariate of Lucca, to another that of Piombino, and so on to the others according to their rank. And by love and fear he induced all of them to swear oaths in his hands. This took up the whole night.

In the morning, with these citizens, the *Anziani* and his troops, and calling himself doge, Giovanni rode through the city and was made lord by popular acclamation. And no one received a single blow. He took possession of the Palace, had all the troops swear in his hands, and, to show that he had come to government and taken the title gently, not as a tyrant, he elected sixteen families of *popolani* of middling rank, and made them his kin or partners, adopting with them a new coat of arms, of a golden leopard rampant on a red field. And he gave to understand that, from year to year, one of them, whoever had the most votes, would be made doge. And so, following the advice of Count Guido da Montefeltro to Pope Boniface,[25] the promises he made were large and long, but his fulfilment of them was narrow and short, for of what he promised he delivered nothing. Instead, as days

---

24 The famous English commander then in charge of mercenaries in Pisan service.

25 'Long promise and short keeping' was Guido da Montefeltro's political/military advice to Pope Boniface in Dante's *Divine Comedy, Inferno*, XXVII, 85–111.

progressed, he took the Signoria as a tyrant, left off the title of doge and had himself called lord. And if ever there was a disagreeable lordship, full of haughtiness, this was it, in Giovanni's ornaments and in his riding with a golden sceptre in his hand. And when he returned to the Palace, he stood in the windows, to show himself to the people, as when relics are displayed, with golden hangings, resting his elbow on cushions of cloth of gold. And he wanted, whenever matters had to be expounded before him, that this be done kneeling down, just as before the pope or emperor; and other such things even more vain.

102 A shortlived 'tyranny': Fermo, 1376–80

A year after rebelling against papal government (December 1375), Fermo found itself unable to resist the military power of Rinaldo da Monteverde, who had returned to the town after the revolt. He, however, was unable to prolong his rule and fell victim to humiliating popular justice, in another example of *pittura infamante* [15]).

Cronache della città di Fermo, ed. G. De Minicis (Florence, 1870), pp. 5–8.

1376, 22 December: The *popolo* of Fermo, through their nine captains and the standard-bearer of justice, reluctantly submitted to the lordship of Rinaldo da Monteverde, And in a council meeting, Vanni Vannucci was made representative to assign the sceptre[26] to the Captain and Standard-bearer, and so there in the council, Vanni assigned it to Rinaldo, and Vanni di Andriolo was the counsellor who spoke in favour of this decision in the debate ...

1379, 25 August: On St Bartholomew's day, there was a revolution in the city of Fermo, a city oppressed by the yoke of the tyrannical viciousness of lord Rinaldo da Monteverde. Lord Rinaldo was at that time in Monte Santa Maria, and had with him count Corrado and his men, a good thousand knights, conducting a campaign in Puglia ...

12 December: Fermo made an alliance with Ancona, Recanati and Ridolfo da Camerino for a year, with Fermo being obliged to maintain a force of fifty lances for the year, Ancona also fifty and Ridolfo da Camerino and Recanati twenty. And this they did on account of Rinaldo da Monteverde, who had come back from Puglia and was living at Monte Santa Maria with count Corrado, 1,500 knights and as many infantry ...

26 *baculum.*

1380: On the last day of May: lord Rinaldo, his wife Lucchina, his servant Angelella ... his legitimate sons Mercennario and Lucchino and his small bastard sons ... and many other followers of lord Rinaldo were, by virtue of God Almighty, captured in the keep of Montefalcone, in the following fashion: Egidio da Monturano and Buonaccorso, who were with lord Rinaldo, were paid 1,000 ducats between them by the commune of Fermo, and 5 ducats for each month they wished to remain in Fermo, and as traitors they surrendered the keep to the commune of Fermo ... On Saturday, 2 June, lord Rinaldo, with all the above named, was brought to the city of Fermo ... each was borne facing backwards on an ass, with a crown of thorns on their heads, and were conveyed before the Priors of Fermo, to great rejoicing. And each district of Fermo, the youths and others, had new clothes made, each district of a different colour, and when all the companies were in the piazza of San Martino, dancing in joy with the Priors, Rinaldo and his sons Mercennario and Lucchino, were beheaded in the presence of all. Others, including Nicola di maestro Federico and the son of Giacomo da Pisa, were hanged then on the same day, and others in the following days were hanged and decapitated.

1381, 25 February: The heads of lord Rinaldo, once tyrant, and of his sons, were sculpted on a stone, which was set up in the piazza San Martino, where they had been beheaded, and alongside the mouth of the sculpted head of Rinaldo were the following verses: 'I was a bad and cruel tyrant', and 'Only for the wrongdoing of me and Lucchina/ Do you, my dear sons, suffer punishment'.

103 A long-lasting lordship: Ferrara, 1264

a. *Statuta Ferrariae anno MCCLXXXVII*, ed. W. Montorsi (Ferrara, 1955), pp. 5–7 (I.1).

To the honour of God and the holy and undivided Trinity, to the praise of his mother the Virgin Mary and in veneration of St George and all saints, and to the good *status* of this city ... in order that beneficial provision be made for this city, not only for the present but also for the future, we Pietro count of Carrara, the podestà of Ferrara, in a full assembly of each and every [male person] of the city of Ferrara, in the piazza, convened at the customary sound of bells, by the will, consent and order of the whole commune of Ferrara and of each and every person of Ferrara present in this assembly, we together with everyone of that assembly, on behalf of the commune of Ferrara, establish and order, to be observed by us and our heirs and successors in perpetuity ... that the magnificent and illustrious lord, Obizzo, grandson and heir of the magnificent lord ... Azzo, by the grace of God and the pope, marquis of Este and of Ancona ... should be the governor, rector, and general and perpetual lord of the city of Ferrara and its district, in all matters to be provided, corrected and reformed there, at his arbitrary will. And he should govern the jurisdiction, power and dominion ... of the city, and have the power to add, do, order, provide and dispose as he pleases and as seems beneficial to him, and generally he can do and dispose in all things as perpetual lord of the city, at his pleasure ... All of this is to apply not only in the person of the lord Obizzo d'Este, for his lifetime, but also, after his death, we want his heir to take his place as governor, rector and general lord ... And if any people at any time attempt to break, change or infringe any of the above, they are *ipso iure*, as desecrators of the city of Ferrara, to be banned in perpetuity, and all their property is to be forfeited to the commune of Ferrara ... and if they ever come into the hands of the commune at any time, they are to be punished with death. All of the above we order ... to be observed immutably, absolutely and perpetually by us, our heirs, descendants and successors ... And by the present statute ... we derogate from all other statutes, ordinances, councils and public debates. Moreover, in the said assembly, Master Appollonio, notary, as syndic lawfully appointed by the community and assembly on behalf of the commune of Ferrara ... promised to the lord Obizzo d'Este ... to keep and have all the above unchangeably ... and not to contravene in any way or form ... and to ensure its greater, perpetual durability ... he swore on the gospels, on the souls of the said Pietro podestà of Ferrara and of all present in the assembly, to observe and fulfil all of the above ... This statute ... was published, made, promised and confirmed ... on 17 January 1264.

b. *Chronica parva ferrariensis*, in *RIS*, ed. L. A. Muratori, vol. 8 (Milan, 1726), coll. 487–8.

[1264] When Azzo d'Este died, his funeral was prepared at San Francesco, and his body was borne there with suitable pomp. The cheeks of the pining citizens were wet with mourning and genuine tears. Even citizens who had supported the rival faction mourned Azzo with tears and exclamations, declaring 'This man was not cruel, but kind and pious'. Once Azzo's body was placed in the church, but not yet in its tomb, everyone at once returned to the piazza, where there was an armed band of citizens – by order, others were forbidden to take up arms. This was on 17 February 1264 ... and an assembly of citizens was summoned by bells and criers, and everyone attended, not just citizens but also a crowd of travellers and those who were sent for as a garrison. Then the leaders from several cities near Ferrara spoke to the pressing crowd. Aldigerio da Fontana spoke ... saying *inter alia* (and I was present as a young man) 'The friends of our faction should not fear, nor should our enemies be glad at the burial of Marquis Azzo, or conceive hope of his properties. For there survives his descendant, the young man here, of fine natural qualities, of whom much may be hoped. Indeed, if offspring suitable for leadership from the Este family were lacking, we should create a ruler out of straw!' Altogether the crowd cried out its agreement, especially those who possessed the property of exiles, or had become rich in privileges, or hoped to be. Once silence returned, a syndic was appointed to confer lordship of the city of Ferrara on Obizzo, who was then in his seventeenth year. The syndic conferred on Obizzo full lordship, such that he could do anything, just or unjust, as he wished. More power was thus given to this new lord than everlasting God has, who can do no injustice. Everyone then left the meeting, its business done, and those who had come as guards went home.

104 Consolidation of a lordship: Verona, 1295

Gli statuti veronesi del 1276, vol. 2, ed. G. Sandri (Venice 1959), pp. 59–61 (later additions to the statutes).

To the honour of Almighty God and his mother the Virgin Mary, of the holy body of the blessed Zeno and of all the saints, and to the honour, increase and good *status* of the lords Alberto and Bartolomeo della Scala, general lords of the *popolo* and city of Verona. These are the statutes and ordinances newly made by the elected statute-makers ... and read, approved and confirmed in the Council of the guild leaders and the Council of 800 ... on 27 November 1295, before the podestà, and the lords Alberto and Bartolomeo della Scala ...

First, we establish and ordain that whoever plots, conspires or consents publicly or privately in removing or diminishing anything of the lordship, captaincy and rectorate of the city of Verona of the lords

Alberto and Bartolomeo della Scala ... or of their honour and jurisdiction, or presumes to commit anything in deed, writing or any other
way against the persons of the lords and their sons, in any manner
that can be imagined ... immediately ... the podestà is to raze his house
to its foundations, uproot his trees and vines, confiscate his property
... And if he comes into the hands of the commune of Verona, he is to
be dragged through the city at a horse's tail, placed in a cask full of
nails,[27] and tied to a bridge over the Adige, where he is to remain until
he dies, and then he is to be hanged ...

Item, we establish and ordain that two bells, one large and one small,
are to be placed at the top of the lords' palace ... and they are to be
rung on the following occasions: If (which God avert) it happens that
fire should break out in the city or suburbs, the small bell is to be
rung, at the sound of which all the soldiers of Verona, horse and foot,
are to come with their arms and horses, to the lords' piazza, as are
those of the guilds elected by the lords, and no others, on pain of an
arbitrary penalty ... Meanwhile to the site of the fire should go the
podestà's staff, the criminal judge ... porters with wine-casks and
those of the district where the fire is, and of the four neighbouring
districts, and those of the family in whose house the fire is ... At the
sound of the large bell, which is to be rung either for fire or for
disturbance, all the guild leaders are to come, with their flags and all
[the members] of their guilds, and all the foot- and horse-soldiers,
with their arms and horses, in order to do and perform all the lords'
orders ... If any guild leader or any [member] of a guild or of the
knights or *popolo* then goes to the house of any magnate, he is to be
punished in his person and property at the discretion of the podestà
and lords.

105 Political spectacle: Florence and Ferrara

Both republics and 'despotisms' used spectacles and street theatre as means of
celebrating their rule and consolidating adhesion to it. Modes, however,
varied, as shown in these contrasting extracts: republics slowly developed a
cult of liberty,[28] while lordships celebrated the magnificent deeds of their
dynasties.

a. *Diario d'anonimo fiorentino*, p. 325.

27 *clois.*
28 Jones, *City-State*, p. 333.

Today, 21 November 1376, a joust was announced in Florence, in the name of God and on behalf of a beautiful girl called Lady Liberty: it was announced that on 7 December in Piazza Santa Croce she would hold a joust open to all-comers who wished to joust for her love. And whoever did best, of all the jousters, would receive a fine lance and garland from Lady Liberty, in honour of the *popolo* of Florence and of the Guelf Party.[29]

b. A. Stella, 'Testi volgari ferraresi del secondo Trecento', *Studi di filologia italiana*, 26 (1968), pp. 248–9.

31 March 1391: Marquis Alberto d'Este returned safe and sound to his city of Ferrara.[30] For this reason a great crowd of citizens on horseback, on foot and in boats went to meet him at the Torre della fossa, with dancing and celebration. Among them were nine companies of celebrants,[31] all dressed in fine clothes. And the honourable company of butchers was the first to reach him at the Torre della Pontonara, receiving him with great joy and festivity. They celebrated for three days, changing their clothes twice. The companies who celebrated were these: the notaries, merchants, drapers, spicers, tailors, goldsmiths, butchers, furriers, and second-hand clothes dealers. The bankers in addition to the celebrating, offered a prize of a silk *palio* for the best celebrants, and this was awarded to the butchers by the marquis, as they were the bravest and most valiant of all the companies. The celebration of the marquis' return continued for ten days, during which time the shoemakers mounted a race for the prize of a scarlet *palio* lined with fur, and the wool merchants one for a parti-coloured *palio*. The mercers held two races, one for men and one for women, the fishers held another for men, and the masons one for donkeys.[32] The carpenters built a wonderful wooden castle on a cart – it was decorated alot at the top, and around it was a very urbane[33] company, including two men dressed as giants. The marquis made them a gift of a silk *palio*.

29 For the political context, see G. A. Brucker, *Florentine Politics and Society, 1343–1378* (Princeton, 1962), pp. 313–14.

30 The marquis, lord of Ferrara, was returning from a pilgrimage to Rome, having obtained several important grants and concessions from the pope, including a licence to establish a university in Ferrara. See, most recently, C. M. Rosenberg, *The Este Monuments and Urban Development in Renaissance Ferrara* (Cambridge, 1997), pp. 25–7.

31 *bagordaduri*.

32 For similar races in Ferrara, see D. Shemek, 'Circular definitions: configuring gender in Italian Renaissance festival', *Renaissance Quarterly*, 48 (1995).

33 *cevile*.

106 Good government under lords: Milan

Though obviously propaganda for monarchy, Fiamma's description of
Lucchino Visconti does conform to contemporary ideals of noble conduct.[34]

Gualvanei de la Flamma, *Opusculum de rebus gestis ab Azone, Luchino et Johanne
Vicecomitibus*, ed. C. Castiglioni, in *RIS*, vol. 12, pt. 4, (Bologna, 1938), pp.
34–5, 43–5.

1339 ... While the archbishopric of Milan was vacant, and after the
death of the illustrious prince Azzone Visconti, all the people, officials
and nobles of the city of Milan unanimously chose as general lords of
Milan and its *contado* the two sons of the great Matteo Visconti, that
is the reverend Giovanni, bishop of Novara, who later became archbishop of Milan, and his brother Lucchino, nobleman and knight ...

Lucchino was and is a man exceptionally handsome in body and
face, well-proportioned in all parts, healthy and sound. He took to
wife the noble lady Violante, daughter of the marquis of Saluzzo, by
whom he had a daughter ... Lucchino was knighted while still a boy
and was made lord of Pavia: there he built a very strong castle and
successfully exercised his lordship of the city for a long time. Then he
was made lord of Milan, Brescia, Como, Bergamo, Lodi, Piacenza,
Novara, Vercelli and Cremona. He added the city of Asti to his lordship, where he ordered a strong castle to be built ... He assembled an
army of knights, foot-soldiers and archers, and he dealt blows to the
regions of Italy; he never ceased from warfare and, fortunate in war,
he was feared beyond measure by his enemies. He largely suppressed
the game of dice. He severely punished adulterers. He had the city
streets paved.[35] At times of famine he had over 40,000 paupers fed at
public expense. He forced Pavia to obey him and compelled them to
raze their walls to the ground with their own hands. He had
outstanding habits ... No one has ever served justice and peace better.
He was of constant heart and true to his word, for, whatever he
promised, he delivered. In the best way possible he preserved the
revenues and properties of the [civic] commune, and abstained from
levying tribute ... Everyday he carefully heard the cases of poor
women and treated[36] thirty paupers to the best food at the table in his
palace. He devoutly heard or said mass and the office of the Blessed

34 P. Contamine, *La noblesse de la royaume de France* (Paris, 1997).

35 *adequari.*

36 *pavit.*

Virgin Mary every day. On prohibited days and Saturdays he ate nothing but Lenten food. His magnificence was shown in his horse-manship and horse-trappings, in his hawks, falcons, sparrowhawks, and large dogs, in his knights, squires, lute-players, jesters and his exceedingly large entourage. He built many castles and palaces in city and *contado* and across Lombardy ...

These two lords of Milan, Giovanni bishop of Novara, and his brother Lucchino, introduced many praiseworthy laws and statutes to be inviolably observed:

The first law was that all the cities subject to them, without any exception of persons, should be a safe residence for their citizens, and that all exiles should return to their homelands ...

The second law was to make the roads and highways, especially in the Val Ticino, secure as never before, for a second podestà was appoin-ted, who had power of life and death beyond the city gates and through-out the *contado* – a man called Zuzius, a marvellous man, exceedingly terrible to robbers, who patrolled day and night, seeking thieves and robbers, and he cleansed the whole of our territory of marauders.

The third law was that no man or clan[37] should rise up against another clan or issue a challenge to arms or make any disturbance; this was not the case in the past, when a man would for nothing in his own affair challenge another, causing wounds and expense ... whereas he would not even venture to draw his sword on behalf of the commune.

The fourth law was that no man, no matter how powerful or noble, should dare to insult or injure any *popolano*; this was not the case in the past, when a fishmonger with his fish or a merchant with his ... goods would be despoiled while travelling through the villages or castles or bridges of our *contado*. All such incidents ceased and every traveller now travels safely.

The fifth law is that the people should not go to war, but should attend to their business at home. This was not the case hitherto, because each year, especially at time of harvest and vintage, when kings usually go to war, the people, leaving their crafts with much risk and expense, were engaged in sieges and incurred losses, especially because such military operations took up much time.

The sixth law is that the houses of exiles or traitors are not destroyed, but preserved for the common good – which was not done before, rather almost for nothing houses were razed, which disfigured the city and incurred manifest infamy ...

37 *parentela.*

And these two lords also endeavoured to eliminate evil customs:

The first evil and detestable custom was that every year, without any apparent cause or necessity, a tax would regularly be imposed, around the beginning of Lent, and sometimes twice a year, which burdened the people and nobles beyond measure. This evil custom has been eliminated, for these two lords have imposed no burden or exaction, nor intend to, unless enemies invade from outside, or in order to settle the debts of the commune, or to acquire some privilege of common benefit.

The second evil custom was that almost the whole of our *contado* was subordinated to various lords, who had rights of lordship and profit-taking,[38] and though the *contado* was already greatly burdened by the commune, this other lordship was heavier and more costly. This custom has been eliminated, for all the *contado* is [now] subject only and immediately to the commune, which contributes to peace for it is burdened neither by the commune nor by individual lords.

The third evil custom was that the commune's revenues were dissipated unduely, because large stipends were given to jesters and musicians, to women and vile people, and these expenses amounted to over 30,000 florins per year. Thus citizens were despoiled and the unworthy were maintained. This custom these two lords removed, and they provide for their own citizens out of their own revenues ... And this custom is eliminated, for today over 6,000 people from Milan hold offices and lead decent lives on public funds.

The fifth [*sic*] evil custom was that court officials freely insisted on tributes, so much so that even base and poor court servants were quickly enriched. And this evil custom is removed because court officials, exposed to various tortures and keen investigations, return all their illicit gains and extortions ...

The sixth evil custom was that murderers, thieves, robbers and many criminals were pardoned and released for a price or on petition. And this custom is removed because it is almost impossible for criminals to escape, through faction, friendship, payment or favour. And, as is generally said, in this city justice has never been observed as it is now.

The seventh evil custom was that if it was sometimes necessary to impose a tax, as was the case in the third year of their lordship on account of the debts arising from the famine the previous year, from court expenses and military preparations, it was assessed, imposed

38 *fructus.*

and collected with great care and attention, equally according to wealth, with no exception of persons. This was badly observed in the past, when taxes were neither equally assessed nor equally collected.

107 The end of communal liberty I: Pisa, 1406

In order to win control of Pisa, Florence had to satisfy the interests of two foreign lords, as well as those of Giovanni Gambacorta, temporarily lord of Pisa in 1405–6 (though few of Florence's promises to the latter were fulfilled). Unlike Venice (next document), Florence did not negotiate with Pisa itself, and this explains the high-handed Florentine treatment of Pisa after 1406.

G. O. Corazzini, *L'assedio di Pisa (1405–6): Scritti e documenti inediti* (Florence, 1885), pp. 4, 6, 7, 9, 18, 25, 26, 29, 50–1, 139–53.

a. *Cronaca di ser Nofri di ser Pietro delle riformagioni.*

On 5 September 1402, the duke of Milan died and left his bastard son Gabriele Maria as lord of Pisa; he came from Lombardy, and with great honour the Pisans received him as lord ... and so he remained until 1405 ... In July 1405 the Pisans, shouting 'Viva the *popolo*, death to the tyrant!', took the city and Gabriele Maria left with his troops ... and Florence arranged to buy Pisa from him. And Messer Boucicaut, lord of Genoa and lieutenant of the king of France, with the agreement of the royal council in Paris, sold it to Florence, with the consent of Gabriele Maria ... for 200,000 florins ... On Sunday 30 August 1405, possession of the citadel of Pisa was taken on behalf of the commune of Florence, and on Monday the troops of Messer Boucicaut freely left it to them ... [But] on Sunday evening, 8 September, the citadel of Pisa was lost and was taken by the Pisans ... as a result of negligence; at which loss all the city of Florence was deeply pained and saddened, as much for shame as for the expense that followed ...

In 1405 the Raspanti, who had become the rulers of Pisa, sent for all the exiles, specifically for the Gambacorta, and they came to Pisa, and all made peace together of all injuries received, and they concluded marriages, and they took the body of Christ and made great oaths to behave as brothers. But it took only a few days for them to betray each other and for Giovanni Gambacorta to be made lord; and he soon had some good citizens of Pisa beheaded and killed ... In October, Giovanni had Messer Giovanni dell'Agnello beheaded, even though they had made peace together, and this was regarded as a great betrayal ...

February 1406 [Florence]: the following citizens were elected as the new Ten [the war committee] because Messer Rinaldo Gianfigliazzi and his companions ended their term of office as the Ten on 1 March: Bartolomeo Corbinelli, Gino Capponi, Lapo Sirigatti, Lotto Castellani, Niccolò Davanzati, Bernardo Cavalcanti, Maso degli Albizzi, Nofri Bischeri and Andrea dal Pino. And they met many times, before their term of office began, to lay the necessary plans for Florence to achieve its objective of taking Pisa, because the outgoing Ten were leaving the war in disorder ... The new Ten, seeing ... that Pisa could never be had except by siege, decided to encamp an army before Pisa ... and to supply the army from the sea through Livorno ...

b. Terms of surrender of Pisa, 1406.

To the honour and glory of God, the blessed Mary his ever-virgin mother, and St John the Baptist protector and defender of the city and commune of Florence ... Bartolomeo Corbinelli, Gino Capponi and Bernardo Cavalcanti, members of the Ten, and Matteo Castellani, commissioner of the commune of Florence ... for the first part, and Bindo Brachi, citizen of Pisa, commissioner and proxy ... of the magnificent lord Giovanni Gambacorta, captain and defender of the Pisan *popolo* ... for the other part, have concluded, made and contracted between them ... the following treaties, agreements and terms ...

1. That Messer Giovanni ... will give and consign entry to Pisa to the said [Florentine] envoys and commissioners ... through one or more gates of the city ... and will give and consign ... all the passwords of the castles in the Pisan *contado* ... and will effectively ensure that none of his kinsmen will make ... any rebellion or opposition to the delivery of any place to them ...

6. That the city of Pisa is to be preserved from all robbery, homicide, theft, burning, assault ... and likewise its citizens and inhabitants ...

7. That the *anziani* are to remain and to have [control of] the expenditure in the city of Pisa of its revenues and gabelles ...

8. That the rebels, named at the end of this clause, are to remain rebels in perpetuity, they and their sons already born, and that they may at no time be pardoned ... and that their properties may be distributed by Messer Giovanni Gambacorta in the year that follows, and against such distribution no opposition may ever be made [A list of thirty-two named individuals follows, along with all members of four families including the dell'Agnello].

9. Nothing may ever be said to the Gambacorta regarding anything done in the city or *contado* of Pisa during Messer Giovanni's rule ... but the Gambacorta, each of them, are to be treated as fully absolved of such actions ...

11. That none of the family of the Gambacorta may be pursued in city or *contado* for any debt contracted up to the present, except for those they owe to citizens of Florence ...

12. That all the Gambacorta and their sons are to be understood to be citizens of Florence in perpetuity, and are to be treated and regarded, they and their descendants in the male line, as native citizens ...

14. That the commune of Florence will give to the Gambacorta three houses in the city of Florence for their residence, honourable and appropriate to their status.

15–16. That Messer Giovanni and ten of his servants may carry any type of weapon in the city and *contado* of Florence ... freely and without penalty ... and likewise Messer Bartolomeo, Messer Francesco and each of the sons of Gherardo and Lorenzo Gambacorta, with five servants each ...

18. That Messer Giovanni ... is to be given 50,000 florins ... in cash, that is, 20,000 now, once Florence has possession of the city of Pisa ... and 15,000 in six months' time, and 15,000 in a year's time ...

19. To bishop Gambacorta[39] will be given the bishopric of Florence, that is, that the commune of Florence should ensure that he has the bishopric within the coming year ...

21. That in place of lands in the Valdera, which are to be consigned [to Florence] ... the following lands are to be given by Florence to Giovanni Gambacorta ... Bagno,[40] Rocca sopra Bagno, Castel Benedetto, Corzano with the castle at Sampietro, Careste, Facciano, Rondinaia, Valdagieto, Castel dell'Alpe, Larciano ... and that Messer Giovanni is required to give and offer each year, on St John the Baptist's day in June, at the church of San Giovanni in Florence, one *palio*, on which at least 25 florins is to be spent ...[41]

---

39 Presumably Lotto Gambacorta, who was bishop of Pisa, 1381–94, before being transferred to Treviso. He died in 1409 without becoming bishop of Florence: P. B. Gams, *Series episcoporum ecclesiae catholicae* (repr. Graz, 1957), pp. 762, 804.

40 This was Bagno di Romagna on Florence's borders with Romagna. Florence had conquered Bagno from its local counts, allies of the Visconti, in 1404. The Gambacorta retained it until 1453: F. Mancini and W. Vichi, *Castelli, rocche e torri di Romagna* (Bologna, 1959), p. 189.

41 See [26].

23. That all members of the Gambacorta family are, for all time, free and exempt from all burdens, material and personal, imposed by the cities of Florence and Pisa, except for gabelles.

108 The end of communal liberty II: Padua, 1405

Galeazzo e Bartolomeo Gatari, *Cronaca carrarese*, ed. A. Medin and G. Tolomei, in *RIS*, vol. 17, pt. 1 (Città di Castello, 1909–31), pp. 571–9.

Giovanni di Beltramino from Vicenza ... was the greatest, proudest fighter in the whole of this war, in damaging the Paduan countryside, burning, robbing and plundering, with a crowd of vile Vicentines ... Giovanni warily sought out and negotiated with some of the guards of the Santa Croce gate-tower, promising them a large sum of money if they let him scale the wall there. They agreed. So the following night, 17 November 1405 ... Giovanni and his company of men came quietly to the wall with ladders, and scaled and mounted the wall, all in the sight of the conniving guards ... They seized the tower and its barbican, and repaid the guards by killing them. Having consolidated their position, they then began to shout 'Marco, Marco!'.[42] ... Soon there was a large body of troops from the Venetian army inside the *borgo Santa Croce*, ransacking it. Throughout the city the bells were ringing the alarm, calling the citizens to take up arms to defend the city; but the citizens were already armed and all guarding their own houses. Seeing this, Francesco da Carrara sent to the Venetian army for a safe-conduct, and then went to parley with them outside the Ognissanti gate ... 'My lords', Francesco da Carrara said, 'I am prepared to give you my city, but what terms will you give me?' They replied: 'My lord, it is not for us to give you any terms, or to promise . them, for the Venetian government [*Signoria*] has not given us the freedom to do so, but you can give us the city and then seek terms from the *Signoria*.' Francesco da Carrara replied that he would do nothing and would return to the city ... At this point Messer Galeazzo Gonzaga [commander of the Venetian army] intervened, saying 'My lord, there is another way forward, which is that you surrender the castle to the Venetians here, and keep the city until you reach an accord with the *Signoria*.' Francesco da Carrara replied: 'Captain, if you want the city and castle, I am happy to give them to you [personally], if you give me your word to return them if I cannot

42 The shout supporting Venice, whose patron was Saint Mark.

reach agreement with the *Signoria.'* Galeazzo was happy with this and gave his word, and so Francesco da Carrara gave him the castle and returned to the city. There he met his citizens to agree matters with them, and he had a safe-conduct for eight citizens to go to Venice to request certain terms for the commune from the *Signoria* ...

[For what follows] you need to know that in the period when the city of Padua was at the height of its victories against its enemies, imposing its lordship on them and subjecting every tyrant ... it had a custom, when the Paduan *popolo* went on any military expedition, of taking with them a large cart [called a *carroccio*], like those the Romans used for their citizens' triumphs on the Campidoglio. And on this cart were carried the magnificent banners of the commune of Padua. The cart was all gilded and of great value, and was always drawn by four large white war-horses ...

[After the agreement between Francesco da Carrara and Galeazzo Gonzaga] entry and exit into and out of Padua was free to anyone from the Venetian army, so that, that evening, Giovanni di Beltramino, entered with perhaps twenty servants, and took lodgings. On the following night, 17 November, he went to the cathedral, where the *carroccio* was, and with his men broke up the *carroccio* with axes, and scattered it on the ground, to the shame and dishonour of the Paduans ...

Two ambassadors were appointed by Francesco da Carrara to go to Venice to negotiate terms ... but at Venice the *Signoria* refused to hear them or to give them any hope. Ambassadors were also appointed by the commune of Padua ... who went to Venice with some terms, such as that the Venetian *Signoria* should promise to observe the statutes of the commune and all its good customs, that the wool guild's statutes should be observed, that the *Studio* should be confirmed at Padua, and so on. They went to Venice, were brought before the *Signoria*, and told to ask what the commune wanted, but not to mention their lord Francesco da Carrara at any point ... And they obtained all that they asked for ...

While the ambasssdors were in Venice, Francesco da Carrara left Padua with his son, Francesco III, and went to parley with Galeazzo Gonzaga ... and this was on 19 November. Once he had left the city, Messer Francesco Dotto ... with perhaps twenty citizens and a banner of San Marco, ran armed to the piazza shouting 'Viva San Marco and death to the da Carrara!' Then they sent message to the Venetian army to come and take the city. And so the Venetian commissioners, with Galeazzo Gonzaga and the banners of San

Marco entered by the Ognissanti gate with many men-at-arms, and came to the piazza ... entered the lords' palace and took up lodging there. Then Messer Galeazzo returned to the army encampment, urging Francesco da Carrara not to come back into the city, because the *popolo* was very disturbed against him, and he recommended that he go to Venice and throw himself on the mercy of the *Signoria*. Francesco replied, 'How can I ask for mercy when they will not receive my ambassadors? You gave me your word, and I trusted you' ... Eventually, Francesco and his son decided to go to Venice ... and they left on 28 November ... and arrived on 29th. So many boats came to meet them that you could not see the water. And the shouting for his destruction was so great that when the Jews had shouted 'Crucify him, crucify Jesus of Nazareth', it was nothing compared to this. Because of the shouting, Francesco and his son were very afraid, and disembarked at San Giorgio, spending the night there ... Then the *Signoria* sent for him and his son, and he went, accompanied by an incredible number of people. Brought before Doge Michele Steno, they both fell to their knees at his feet, before at length getting up and sitting beside him ... The doge spoke many words, especially regarding the goodwill that Venice had once had towards him ... Francesco made no reply to this, other than to say that he asked for pardon and mercy ... After this, the *Signoria* sent him back to San Giorgio, where he stayed for many days. The *Signoria* was all day in great discussion over what to do with Francesco da Carrara ... some said that he and his sons should be confined to Candia, others to Cyprus, and yet others in prison. Finally, after much discussion, they decided to make a large cage in the room leading to the *Toresella* in the Doge's Palace, and to put him in it with his sons, and to arrange for six gentlemen to go there every day for his company, and for him to be attended by four of his own servants, and to have such provision that he could live honourably ...

With the city of Padua now well pacified, Venice assisted it by supplying food in abundance, which for a year was sold cheap to anyone who wanted it. The Paduans were thus treated with great humanity. In return, it was decided among the citizens to send a noble embassy to the doge ... to present him with the honour of his city of Padua. Sixteen ambassadors were appointed, and, dressed in finest scarlet ... they left Padua on 2 January ... On 4 January they were presented to the *Signoria* on a great platform erected on the Piazza San Marco: our ambassadors were all on horseback, and were preceded by their numerous servants dressed in green cloth and with many musical instruments. After a magnificent address by Messer Francesco Zabarella, the banner of the Paduan *popolo* was given to the doge, [followed by] ... the sceptre[43] of lordship ... the keys, and ... the commune's seal; and with this, the celebration was over. After dinner, our ambassadors held a fine joust, for the prize of a *palio* of red silk lined with squirrel-fur, and this was won by Messer Palamino Vitaliani ...

When the war was over, Messer Giacomo dal Verme, an enemy of the whole Carrara family, came to Venice and was honourably received by the *Signoria* ... and he so used his acumen with the *Signoria*, showing them the many reasons why the lives of the da Carrara were very dangerous to them ... for if Francesco lived he would doubtless escape and could always seek his revenge ... and claiming that the old proverb was true: that a dead man fights no more war. So, I advise you, he concluded ... to take their lives. On account of which the Council of Ten immediately decided that Francesco da Carrara and his sons had to die.

43 *bacchetta.*

FURTHER READING

Bowsky, W. M., *A Medieval Italian Commune: Siena Under the Nine, 1287–1355* (Berkeley and London, 1981)

Dean, T. and C. Wickham (eds), *City and Countryside in Late-Medieval and Renaissance Italy: Essays presented to Philip Jones* (London, 1990)

Epstein, S. A., *Genoa and the Genoese, 958–1528* (Chapel Hill and London, 1996)

Hyde, J. K., *Padua in the Age of Dante* (Manchester, 1966)

— *Society and Politics in Medieval Italy: The Evolution of the Civil Life, 1000–1350* (London, 1973)

Jones, P. J., *The Italian City-State: From Commune to Signoria* (Oxford, 1997)

Klapisch-Zuber, K., *Women, Family and Ritual in Renaissance Italy* (Chicago and London, 1985)

Lambert, M., *The Cathars* (Oxford, 1998)

Larner, J., *Culture and Society in Italy, 1290–1420* (London, 1971)

— *Italy in the Age of Dante and Petrarch* (London, 1980)

Romano, D., *Patricians and Popolani: The Social Foundations of the Venetian Renaissance State* (Baltimore, 1987)

Waley, D., *The Italian City Republics*, 3rd edn (London, 1988)

— *Siena and the Sienese in the Thirteenth Century* (Cambridge, 1991)

INDEX